Learn MonoGame the Easy Way

A Practical Guide to 2D & 3D Game Development with C#, .NET, and Reusable Game Systems

ERIC T. COTNER

Preface

Game development has never been more accessible than it is today, yet many beginners still find themselves overwhelmed by complex engines, massive toolsets, and endless workflows. I wrote this book to solve that problem—to show that you can build real, polished games without being buried under layers of editor windows, plug-ins, or complicated interfaces. MonoGame gives you power and control, but more importantly, it lets you learn game development from the inside out. This book is designed to make that journey simple, clear, and rewarding.

Learn MonoGame the Easy Way grew from years of teaching, building, and breaking games. I've watched countless learners struggle with the same early challenges: where to start, how to structure a project, why a sprite won't render, and how to keep a game from turning into an unmanageable pile of code. What they needed wasn't just documentation—it was a guided path. A resource that teaches not only how MonoGame works, but how to think like a game developer.

That is the purpose of this book.

Every chapter focuses on practical, real-world game development. You will build complete systems—rendering pipelines, input handling, animations, audio, UI, physics, cameras, and entire reusable architectures that you can carry into any project. You will create both 2D and 3D experiences, using C# and .NET in a way that feels natural and efficient. You will learn how to design clean game loops, manage assets, optimize performance, and ship games confidently.

This is not a book that overwhelms you with theory or leaves you copying code mindlessly. Instead, each concept is explained clearly, applied immediately, and reinforced through hands-on examples. Whether you have never built a game before or you're transitioning from another engine, you will find a smooth learning curve, a friendly tone, and a practical roadmap from "I've never opened MonoGame" to "I can build complete games on my own."

My hope is that by the time you turn the final page, you will feel empowered—not just with skills, but with the confidence to bring your own ideas to life. MonoGame is a tool used by studios, hobbyists, and indie creators worldwide. Now, it's your turn to join them.

Let's build something amazing together.

— ERIC T. COTNER

Table of Contents

Introduction

Welcome! In this book, you'll start creating real games from day one. I'll show you how to set up MonoGame on your PC or Mac, get your first project running, and understand the workflow that professional developers use. By the end of this introduction, you'll be ready to start coding your first game.

What is MonoGame & Why Use It

If you want to build games with C# — whether simple 2D or full 3D — but you don't want to be locked into a heavy, opinionated engine, then MonoGame is a brilliant choice. MonoGame is a free, open-source game-development framework that gives you the building blocks: rendering (2D and 3D), input handling, audio, asset/content management, and math utilities tailored for games.

Think of MonoGame like a "game-toolkit." It doesn't force you into a particular editor or tool; instead it hands you the toolbox and lets you assemble your game exactly how you want. That means freedom — you decide your project structure, your workflow, your tools, your art pipeline. It's a "bring-your-own-tools" philosophy, which appeals especially if you like control and flexibility.

Because it's based on .NET and C#, if you already know (or are learning) C#, you're in good shape. You don't need to learn a brand-new scripting language or proprietary engine scripting system. MonoGame fits smoothly into .NET workflows.

Finally — and perhaps most importantly — MonoGame is **cross-platform**. That means games you build with it can run on

Windows, macOS, Linux — and, with the right setup, mobile platforms like Android and iOS

In short: MonoGame offers you power, flexibility, and freedom — all while staying lightweight and accessible. It's ideal for hobbyists, indie developers, learners, or anyone who wants to build games without the overhead (or constraints) of a full game engine.

Who This Book Is For & Prerequisites

This book is for **you** — whether you're an absolute beginner in game development, someone who knows C# but hasn't built a game before, or even an experienced developer wanting to master cross-platform, efficient game development with full control.

What you need to know (or are willing to learn):

- Basic programming concepts: variables, functions, object-oriented programming, loops, conditionals. MonoGame itself uses these concepts — so a basic comfort with C# (or another .NET language) helps.
- Willingness to code. MonoGame doesn't give a drag-and-drop editor or visual scripting. Everything is code-first. If you're comfortable writing code (or want to become comfortable), you'll fit right in.
- A computer (PC, Mac or Linux), and willingness to install a few development tools (SDKs, libraries, IDE or code editor).

I designed this book so even if you've never coded a game before — but you know (or are learning) C# — you can follow along. If you've built console apps or desktop apps, this will feel familiar — just with extra graphics, audio, input, and real-time loops.

Even if you've used other engines, this book will help you appreciate what MonoGame does differently: how it gives full control, flexibility, and portability — and how you can harness those strengths to build games that are yours, from the ground up.

How This Book Is Structured & How to Use It

This book is built like a **journey from zero to game**. Each chapter builds on what came before — from setting up your tools, to rendering graphics, handling input, managing game objects, to building full games, and even deploying them across platforms.

I've avoided heavy theory: you won't find long academic chapters. Instead, each section is **practical**, **hands-on**, and **actionable** — designed so you can follow along and build real things as you learn.

Most chapters end with a small "mini-deliverable" — something you build that actually runs. Later chapters combine earlier pieces into **full game projects**: by the end, you'll have at least one complete game under your belt.

You can treat this book like a **guided workshop**.

- **Read a section**,
- **Follow along to build**,
- **Experiment with variations**,
- **Use what you learn as a base for your own ideas**.

If you skip ahead — that's okay too. Each chapter is somewhat self-contained (after setup); so if you already know sprites and input but want to dive into 3D or shaders, you won't have to read the whole book first.

Setting Up Your Development Environment (Windows, macOS, Linux, IDEs)

Before we build games — we need a working setup. This section walks you through getting MonoGame running on your machine. Whether you're on Windows, macOS or Linux — I've got you covered.

What you'll install / configure:

- A .NET SDK (MonoGame works with .NET — the version recommended recently is .NET 9, though earlier versions may work depending on your setup)
- MonoGame project templates (so you can start new games quickly)
- An IDE or code editor of your choice: on Windows, many use Visual Studio; on macOS and Linux, Visual Studio Code or Rider are popular; but if you're comfortable with a code editor + command line, that works too.

Why this setup matters now: once you have this environment ready, you'll be able to follow everything in the book — from loading sprites to building full 2D or 3D games — without roadblocks or configuration headaches.

What you'll have by the end of this chapter: a working development environment, ready to compile and run MonoGame projects. You'll be ready to start building your first game skeleton — and that's where the fun begins.

Final Thoughts for You (Reader)

Starting game development can feel overwhelming — there are so many engines, tools, languages. But MonoGame strips away the fluff: you get clean, well-designed building blocks, the power of C#, and full control.

In this book, I'm your guide: I'll help you navigate setup, avoid common pitfalls, and build real games step by step.

If you're ready, let's jump in — and begin building games that are truly yours.

Chapter 1: Getting Started with MonoGame

You'll install MonoGame, set up your environment, and create your very first project. You'll see how the game loop works and understand how your game updates and draws frames. By the end, you'll have a working game skeleton you can immediately expand.

1.1 Installing MonoGame & .NET

This is where your journey begins. Before you can write any game code, you need to put the right tools in place: the .NET SDK (the foundation) and MonoGame (the game framework). Once you're set up, you'll be ready to launch your first game skeleton with just a few commands.

Why .NET First — and Which Version to Use

MonoGame builds on top of .NET. That means you need a working .NET SDK installed before you can use MonoGame. Right now, the recommended version of .NET for MonoGame is **.NET 9**.

Even if a previous .NET version is installed, installing the SDK ensures you have all necessary libraries, command-line tools, and runtime components required to compile and run games.

Once .NET SDK is installed, your system will understand commands like `dotnet new` ... — which you'll use to scaffold MonoGame projects.

Step 1: Install .NET SDK

Depending on your platform, the installation process will vary:

- On **Windows**: download the `.NET 9 SDK` installer from the official .NET site, run it, and complete the setup. Once done, open a **new Command Prompt** and type `dotnet`. If it prints usage information rather than an error, you're good.
- On **macOS or Linux**: download the matching installer or use your OS package manager if available. On Linux (e.g. Ubuntu), you can install via standard package commands. After installation, open a **Terminal** and run `dotnet` to verify the install.

After this, your machine is ready to compile C# code and build .NET projects.

Step 2: Install MonoGame — Using the .NET CLI Templates

With .NET ready, installing MonoGame is simple and cross-platform. Instead of messing with complicated installers, MonoGame offers project templates via the .NET CLI.

Open your terminal (or Command Prompt) and run:

```
dotnet new install MonoGame.Templates.CSharp
```

This command downloads and registers the official MonoGame templates so you can create new MonoGame projects with a single `dotnet new` command.

Once installed, you can verify the templates by listing all available project templates:

```
dotnet new -l
```

You should see several entries starting with `mg`, such as `mgdesktopgl`.

Step 3: Create Your First MonoGame Project (Platform-agnostic)

Now that MonoGame is installed, you can scaffold a new game project. Suppose you want to build a simple desktop game. In your terminal, navigate to a folder where you keep development projects, then run:

```
dotnet new mgdesktopgl -o MyFirstGame

cd MyFirstGame
```

This creates a new folder named `MyFirstGame`, with all the necessary files for a basic MonoGame app, using the "DesktopGL" template (which works on Windows, macOS, and Linux).

Once generated, open the project in your code editor — or continue in the terminal.

To run the game, type:

```
dotnet run
```

If everything is correct, you should see a blank game window appear (MonoGame's default starting window). This confirms your environment is properly set up: .NET, MonoGame, and the project all working together.

Optional — If You Use Visual Studio (Windows) or Visual Studio Code / VS Code / Rider

If you prefer a full-featured IDE instead of CLI + editor, you can also use **Visual Studio 2022**, **Visual Studio Code (VS Code)** or other editors.

For Visual Studio: after installing the .NET SDK, you can add the official MonoGame extension, which installs GUI-based project templates. After that, you can create a new MonoGame project via "New Project → MonoGame" and run it with the IDE's Play/Run button.

If you use VS Code (or Rider / any text editor), the CLI method described above works perfectly — plus you get lightweight editing, full cross-platform support, and simple version control friendliness.

What You Should Have by the End of This Section (Your First Milestones)

By the time you finish this section, you will have:

- A working .NET SDK installed on your machine.
- The MonoGame templates registered to your .NET environment.
- A brand-new MonoGame project scaffolded and ready to code.
- A running MonoGame "empty" game window confirming that everything works.

This gives you the foundation you need for everything that follows — rendering graphics, handling input, building game logic, and more.

Troubleshooting (Common Issues & What to Do)

Sometimes things don't go smoothly. For example: if after running `dotnet run` nothing happens, check that your .NET SDK paths are correctly configured. On Windows, ensure you opened a *new* Command Prompt after installation. On macOS/Linux, ensure `dotnet` is in your shell's PATH.

If the MonoGame templates don't show up after installation, try reinstalling them (`dotnet new install MonoGame.Templates.CSharp`) or verify you have the latest .NET SDK version.

If you prefer a full IDE like Visual Studio and templates don't appear in the "New Project" dialog, you may need to install the MonoGame extension manually (or run Visual Studio as administrator).

That's it — you're ready. With .NET and MonoGame installed, and your first project up and running, you've laid the foundation for everything else in this book.

When you're ready, we'll move on to **drawing sprites and rendering 2D graphics** — where your game will start to look like a real game.

1.2 Creating Your First Project (2D Template) — Practical Guide

Now that you've installed .NET and MonoGame, it's time to **create a real 2D project** and start experimenting. This section will guide you step by step, showing code you can run immediately, helping you see results fast.

Step 1: Scaffold a New 2D Project

Open your terminal (macOS/Linux) or Command Prompt (Windows) and navigate to the folder where you want your project. Run:

```
dotnet new mgdesktopgl -o MyFirst2DGame

cd MyFirst2DGame
```

This creates a folder MyFirst2DGame with the basic MonoGame structure:

```
MyFirst2DGame/
├── Content/
├── Game1.cs
├── MyFirst2DGame.csproj
└── Program.cs
```

- **Content/**: where your sprites, textures, fonts, and audio assets go.
- **Game1.cs**: the main game class; contains the core game loop.
- **Program.cs**: the entry point that starts your game.

- **MyFirst2DGame.csproj**: the project file that defines dependencies and build settings.

Step 2: Run the Blank Game Window

In the terminal, type:

```
dotnet run
```

A window should appear with the default blue background. This confirms that your game loop is running, and MonoGame is ready.

Step 3: Examine Game1.cs — Your First Code

Open **Game1.cs** in your editor. You'll see something like this (simplified):

```
using Microsoft.Xna.Framework;

using Microsoft.Xna.Framework.Graphics;

using Microsoft.Xna.Framework.Input;


namespace MyFirst2DGame

{

    public class Game1 : Game

    {

        private GraphicsDeviceManager _graphics;

        private SpriteBatch _spriteBatch;
```

```csharp
public Game1()

{

    _graphics = new
GraphicsDeviceManager(this);

    Content.RootDirectory = "Content";

    IsMouseVisible = true;

}


protected override void Initialize()

{

    // Called before the game starts running

    base.Initialize();

}

protected override void LoadContent()

{

    _spriteBatch = new
SpriteBatch(GraphicsDevice);

    // Load your textures and assets here

}

protected override void Update(GameTime
gameTime)

{

    // Check for exit
```

```csharp
            if
(Keyboard.GetState().IsKeyDown(Keys.Escape))

                Exit();


        base.Update(gameTime);

    }

    protected override void Draw(GameTime
gameTime)

        {


GraphicsDevice.Clear(Color.CornflowerBlue);

        _spriteBatch.Begin();

        // Draw your sprites here

        _spriteBatch.End();


        base.Draw(gameTime);

    }

  }

}
```

What this does:

- Initialize(): run setup logic before the game starts.
- LoadContent(): load sprites, fonts, and audio here.
- Update(): handle input, game logic, and movement every frame.
- Draw(): render graphics every frame.

- `GraphicsDevice.Clear(Color.CornflowerBlu e)`: clears the screen to blue each frame.
- `SpriteBatch`: used to draw 2D textures on screen.

At this stage, the game window is blank. Next, you'll add your first visual elements.

Step 4: Add a Simple Sprite — First Visual

Create a new image file (e.g., **player.png**) and put it in the Content folder. For now, it can be a simple colored square.

Modify `LoadContent()` to load the texture:

```
private Texture2D _playerTexture;

private Vector2 _playerPosition = new
Vector2(100, 100);

protected override void LoadContent()

{

    _spriteBatch = new
SpriteBatch(GraphicsDevice);


    // Load the texture

    _playerTexture =
Content.Load<Texture2D>("player"); // omit
.png

}
```

Update Draw() to render it:

```
protected override void Draw(GameTime gameTime)
{
    GraphicsDevice.Clear(Color.CornflowerBlue);

    _spriteBatch.Begin();

    _spriteBatch.Draw(_playerTexture,
_playerPosition, Color.White);

    _spriteBatch.End();


    base.Draw(gameTime);
}
```

Now, when you run dotnet run, your window will display a single sprite at (100, 100). Congratulations — you have a moving 2D canvas and a visible sprite.

Step 5: Move Your Sprite with Keyboard Input

Update Update() to make your sprite move with arrow keys:

```
protected override void Update(GameTime gameTime)
{
    var keyboardState = Keyboard.GetState();
```

```
if (keyboardState.IsKeyDown(Keys.Escape))

    Exit();

if (keyboardState.IsKeyDown(Keys.Up))

    _playerPosition.Y -= 3;

if (keyboardState.IsKeyDown(Keys.Down))

    _playerPosition.Y += 3;

if (keyboardState.IsKeyDown(Keys.Left))

    _playerPosition.X -= 3;

if (keyboardState.IsKeyDown(Keys.Right))

    _playerPosition.X += 3;

base.Update(gameTime);

}
```

Now, you can move your sprite around the screen. You're officially controlling your first game object in MonoGame!

Step 6: What You've Learned

At the end of this section, you have:

1. Installed MonoGame and .NET, created a 2D template project.
2. Run a working game window.
3. Loaded a sprite and drawn it on the screen.
4. Moved the sprite using keyboard input.

This gives you a **hands-on foundation** for everything in the book: rendering graphics, handling input, and building game logic. The next chapter will expand on this by teaching **sprites, textures, and animation**.

1.3 Understanding the Game Loop: Update & Draw

When you run a MonoGame game, what actually happens behind the scenes is a continuous loop — the "game loop." As long as your game runs, MonoGame keeps repeating that loop: update the game's state, then draw the game. This is the heart of every real-time game.

The core class — usually called `Game1`, inheriting from MonoGame's `Game` base class — defines two methods you care most about: `Update(GameTime gameTime)` and `Draw(GameTime gameTime)`. MonoGame calls these over and over again. `Update` is where you calculate logic: reading input, moving characters, checking collisions, updating game state. `Draw` is where you render — draw sprites, backgrounds, UI — based on the current state.

By default, MonoGame runs this loop at a fixed rate: 60 frames per second (fps). That means ideally `Update + Draw` run every ~16.67 ms.

Here's what a minimal skeleton looks like to show this clearly:

```
using Microsoft.Xna.Framework;

using Microsoft.Xna.Framework.Graphics;
```

```csharp
using Microsoft.Xna.Framework.Input;


namespace MyFirstGame

{

    public class Game1 : Game

    {

        GraphicsDeviceManager _graphics;

        SpriteBatch _spriteBatch;


        public Game1()

        {

            _graphics = new
GraphicsDeviceManager(this);

            Content.RootDirectory =
"Content";

            IsMouseVisible = true;

        }


        protected override void Initialize()

        {

            // Put any non-content
initialization logic here
```

```csharp
        base.Initialize();

    }


    protected override void LoadContent()

    {

        _spriteBatch = new
SpriteBatch(GraphicsDevice);

        // Load textures, fonts, audio
here

    }


    protected override void
Update(GameTime gameTime)

    {

        // Example: exit the game when
Escape is pressed

        if
(Keyboard.GetState().IsKeyDown(Keys.Escape))

            Exit();

        // [Game logic goes here]


        base.Update(gameTime);          }
```

```
        protected override void Draw(GameTime
gameTime)

        {

GraphicsDevice.Clear(Color.CornflowerBlue);


            _spriteBatch.Begin();

            // [Rendering code goes here]

            _spriteBatch.End();


            base.Draw(gameTime);

        }

    }

}
```

When you run this, MonoGame opens a window and starts the loop. Internally, MonoGame does:

- Call Update(...) — process input, update state.
- Then call Draw(...) — render based on the latest state.
- Repeat.

That's why even before you add sprites or game logic, you got that blank window earlier — the loop is working.

Why Separate Update and Draw?

It might be tempting to mix logic and rendering, but separating them brings clarity, performance, and consistency.

In `Update`, you focus purely on game state and logic: where objects move, how they interact, user input, physics, timers. In `Draw`, you take the resulting state and render — draw sprites, backgrounds, UI, effects.

This separation helps ensure that logic doesn't accidentally depend on rendering speed. For example, if your game slows down and doesn't render as often, logic still runs correctly (if you code it properly).

Also, because MonoGame supports a *fixed-step* loop by default — meaning `Update` is invoked at fixed intervals — you can write movement or physics updates that rely on consistent time units. For instance, if you want a sprite to move at 100 pixels per second, you'd calculate movement as velocity × elapsed time. Your game will behave the same regardless of machine speed (within reason).

Modifying Loop Behavior — Fixed-step vs Variable-step

MonoGame's default setup uses a fixed-step loop calling `Update` roughly 60 times per second. If your `Update` takes too long (e.g. heavy logic), MonoGame will sometimes skip a `Draw` to catch up.

If you want — for example, for physics-heavy games or variable frame-rate rendering — you can switch to a *variable-step* loop by setting `IsFixedTimeStep = false`. In that case, `Update` and `Draw` are called as fast as possible; and you must be careful to base movement/animation on the elapsed time provided by `GameTime`.

Practical Example: Moving a Sprite Smoothly Using GameTime

Here's how to use the game loop properly to move a sprite at a consistent speed, no matter the frame rate:

```
Texture2D _player;

Vector2 _playerPosition = new Vector2(100, 100);

float _playerSpeed = 150f;    // 150 pixels per second

protected override void LoadContent()

{

    _spriteBatch = new SpriteBatch(GraphicsDevice);

    _player = Content.Load<Texture2D>("player");

}

protected override void Update(GameTime gameTime)

{

    KeyboardState keys = Keyboard.GetState();

    float delta =
(float)gameTime.ElapsedGameTime.TotalSeconds;

    if (keys.IsKeyDown(Keys.Left))

        _playerPosition.X -= _playerSpeed * delta;

    if (keys.IsKeyDown(Keys.Right))

        _playerPosition.X += _playerSpeed * delta;

    if (keys.IsKeyDown(Keys.Up))

        _playerPosition.Y -= _playerSpeed * delta;

    if (keys.IsKeyDown(Keys.Down))
```

```
        _playerPosition.Y += _playerSpeed * delta;


    base.Update(gameTime);

}


protected override void Draw(GameTime gameTime)

{

    GraphicsDevice.Clear(Color.CornflowerBlue);

    _spriteBatch.Begin();

    _spriteBatch.Draw(_player, _playerPosition,
Color.White);

    _spriteBatch.End();

    base.Draw(gameTime);

}
```

In this example, `_playerPosition` is updated every frame, but movement is scaled by `delta` — the time elapsed since last update. This ensures that the sprite moves at roughly 150 pixels per second, regardless of frame rate fluctuations.

Using this approach will make your game feel smooth, consistent, and fair — whether it's running on a high-end PC or a modest laptop.

What's Next — Why This Matters

Now that you understand how MonoGame's game loop drives the flow — update logic, then render — you have the foundation for everything: movement, input, physics, animation, rendering, UI, and more.

In the next chapters, you'll use this loop as your canvas: you'll load textures, draw sprites, handle input (keyboard, mouse, gamepad, touch), animate objects, build game objects, and combine them into playable games.

Understanding the loop ensures you place code in the right place: logic in `Update`, rendering in `Draw`, resource loading in `LoadContent`, initialization in `Initialize`. That discipline pays off as your game grows in complexity.

Get comfortable with this pattern now — it's the heartbeat of every MonoGame game you'll ever build.

1.4 Project Structure & Best Practices

When you build games with MonoGame, how you organize your files — code, assets, content, configuration — matters a lot. A clean, consistent project structure helps you avoid chaos as your game grows, makes debugging easier, and allows you to reuse or extend parts of your game later. In this section, we'll shape a recommended folder layout, coding practices, and explain why they matter.

A Recommended Project Layout

Start by thinking of your project as having two main parts: the game code, and the game content (assets: images, audio, fonts, etc.). Here's a layout that works well for many 2D games:

`MyGame/`

```
├── Content/              ← content-pipeline folder
(raw + processed assets)

│    ├── images/

│    ├── audio/

│    ├── fonts/

│    └── effects/         ← shaders or
post-processing assets, if any

├── src/                  ← your C# source code (game
logic)

│    ├── Scenes/          ← game states/screens
(Menu, Game, Pause, etc.)

│    ├── Entities/        ← player, enemies, NPCs,
game objects

│    ├── UI/              ← UI code: menus, HUD,
buttons, text rendering

│    ├── Systems/         ← helpers: input, audio
management, resource loading

│    └── Game1.cs         ← main game class (or entry
class)

├── GameName.csproj       ← project file

└── README.md             ← project notes,
instructions, version, contact, license
```

In this layout, the Content/ folder holds all game assets —
images, audio, fonts, shaders — organized by type, so they're easy
to find. Using folders like images/, audio/, fonts/ helps you
and anyone else working on the game know exactly where assets
live.

The `src/` folder is where all source code lives: game logic, object definitions, UI, scene management, systems. Organizing code by functionality (scenes, entities, UI, systems) makes it easier to find and maintain as the project grows.

Putting the main game class (e.g. `Game1.cs`) at the root of `src/` gives a clear entry point for your game logic. A README file helps document what the project is, how to build/run it, and any dependencies — useful especially if you share or come back to the project later.

This structure separates **content** (assets) from **code**, keeps things modular, and prevents your project folder from becoming a tangled mix of unrelated files.

Using MonoGame's Content Pipeline — Keep Content Organized

MonoGame provides a content pipeline (via the `.mgcb` file) to process and package assets (textures, audio, fonts, etc.) into optimized format for runtime. Using this pipeline helps ensure faster loading, optimized memory use, and consistent asset handling across platforms.

Inside your `Content/` folder, set up subfolders like `images/`, `audio/`, `fonts/`, etc. Then in the pipeline tool (or via your build setup), add these asset files and build the content. At runtime you load them with the provided `ContentManager`. Since the pipeline compiles the assets, the game loads optimized versions — which improves performance and cross-platform compatibility.

For example, if you add `Content/images/player.png`, in code you can load it with just `"images/player"` (without file extension) — MonoGame handles the rest.

Modular Code — Divide Responsibilities Clearly

As your game grows beyond a simple demo, you'll want to avoid stuffing everything into `Game1.cs`. Instead, distribute responsibilities into modules: input handling, audio, UI, scenes, entities, game logic.

For instance: create an **InputManager** class under `src/Systems/` — responsible for reading keyboard, mouse, or controller state and exposing a simpler API to the rest of your code. Similarly, an **AudioManager** can manage playing sounds or music, muting, volume control, etc. Having dedicated modules keeps code organized, avoids duplication, and makes maintenance easier.

If you anticipate working on multiple game projects (or building several games over time), consider isolating reusable parts (input, audio, UI, scene management) into a separate library (class library) — then reference that library from each new game project. This reduces duplication and gives you a "starter kit" you can bring into new projects. Moderately advanced MonoGame projects use exactly this pattern.

Scene / State Management — Keep Game States Separate

Games often have more than one "state": menus, gameplay, pause screen, game-over screen, etc. To avoid messy code and tangled logic, structure each state (scene) as its own module — a class that manages its own update/draw logic, input, and assets. For example, have folders under `src/Scenes/` such as

MainMenuScene.cs, GameplayScene.cs, PauseScene.cs.

When switching scenes, unload the old scene's content (if appropriate) and load the new one. This keeps memory and assets managed carefully, helps avoid bugs, and makes code easier to follow.

Code Naming and Asset Naming Conventions — Be Consistent and Clear

When naming code files, classes, assets — choose clear, descriptive names. For example, instead of Img1.png, name it Player_Hero.png or Background_Level01.png. Instead of GameMain.cs, name your main class after the game or the role, like MyGame.cs or GameCore.cs.

In code, maintain consistent naming for classes: each major concept (player, enemy, UI, audio manager) gets its own class. Use namespaces that reflect folder structure (e.g. MyGame.Scenes, MyGame.Entities, MyGame.Systems). This way, when the project grows, everything remains organized and intuitive.

Using a Class Library for Shared or Reusable Components

If you expect to build multiple games, or want to build a home-grown "engine" on top of MonoGame, a class library is a powerful tool. Create a MonoGame Class Library project to hold shared components — like input, audio, UI, entity base classes — then reference this library from each game project. That way, you avoid repeating work each time you start a new game.

Inside the library, keep only reusable code: do not include project-specific assets, or game-specific classes. This keeps the library clean. Then in each game, you add only the code and assets unique to that game.

Build & Distribution Readiness — Preparing for Deployment

Once your game logic and assets are well organized, you'll eventually want to build or publish the game. It helps if your project structure is clean because you'll often need to package executable files, assets, and dependencies together.

When using MonoGame with .NET, one recommended approach is to use self-contained deployments. This packages the .NET runtime together with your game, ensuring players don't need to have .NET installed. That means your project's folder structure and asset pipeline must be clean and organized — so the packaging process picks up exactly what's needed.

A clean structure also makes it easier to manage version control, diff changes, and collaborate with others — whether you're adding new content, refactoring code, or building new features.

Why This Discipline Matters — Long-Term Payoff

At first, when your project is small (just a sprite or two), you might not notice a messy structure. But as you add more sprites, audio files, fonts, UI, entities, logic — things get messy quickly. Without a clear structure, you end up spending more time finding files, debugging, fixing collisions between names or assets, or dealing with messy dependencies.

By starting with a clean project layout and disciplined practices early — modular code, consistent naming, separation of content and code — you save yourself future headaches. You make the project scalable, maintainable, and easier to extend.

Later, when you build a second game (or expand the first), you can re-use modules, maintain shared libraries, and focus on game design — not on housekeeping.

Practical Example — Minimal Project Skeleton to Start With

Here's a minimal `MyGame.csproj` plus folder layout showing how your initial files could look when you start a new project using good structure:

```
MyGame/

  Content/

    images/

    audio/

    fonts/

  src/

    Scenes/

      SplashScene.cs

      MenuScene.cs

    Entities/

      Player.cs

      Enemy.cs
```

```
Systems/

    InputManager.cs

    AudioManager.cs

  UI/

    HUD.cs

  Game1.cs

MyGame.csproj
```

In Game1.cs, you set up the game, initialize systems, and delegate update/draw calls to active scene:

```
// in Game1.cs

protected override void Update(GameTime gameTime)

{

    _currentScene?.Update(gameTime);

    base.Update(gameTime);

}

protected override void Draw(GameTime gameTime)

{

    GraphicsDevice.Clear(Color.Black);

    _spriteBatch.Begin();

    _currentScene?.Draw(gameTime, _spriteBatch);

    _spriteBatch.End();

    base.Draw(gameTime);
```

}

Each scene (e.g. `MenuScene`, `GameplayScene`) lives in its own file under `src/Scenes/`, with its own `Update` and `Draw`logic. Asset folders align with the content pipeline. Systems like input and audio are in `src/Systems/` — reusable across scenes.

As you build more features — UI, entities, levels, audio — your project stays clean and manageable.

Summary

A well-structured project makes a huge difference. By separating code and assets, organizing by functionality, using the content pipeline properly, and modularizing code, you set yourself up for scalable, maintainable games. Whether you build a tiny prototype or a full-fledged game, this foundation will pay off — making development smoother, debugging easier, and future expansion much simpler.

When you're ready, we'll move next into working with sprites, textures, and 2D rendering — and you'll immediately see the benefit of having a clean project structure underneath.

1.5 Running & Debugging Your First Game

Once you've created your first MonoGame project, the next big step is to run it — and to learn how to debug it when things go wrong. Running and debugging are your tools to verify that everything is wired up correctly (graphics, game loop, asset pipeline) and catch mistakes early. In this section, we'll show you how to run your game from the command line or inside an IDE, how to debug it, and what to check if things don't run as expected.

Running Your Game — First Test

Assuming you created a project using the template (for example `mgdesktopgl`) and your terminal is inside the project folder, simply type:

```
dotnet run
```

MonoGame will build the project (compile your C# code, process content, link things), then launch a window. You should see a basic game window — typically with a plain background (MonoGame's default "Cornflower Blue"). That window is your blank canvas. If you see it, congratulations: your environment is set up correctly, the game loop is running, and everything is wired correctly (graphics device, content pipeline, project structure).

If you prefer using an IDE, open the project (e.g. in Visual Studio Code, Visual Studio 2022, or Rider). In Visual Studio, you can press **F5** (or choose Run → Start Debugging). In VS Code, after the first build, you may need to let the editor generate the debug configuration (often via ".NET Generate Assets for Build and Debug") — then press F5 to start your game with debugging attached. Once started, you'll see the same window.

Running the game successfully confirms everything is ready: .NET runtime, MonoGame framework, project structure, and build tools are cooperating.

A Minimal Example That Runs

Inside the default project you get from the template, there is typically a class (often Game1.cs) that looks similar to this:

```
using Microsoft.Xna.Framework;

using Microsoft.Xna.Framework.Graphics;

namespace MyFirst2DGame

{

    public class Game1 : Game

    {

        private GraphicsDeviceManager _graphics;

        private SpriteBatch _spriteBatch;


        public Game1()

        {

            _graphics = new
GraphicsDeviceManager(this);

            Content.RootDirectory = "Content";

            IsMouseVisible = true;

        }

        protected override void LoadContent()

        {

            _spriteBatch = new
SpriteBatch(GraphicsDevice);

        }
```

```
        protected override void Update(GameTime
gameTime)

        {

            base.Update(gameTime);

        }

        protected override void Draw(GameTime
gameTime)

        {

GraphicsDevice.Clear(Color.CornflowerBlue);

            base.Draw(gameTime);

        }

    }

}
```

If you run this (via dotnet run or your IDE), you'll get a blank, blue screen. That's normal. Behind the scenes, MonoGame has created a window, initialized graphics, and set up the game loop (update + draw). This minimal project is your "hello world" — it verifies that everything is functioning, even before you add sprites, input, assets, or logic.

Debugging — Finding & Fixing Issues Early

When you start building games, you'll often make mistakes — wrong file paths, missing assets, code typos, null references, or unexpected behavior. Good debugging setup helps you catch these early.

If you run via an IDE (e.g. Visual Studio or VS Code with debugging configured), you can set breakpoints inside methods like LoadContent, Update, or Draw. For example, you could put a breakpoint at the start of LoadContent, or after loading a texture, and inspect variables (texture variables, content paths, etc.). If an exception occurs — say a missing asset — the debugger will pause at the error and show you a stack trace.

In VS Code with MonoGame, you might need to ensure the .vscode/launch.json and .vscode/tasks.json files are set up (this often occurs automatically when you first press F5 after opening the project). Then use the debug play button to run with debugging attached.

Another simple but effective debugging technique is to log to the console (or debug output) — e.g.:

```
System.Diagnostics.Debug.WriteLine("Loading
content...");

var texture = Content.Load<Texture2D>("player");

System.Diagnostics.Debug.WriteLine("Texture loaded: "
+ (texture != null));
```

Then check the debug output or console window to see if your assets loaded correctly. This is especially useful if you try to load assets and nothing appears, or you get silent failures.

Common Problems & What to Check

If the game fails to launch (no window appears), or crashes immediately, common causes include:

- The MonoGame templates weren't installed properly before project creation. Try reinstalling them.

- The content pipeline hasn't built assets properly (especially if you manually add assets). Make sure your `.mgcb` file was built, and the content was processed.
- Wrong asset path or name when loading (e.g. wrong string passed to `Content.Load<Texture2D>`). Remember to omit the file extension and use the correct relative path.
- On some systems or backends, graphics device or driver issues can prevent the window from opening — especially with DesktopGL on certain Linux / macOS setups. In such cases, verifying your graphics drivers or using a different backend can help.

If you are debugging and hit an exception, examine the stack trace to see exactly where (which method, which line) the error occurred. Then confirm your asset paths, variable values, and project setup.

What This Means for You Now

By now you should be able to run and debug your first MonoGame project. You have confirmed the essential plumbing works: .NET runtime, project structure, graphics initialization, game loop, and build system. This foundation means you can confidently move forward.

In the coming chapters, when you load textures, handle input, draw sprites, and build game logic — you'll have this "working base" beneath you. If anything stops working, you know the source of truth: a clean project + working game loop + debug tools = you can track down issues quickly.

Let's move on — next up: working with sprites, textures, and actual 2D rendering, so you start seeing your first visuals.

Chapter 2: Sprites, Textures & 2D Rendering

You'll load images, draw sprites, and animate characters. You'll also handle different screen sizes and optimize your assets for performance. By the end, your games will look professional and run smoothly.

2.1 Loading Textures & Assets (MGCB / Content Pipeline)

In a game, art assets — images, sprites, sounds, fonts — are just as important as the code. But raw files like `.png`, `.jpg`, or `.wav` aren't always ready for optimal use by the graphics card or audio system. That's where the MonoGame Content Pipeline (and its tool, the MGCB Editor) come in: they take your raw assets, pre-process them into a format optimized for gaming, and make them easy to load at runtime using MonoGame's built-in asset loader.

Using the Content Pipeline is the recommended way to manage assets in MonoGame — it produces efficient binary asset files, automatically includes them in your build, and ensures that when you deploy your game to different platforms (desktop, mobile, etc.), asset loading stays consistent.

Preparing your asset and adding it with the MGCB Editor

First, pick an asset you want to add — e.g. a sprite image. Save a `.png` file (say `player.png`) somewhere on your machine.

Open your game project, then locate the Content/Content.mgcb file (this is created automatically when you use a MonoGame template). Double-click (or right-click → "Open in MGCB Editor") to open the MGCB Editor. In that editor, choose "Add Existing Item", navigate to where you placed player.png, and add it — make sure you choose "copy the file to the directory" so the asset lives inside your project's content folder rather than referencing an outside path. Then **save** the .mgcb file.

With that done, when you build your project (via IDE or dotnet build / dotnet run), MonoGame's build tasks will automatically process that .png into an optimized internal asset file (with .xnb extension), and copy it to the output folder for your game — ready for runtime asset loading.

Loading and using the texture in code

Once you've imported and built the asset via MGCB, you can load it in your game code. In your Game1 class (or whichever class you use), declare a field:

```
private Texture2D _playerTexture;
```

Then in LoadContent() method, load it via the Content manager:

```
protected override void LoadContent()

{

    _spriteBatch = new SpriteBatch(GraphicsDevice);

    _playerTexture =
Content.Load<Texture2D>("player");   // No file
extension
```

```
}
```

Finally, in your Draw() method, draw it on screen:

```
protected override void Draw(GameTime gameTime)

{

    GraphicsDevice.Clear(Color.CornflowerBlue);

    _spriteBatch.Begin();

    _spriteBatch.Draw(_playerTexture, new
Vector2(100, 100), Color.White);

    _spriteBatch.End();


    base.Draw(gameTime);

}
```

When you run the game, you should now see your sprite (from player.png) visible at position (100, 100).

This workflow — MGCB → build → Content.Load → draw — ensures your assets are pre-processed once, optimized for performance, and managed consistently.

Why the Content Pipeline (instead of loading raw files directly)

You *could* bypass MGCB and load raw .png or .wav files at runtime using lower-level methods (like Texture2D.FromFile(...)). But that approach has drawbacks: raw image formats are typically compressed (PNG, JPEG), so at runtime the GPU must decompress them, which increases memory usage and can affect performance; worse, results might be inconsistent across platforms.

With the Content Pipeline, assets are processed ahead-of-time, converted into GPU-friendly formats (e.g. compressed textures, pre-processed audio), and included in the final build — so runtime loading is faster, more predictable, and more efficient.

Managing different types of assets

The Content Pipeline supports more than just textures. You can add audio (sound effects, music), fonts (via `.spritefont`), shaders/effects, and more. Each asset type is processed with suitable importers and processors internally. When you add them via MGCB Editor, they get compiled appropriately. At runtime, loading is as simple as `Content.Load<SoundEffect>("audio/jump")`, `Content.Load<SpriteFont>("fonts/main")`, etc.

What could go wrong — common pitfalls and how to avoid them

A common mistake is to add an image file to your project folder without adding it through the MGCB content project — then trying to `Content.Load<Texture2D>("Images/ship.png")`. That will fail, because the ContentManager only looks for compiled `.xnb` assets based on the content pipeline. To avoid this, always use the MGCB Editor (or manually edit `.mgcb`) and rebuild assets.

Another issue: when naming the asset path in `Content.Load`, never include the file extension. If you added `player.png` via MGCB, use `"player"` (or `"folderName/assetName"` if inside subfolders) — e.g.

`Content.Load<Texture2D>("images/player")`. The ContentManager expects the compiled asset name (without `.xnb`).

Also be mindful of saving the `.mgcb` after adding assets. If you forget to save, build will not include the new asset — leading to runtime "asset not found" errors.

Summary — What You've Achieved

At the end of this section, you will have successfully imported a texture into your project, built it via the content pipeline, loaded it in code, and drawn it on screen. You now have a robust, production-ready workflow for managing all your textures, audio, fonts, and more — properly optimized and platform-aware.

With this foundation, you can confidently move to the next chapter: drawing sprites, animations, handling input, and building game logic — all with assets managed cleanly and efficiently.

2.2 Drawing Sprites & Using SpriteBatch

After loading textures and assets using the content pipeline, the next step is to actually draw those assets to the screen — to make your game "visible." In MonoGame, this is done with the `SpriteBatch` class: a simple, efficient way to draw 2-D textures (sprites) and text each frame. Once you understand how `SpriteBatch` works, you can draw backgrounds, characters, UI elements — anything.

Setting up your sprite drawing

Start by making sure your class has a SpriteBatch and a Texture2D field. For example, in your Game1 class add:

```
private SpriteBatch _spriteBatch;

private Texture2D _playerTexture;

private Vector2 _playerPosition = new
Vector2(100, 100);
```

Then inside LoadContent() load the texture you previously added through the content pipeline:

```
protected override void LoadContent()

{

    _spriteBatch = new SpriteBatch(GraphicsDevice);

    _playerTexture =
Content.Load<Texture2D>("player"); // omit file
extension

}
```

With that done, update your Draw() method to render the sprite each frame. Replace or extend the default Draw:

```
protected override void Draw(GameTime gameTime)

{

    GraphicsDevice.Clear(Color.CornflowerBlue);

    _spriteBatch.Begin();

    _spriteBatch.Draw(_playerTexture,
_playerPosition, Color.White);
```

```
_spriteBatch.End();


    base.Draw(gameTime);

}
```

Run your game now — you should see the player.png sprite
appear at position (100, 100) on the screen. That's your first visible
sprite rendered through MonoGame using SpriteBatch.

Understanding how SpriteBatch works & advanced use

SpriteBatch works by batching draw calls — you call
Begin(), then one or more Draw(...), then End() to flush to
the graphics device. This is efficient and designed for 2D games.

The simplest Draw method takes a texture, a position, and a tint
color. Color.White means "draw the sprite as-is, no tint." If you
want, you can draw a part of a texture (for example, from a sprite
sheet) by supplying a sourceRectangle. That rectangle defines
which sub-region of the texture to draw. For instance, if your sprite
sheet contains multiple frames of animation, you can draw just one
frame by specifying the right rectangle.

Here's an example drawing from a sprite sheet:

```
// Assume _spritesheet is loaded via
Content.Load<Texture2D>("mysheet")

Rectangle sourceRect = new Rectangle(0, 0, 64, 64);
// draws top-left 64×64 tile

Vector2 drawPosition = new Vector2(200, 150);

_spriteBatch.Begin();
```

```
_spriteBatch.Draw(_spritesheet, drawPosition,
sourceRect, Color.White);

_spriteBatch.End();
```

That draws just the top-left 64×64 region of the texture at the screen position (200, 150). This is particularly useful for sprite sheets, tile maps, or when you want to reuse a single texture for multiple sprites.

You can also use more advanced overloads of Draw — specifying rotation, scaling, origin, layer depth (for draw order), and sprite effects (flip horizontally/vertically). These give you flexibility for animation, rotation, scaling, layering, and flipping sprites.

For example, to draw a sprite rotated around its center:

```
Vector2 origin = new Vector2(_playerTexture.Width /
2f, _playerTexture.Height / 2f);

float rotation = MathHelper.ToRadians(45);  // rotate
45 degrees

Vector2 position = new Vector2(300, 200);

_spriteBatch.Begin();

_spriteBatch.Draw(

    _playerTexture,

    position,

    null,

    Color.White,

    rotation,

    origin,

    1.0f,          // scale
```

```
    SpriteEffects.None,

    0f              // layer depth

);

_spriteBatch.End();
```

This draws the sprite centered at $(300, 200)$, rotated by 45°, no scaling, normal draw depth.

Best Practices when Drawing Sprites

Do all draw calls inside the Draw() method. The pattern Begin → Draw → End must be maintained; calling Draw outside a Begin/End block will cause errors.

When drawing many sprites (e.g., tile maps, hundreds of entities), try to minimize texture swapping: batch sprites that use the same texture together. If possible, use **sprite sheets** (single textures containing multiple sprites) and draw via sourceRectangle. This reduces overhead and improves performance.

Be mindful of origin, scaling, depth (layering) and draw order if you have overlapping sprites (UI over game world, foreground/background layers, etc.). Use the overloads of Draw or multiple draws with different parameters to control layering, rotation, flipping, scaling, etc.

What This Enables — Building Visual Games

With basic sprite drawing under your belt, you now have the core functionality to render a 2D game: backgrounds, characters, UI, effects. Combining sprite drawing with input, asset loading, and the game loop (Update/Draw) lets you build interactive games.

In upcoming chapters, you'll add sprite animation, input-based movement, collisions, UI elements — all using `SpriteBatch` (and possibly sprite sheets) as your drawing backbone.

By mastering sprite drawing now, you ensure your game logic and visual rendering remain clean, efficient, and manageable — no messy hacks.

2.3 Sprite Animation & Frame Management

Now that you can load textures and draw sprites, the next step is animation — making your characters or objects move visually. In 2D games, animation is usually done with **sprite sheets**: a single texture containing multiple frames of a character or object in different poses. By drawing each frame in sequence over time, you create the illusion of motion.

Understanding Frames & Sprite Sheets

A sprite sheet is simply a grid of frames, where each frame represents one "pose" of your sprite. For example, a character running might have 6 frames arranged horizontally in one image. Each frame has the same width and height. By changing which frame you draw every few milliseconds, you can animate the character.

Suppose we have `player_run.png` with 6 frames, each 64×64 pixels, arranged in a single row. The total image width is $6 \times 64 = 384$ pixels, height 64 pixels.

Setting up animation variables

To animate, we track which frame to display and how much time has passed. Add the following fields to your Game1 class:

```
private Texture2D _playerRunTexture;

private Vector2 _playerPosition = new Vector2(100,
100);

// Animation variables

private int _frameWidth = 64;

private int _frameHeight = 64;

private int _currentFrame = 0;

private int _totalFrames = 6;

private float _timePerFrame = 0.1f;   // 100 ms per
frame

private float _elapsedTime = 0f;
```

Here, _timePerFrame controls the speed of the animation: lower values mean faster animation. _elapsedTimeaccumulates the time since the last frame change.

Loading the sprite sheet

In LoadContent( ), load the sprite sheet:

```
protected override void LoadContent()

{
```

```
    _spriteBatch = new SpriteBatch(GraphicsDevice);

    _playerRunTexture =
Content.Load<Texture2D>("player_run");

}
```

Updating the animation in Update()

The animation frame changes over time. Use the GameTime
parameter in Update to control frame changes consistently,
independent of frame rate:

```
protected override void Update(GameTime gameTime)

{

    float delta =
(float)gameTime.ElapsedGameTime.TotalSeconds;

    _elapsedTime += delta;

    if (_elapsedTime >= _timePerFrame)

    {

        _currentFrame++;

        if (_currentFrame >= _totalFrames)

            _currentFrame = 0;


        _elapsedTime -= _timePerFrame;

    }

    base.Update(gameTime);

}
```

Here, we accumulate elapsed time. When it exceeds _timePerFrame, we move to the next frame and reset the counter. The modulo logic ensures the animation loops indefinitely.

Drawing the current frame

In Draw(), we draw only the rectangle corresponding to the current frame:

```
protected override void Draw(GameTime gameTime)

{

    GraphicsDevice.Clear(Color.CornflowerBlue);

    _spriteBatch.Begin();

    Rectangle sourceRect = new Rectangle(

        _currentFrame * _frameWidth,  // X position
of the frame in the sprite sheet

        0,                                // Y position
(top row)

        _frameWidth,

        _frameHeight

    );

    _spriteBatch.Draw(_playerRunTexture,
_playerPosition, sourceRect, Color.White);

    _spriteBatch.End();

    base.Draw(gameTime);

}
```

This draws only the current frame of the sprite sheet at the specified position. As `Update()` advances `_currentFrame`, the drawn frame changes, creating smooth animation.

Making the animation flexible

You can make the animation system reusable for multiple sprites by wrapping it into an **Animation** class:

```
public class Animation

{

    public Texture2D Texture { get; }

    public int FrameWidth { get; }

    public int FrameHeight { get; }

    public int TotalFrames { get; }

    public float TimePerFrame { get; }

    private int _currentFrame = 0;

    private float _elapsedTime = 0f;

    public Animation(Texture2D texture, int
frameWidth, int frameHeight, int totalFrames, float
timePerFrame)

    {

        Texture = texture;

        FrameWidth = frameWidth;

        FrameHeight = frameHeight;

        TotalFrames = totalFrames;

        TimePerFrame = timePerFrame;
```

```
    }

    public void Update(GameTime gameTime)

    {

        _elapsedTime +=
(float)gameTime.ElapsedGameTime.TotalSeconds;

        if (_elapsedTime >= TimePerFrame)

        {

            _currentFrame = (_currentFrame + 1) %
TotalFrames;

            _elapsedTime -= TimePerFrame;

        }

    }

    public void Draw(SpriteBatch spriteBatch, Vector2
position)

    {

        Rectangle sourceRect = new
Rectangle(_currentFrame * FrameWidth, 0, FrameWidth,
FrameHeight);

        spriteBatch.Draw(Texture, position,
sourceRect, Color.White);

    }

}
```

Then in Game1, you can instantiate:

```
private Animation _playerAnimation;


protected override void LoadContent()
```

```
{

    _spriteBatch = new SpriteBatch(GraphicsDevice);

    Texture2D playerTexture =
Content.Load<Texture2D>("player_run");

    _playerAnimation = new Animation(playerTexture,
64, 64, 6, 0.1f);

}

protected override void Update(GameTime gameTime)

{

    _playerAnimation.Update(gameTime);

    base.Update(gameTime);

}


protected override void Draw(GameTime gameTime)

{

    GraphicsDevice.Clear(Color.CornflowerBlue);

    _spriteBatch.Begin();

    _playerAnimation.Draw(_spriteBatch, new
Vector2(100, 100));

    _spriteBatch.End();

    base.Draw(gameTime);

}
```

This approach allows multiple animated sprites to coexist, each with independent frame counts, speed, and positions.

Summary

Now you know how to animate sprites in MonoGame:

1. Use sprite sheets with consistent frame sizes.
2. Track elapsed time to advance frames smoothly.
3. Draw only the current frame using a `sourceRectangle`.
4. Wrap animation in a reusable class to manage multiple sprites efficiently.

This gives your 2D games life, making characters run, jump, attack, or otherwise move dynamically on screen.

2.4 Handling Multiple Resolutions & Screen Scaling

When you build a game, you never know what screen your player will have: a small laptop, a full HD monitor, or a high-resolution display. You want your game to look right no matter what. By handling resolution and scaling gracefully, you make your game accessible to more players, and avoid stretched or distorted graphics. In this section, you'll learn how to use a "virtual resolution" — a fixed design resolution — and scale your game view to fit the actual screen, using the power of MonoGame.

Why a "Virtual Resolution" Matters

Imagine you design your game for 800 × 600. All your sprites, UI layouts, positions are based on that coordinate space. But what happens if the game runs on a 1920 × 1080 monitor? Without scaling, your game appears tiny or only occupies part of the screen. If you just stretch everything, things look distorted or pixelated. Instead, by using a "virtual resolution," you treat 800 × 600 as your game's internal, logical screen — and scale it to whatever real screen is used. This approach keeps proportions, layout, and logic consistent, regardless of display.

Setting Up a Virtual Resolution with a Transformation Matrix

MonoGame supports screen-scaling via a transform matrix applied to all your sprite rendering. The idea is: draw everything as if on the virtual resolution, then scale up (or down) to the actual window.

First, in your Game1 constructor (or initialization), set your target (virtual) resolution:

```
private const int VIRTUAL_WIDTH = 800;

private const int VIRTUAL_HEIGHT = 600;

private Matrix _scaleMatrix;

public Game1()

{

    _graphics = new GraphicsDeviceManager(this);

    _graphics.PreferredBackBufferWidth =
VIRTUAL_WIDTH;

    _graphics.PreferredBackBufferHeight =
VIRTUAL_HEIGHT;

    Content.RootDirectory = "Content";

    IsMouseVisible = true;

}
```

Then, after either initial setup or whenever window/resolution changes, compute a scale matrix that matches real screen to virtual resolution:

```
private void UpdateScaleMatrix()
```

```
{
    float scaleX = GraphicsDevice.Viewport.Width /
(float)VIRTUAL_WIDTH;

    float scaleY = GraphicsDevice.Viewport.Height /
(float)VIRTUAL_HEIGHT;

    float scale = Math.Min(scaleX, scaleY);

    _scaleMatrix = Matrix.CreateScale(scale, scale,
1f);

}
```

Calling UpdateScaleMatrix() ensures that regardless of the actual window size, draws based on the virtual space will be scaled uniformly (no distortion), and aspect ratio is preserved.

Applying the Scale Matrix in SpriteBatch

Once you have the transformation matrix, pass it to SpriteBatch.Begin(...) so that all your drawing occurs in "virtual coordinates," then gets scaled to the real screen:

```
protected override void Draw(GameTime gameTime)

{

    GraphicsDevice.Clear(Color.Black);

    _spriteBatch.Begin(

        SpriteSortMode.Deferred,

        null,

        null,

        null,

        null,
```

```
        null,

        _scaleMatrix

    );

    // All draw calls here use virtual resolution
coordinates

    // e.g. Draw background, sprites, UI with
positions based on 800x600

    _spriteBatch.Draw(_playerTexture, new
Vector2(100, 100), Color.White);

    _spriteBatch.End();

    base.Draw(gameTime);

}
```

With this in place, if the window is larger than 800×600, the game will automatically scale up; if smaller, scale down — while preserving aspect ratio.

Handling Window Resize and Aspect Ratio Differences

To support window resizing (on desktop), allow the window to be resizable and listen for size change events. In your game constructor:

```
Window.AllowUserResizing = true;

Window.ClientSizeChanged += OnClientSizeChanged;
```

Then define the handler:

```
private void OnClientSizeChanged(object sender,
EventArgs e)
```

```
{

    UpdateScaleMatrix();

}
```

Every time the user resizes the window, the scale matrix recalculates and drawing adapts immediately. This ensures UI and game world always fit properly.

Using a RenderTarget for Fixed-Virtual Resolution (Optional but Powerful)

An alternative approach — especially useful if you want "pixel-perfect" graphics or want to avoid scaling artifacts — is to render your game to a fixed-size RenderTarget2D (matching your virtual resolution), and then draw that render target scaled to fit the screen. This keeps your internal logic fixed, and final output is just a scaled image.

In your Draw method:

```
// First render to virtual-size render target

GraphicsDevice.SetRenderTarget(_renderTarget);

GraphicsDevice.Clear(Color.CornflowerBlue);

_spriteBatch.Begin();

// draw your game scene in virtual coordinates

_spriteBatch.Draw(_playerTexture, _playerPosition,
Color.White);

_spriteBatch.End();

// Reset to back buffer

GraphicsDevice.SetRenderTarget(null);
```

```
GraphicsDevice.Clear(Color.Black);

// Now draw scaled render target to screen

_spriteBatch.Begin(

    SpriteSortMode.Deferred,

    null,

    null,

    null,

    null,

    null,

    _scaleMatrix

);

_spriteBatch.Draw(_renderTarget, Vector2.Zero,
Color.White);

_spriteBatch.End();
```

This method ensures that internal drawing stays consistent, and final screen display is scaled — often cleaner for pixel art or resolution-independent UI.

What to Watch Out For — Common Pitfalls

If you forget to use a scale matrix (or RenderTarget) and simply draw using virtual coordinates on a large screen, your game will appear in the top-left and look tiny. If you scale non-uniformly (different X and Y scales), sprites and UI will stretch weirdly. Always use a single scale factor (same for X and Y) to preserve aspect ratio. Also, when scaling with matrices or render targets, mouse/touch input coordinates will not match screen pixels automatically — you'll need to transform input positions back into virtual coordinate space (using inverse of the scale matrix) to detect clicks or touches correctly.

Another common issue: changing the window size or going fullscreen without recalculating the scale matrix — leading to distorted or cropped graphics. Always update the scale matrix whenever the screen dimension changes (window resize or resolution change).

Why This Matters for You

By building resolution-independent rendering from the start, you save yourself from a world of trouble — no ugly stretching, no UI misplacement, no platform-specific hacks. Your game will look consistent on desktop monitors, laptops, maybe tablets (if you target them), and any resolution players happen to use. This makes your game more professional, accessible, and polished.

With scaling and resolution management working, you can focus on art, gameplay, UI, and logic — without worrying about "will this run correctly on that screen?"

In the next chapter, we'll explore more advanced rendering techniques — layering, parallax, and UI scaling — all building on this resolution-independent foundation.

2.5 Optimizing Texture Usage & Sprite Sheets

When you start building a simple game, you might load each sprite or asset as its own texture and never think twice. But as a game grows — many characters, backgrounds, UI elements, effects — naïvely loading lots of separate textures can quickly lead to performance problems (slow rendering, high memory, long load times). That's where good texture-management practices come in: using sprite sheets (texture atlases), minimizing texture swaps, and batching draw calls carefully.

Why texture optimization matters

Every time you draw something with a different texture than previously drawn, the GPU needs to "swap" textures — unbind the old, bind the new. In a small test that's negligible; in a real game with many sprites per frame this adds overhead and can become a performance bottleneck. MonoGame documentation refers to this as "texture swapping," and warns that many swaps per frame is expensive.

Using a single texture atlas (sprite sheet) containing many sprites means you draw many different sprites while referencing the *same* texture — avoiding repeated binds, enabling batching, and reducing memory/texture overhead.

Moreover, by combining many small images into a bigger one, you reduce file I/O overhead at load time, improve caching, and make asset management easier.

Building a texture atlas / sprite sheet

Let's suppose you have multiple related sprites: e.g. player walk frames, enemy sprites, UI icons, etc. Instead of separate PNGs, pack them into a single atlas. You can use a tool — for example TexturePacker — which arranges and packs sprites efficiently, removes wasted space (empty transparent borders), and outputs a combined texture + metadata (e.g. JSON or atlas info) usable in MonoGame. This reduces memory and optimizes draw performance.

After packing, add the atlas texture via the content pipeline like any other asset. Then in code you refer to sub-regions (frames or sprites) using source rectangles.

Example: Single Atlas with Multiple Sprites

Here's a conceptual example showing how to use a single atlas for multiple sprites (player, background, UI) and draw them efficiently without texture swaps:

```
Texture2D _atlas;

Rectangle _playerSource = new Rectangle(0, 0, 64,
64);

Rectangle _enemySource = new Rectangle(64, 0, 64,
64);

Rectangle _uiIconSource = new Rectangle(128, 0, 32,
32);


protected override void LoadContent()

{

    _spriteBatch = new SpriteBatch(GraphicsDevice);
```

```
    _atlas = Content.Load<Texture2D>("game_atlas");
// atlas.png packed with all sprites

}


protected override void Draw(GameTime gameTime)

{

    GraphicsDevice.Clear(Color.CornflowerBlue);

    _spriteBatch.Begin(SpriteSortMode.Texture,
BlendState.AlphaBlend);


    // draw player

    _spriteBatch.Draw(_atlas, new Vector2(50, 50),
_playerSource, Color.White);

    // draw enemy

    _spriteBatch.Draw(_atlas, new Vector2(150, 50),
_enemySource, Color.White);

    // draw UI icon

    _spriteBatch.Draw(_atlas, new Vector2(10, 10),
_uiIconSource, Color.White);

    _spriteBatch.End();

    base.Draw(gameTime);

}
```

Because all draws reference the same _atlas texture, the GPU doesn't need to re-bind different textures, and the draw calls can be batched efficiently. This is significantly faster than loading and drawing three separate textures (player.png, enemy.png, icon.png).

When to use multiple atlases or split textures

Sprite sheets and atlases are powerful — but don't assume "everything in one big atlas" is always best. Graphics cards have texture-size limits; for large games with many high-resolution textures, packing everything into a single giant atlas may exceed limits or waste memory. Also, logically distinct sets of sprites (e.g. UI vs game world vs background vs high-res photos) might be better maintained in separate atlases for easier asset management and memory control.

A common compromise: group similar sprites (characters, entities) in one atlas; UI elements and backgrounds in others. That way you still minimize texture swaps within each group, while keeping flexibility.

Additionally, MonoGame (via `SpriteBatch`) supports sorting sprites by texture before drawing, which helps minimize swaps when using multiple textures — but it's still more efficient to draw as many sprites as possible from one atlas.

Handling sprite sheets with frame-based animations or many sub-sprites

For animated sprites (walking, running, effects), sprite sheets typically have tightly packed frames. Instead of treating each frame as a separate texture, use a single atlas and reference each frame via source rectangles or dedicated metadata (e.g. data generated by TexturePacker). This way you still enjoy the performance benefits of atlasing while supporting animations and dynamic sprite selection.

If you want to build a reusable system, you can abstract frame definitions in a small helper — for example, a dictionary mapping sprite names or animation names to `Rectangle` frames. Then during rendering or animation you look up the rectangle by key and draw accordingly, keeping code clean and flexible.

Additional Optimization Considerations — Memory, Compression, and Overdraw

Beyond sprite sheets, it's worth thinking about texture size and compression. Use the smallest reasonable resolution for textures that still look good — avoid unnecessarily large textures for small UI icons. This helps reduce memory use, load times, and GPU memory pressure. In cases where your target platform supports compressed textures (or when building for mobile), using compressed texture formats (via the content pipeline) helps reduce memory footprint. The content pipeline automatically handles texture import/processing which often includes compression behind the scenes.

Also, minimize overdraw: avoid drawing sprites far outside the visible screen, avoid excessive transparent pixels, and when possible draw only what's needed. Using sprite sheets helps here too — fewer textures overall means easier culling and better batching.

Summary — What You Gain by Being Smart about Textures

If you follow these practices — using atlases / sprite sheets, batching draw calls, organizing assets sensibly, and avoiding unnecessary textures — you gain smoother rendering, fewer frame drops, lower memory consumption, faster load times, and a cleaner asset workflow. Your game becomes more scalable: whether it's a simple prototype or a full-fledged project with many sprites, it remains efficient and manageable.

From here on, as you build gameplay, animations, UI, levels —
remember that good texture management is as important as good
code structure. It's the foundation of a performant,
professional-looking game.

Chapter 3: Input Handling & Game Controls

You'll make your games interactive by handling keyboard, mouse, touch, and controller input. You'll build a reusable input system so your games respond perfectly to players. By the end, you'll have full control over player interactions.

3.1 Keyboard & Mouse Input

Interactivity is at the heart of every game. To make your game respond to the player, you need to handle input — typically from the keyboard and mouse. MonoGame provides built-in classes that make reading input straightforward, while giving you control over both current states and state changes (like key presses, releases, or mouse clicks).

Handling Keyboard Input

MonoGame's Keyboard class provides access to the keyboard state at any given frame. To read which keys are pressed:

```
using Microsoft.Xna.Framework.Input;

Inside your Update method:

protected override void Update(GameTime gameTime)

{

    KeyboardState keyboardState =
Keyboard.GetState();
```

```
    if (keyboardState.IsKeyDown(Keys.W))

    {

        _playerPosition.Y -= 5; // Move player up

    }

    if (keyboardState.IsKeyDown(Keys.S))

    {

        _playerPosition.Y += 5; // Move player down

    }

    if (keyboardState.IsKeyDown(Keys.A))

    {

        _playerPosition.X -= 5; // Move player left

    }

    if (keyboardState.IsKeyDown(Keys.D))

    {

        _playerPosition.X += 5; // Move player right

    }

    base.Update(gameTime);

}
```

Here, _playerPosition is a Vector2 representing the player's position. Every frame, we read the keyboard state and update the player position accordingly. Using IsKeyDown allows continuous movement while the key is held.

If you need to detect a **single key press event** (not holding), you can track the previous keyboard state:

```
private KeyboardState _previousKeyboardState;


protected override void Update(GameTime gameTime)

{

    KeyboardState currentKeyboardState =
Keyboard.GetState();

    if (currentKeyboardState.IsKeyDown(Keys.Space) &&

!_previousKeyboardState.IsKeyDown(Keys.Space))

    {

        // Space was just pressed

        Jump();

    }


    _previousKeyboardState = currentKeyboardState;

    base.Update(gameTime);

}
```

This pattern is essential for actions that should trigger once per key press, like jumping, shooting, or menu selection.

Handling Mouse Input

Mouse input is equally important — for pointing, clicking, or dragging. MonoGame's Mouse class provides the current state of the mouse:

```
using Microsoft.Xna.Framework.Input;
```

```
Inside Update():

MouseState mouseState = Mouse.GetState();

// Get mouse position

Point mousePosition = mouseState.Position;

// Check for button click

if (mouseState.LeftButton == ButtonState.Pressed)

{

    _playerPosition = new Vector2(mousePosition.X,
mousePosition.Y);

}

// Detect mouse wheel scrolling

int scrollValue = mouseState.ScrollWheelValue;
```

As with the keyboard, to detect a **single click**, store the previous mouse state:

```
private MouseState _previousMouseState;

protected override void Update(GameTime gameTime)

{

    MouseState currentMouseState = Mouse.GetState();


    if (currentMouseState.LeftButton ==
ButtonState.Pressed &&

        _previousMouseState.LeftButton ==
ButtonState.Released)

    {

        FireProjectile();
```

```
    }

    _previousMouseState = currentMouseState;

    base.Update(gameTime);

}
```

This ensures actions happen only once per click, avoiding repeated triggers while the button is held.

Combining Keyboard & Mouse

Games often require simultaneous input from both devices. Simply combine the above patterns in Update():

```
protected override void Update(GameTime gameTime)

{

    KeyboardState keyboardState =
Keyboard.GetState();

    MouseState mouseState = Mouse.GetState();


    // Move player with keyboard

    if (keyboardState.IsKeyDown(Keys.W))
_playerPosition.Y -= 5;

    if (keyboardState.IsKeyDown(Keys.S))
_playerPosition.Y += 5;

    if (keyboardState.IsKeyDown(Keys.A))
_playerPosition.X -= 5;

    if (keyboardState.IsKeyDown(Keys.D))
_playerPosition.X += 5;

    // Shoot towards mouse click
```

```
    if (mouseState.LeftButton ==
ButtonState.Pressed &&

        _previousMouseState.LeftButton ==
ButtonState.Released)

    {

        ShootTowards(mouseState.Position);

    }

    _previousMouseState = mouseState;



    base.Update(gameTime);

}
```

This pattern gives full control for movement, actions, and interactions in your game.

Tips for Smooth Input Handling

1. **Track previous states**: This avoids repeated triggers and enables "just pressed" or "just released" events.
2. **Separate input logic from game logic**: Consider having a dedicated input handler or helper methods if your game grows complex.
3. **Normalize input speeds**: For consistent movement across different frame rates, multiply movement values by gameTime.ElapsedGameTime.TotalSeconds.

Example for frame-rate independent movement:

```
float delta =
(float)gameTime.ElapsedGameTime.TotalSeconds;
```

```
_playerPosition.X += 200f * delta; // moves at
200 units per second
```

What This Enables

Once you master keyboard and mouse input, you can create fully interactive games: moving characters, shooting projectiles, navigating menus, or clicking on objects. It forms the foundation for player control in almost every 2D game.

3.2 Gamepad / Controller Input

In addition to keyboard and mouse, modern games often support **gamepads or controllers**. MonoGame provides a robust GamePad class that allows you to detect button presses, triggers, and analog stick movement for multiple controllers. Supporting gamepads makes your game more accessible and fun for console-style gameplay or PC users who prefer a controller.

Detecting a Gamepad

MonoGame supports up to four controllers, identified by PlayerIndex.One through PlayerIndex.Four. You can check whether a controller is connected and read its current state with the GamePad.GetState() method:

```
using Microsoft.Xna.Framework.Input;

protected override void Update(GameTime gameTime)

{

    GamePadState state =
GamePad.GetState(PlayerIndex.One);
```

```
if (state.IsConnected)

{

    // Controller is connected

    base.Update(gameTime);

}

else

{

    // Optionally fallback to keyboard or
show a warning

    base.Update(gameTime);

}

}
```

The IsConnected property tells you whether the controller is currently connected. You should check this each frame to handle disconnections gracefully.

Reading Button Input

GamePadState provides boolean properties for each button on the controller, such as A, B, X, Y, LeftShoulder, RightShoulder, Start, and Back. You can check if a button is pressed using IsButtonDown():

```
if (state.IsButtonDown(Buttons.A))

{
```

```
    Jump();

}

if (state.IsButtonDown(Buttons.B))

{

    Shoot();

}
```

To detect a single press (i.e., button just pressed this frame), store the previous GamePadState:

```
private GamePadState _previousGamePadState;

protected override void Update(GameTime gameTime)

{

    GamePadState currentState =
GamePad.GetState(PlayerIndex.One);

    if (currentState.IsButtonDown(Buttons.A) &&

        !_previousGamePadState.IsButtonDown(Buttons.A))

    {

        Jump();

    }

    _previousGamePadState = currentState;

    base.Update(gameTime);

}
```

This prevents repeated triggers when a button is held down.

Reading Analog Sticks

Analog sticks provide floating-point values between -1.0f and 1.0f. Use ThumbSticks.Left or ThumbSticks.Right to get X and Y values:

```
Vector2 leftStick = state.ThumbSticks.Left;

// Note: Y-axis is inverted; up = +1, down = -1

_playerPosition.X += leftStick.X * 5f;

_playerPosition.Y -= leftStick.Y * 5f;
```

Multiplying by a speed factor allows smooth, analog movement of your character or camera.

Reading Triggers

Triggers return values between 0.0f (not pressed) and 1.0f (fully pressed). Use them for actions such as shooting, acceleration, or zooming:

```
float rightTrigger = state.Triggers.Right;

if (rightTrigger > 0.1f)

{

    FireProjectile(rightTrigger); // scale power
by trigger pressure

}
```

This provides analog input that can add nuance to gameplay (e.g., partial pressure for slower movement or weaker attacks).

Vibration / Force Feedback

MonoGame allows you to control controller vibration through `GamePad.SetVibration()`:

```
GamePad.SetVibration(PlayerIndex.One, 0.5f,
0.5f); // left and right motors 50%
```

This can enhance gameplay for explosions, hits, or environmental feedback. Don't forget to reset vibration when not needed:

```
GamePad.SetVibration(PlayerIndex.One, 0f, 0f);
```

Combining Controller with Keyboard/Mouse

Many games support multiple input types. Simply combine your existing keyboard/mouse logic with controller input:

```
protected override void Update(GameTime gameTime)

{

    // Keyboard input

    KeyboardState keyboard = Keyboard.GetState();

    if (keyboard.IsKeyDown(Keys.W))
_playerPosition.Y -= 5;


    // Controller input

    GamePadState gamePad =
GamePad.GetState(PlayerIndex.One);

    if (gamePad.IsConnected)

    {

        Vector2 stick = gamePad.ThumbSticks.Left;

        _playerPosition.X += stick.X * 5f;
```

```
    _playerPosition.Y -= stick.Y * 5f;

  }


  base.Update(gameTime);

}
```

This ensures players can seamlessly switch between keyboard/mouse and controller.

Tips for Smooth Controller Input

1. **Dead Zones**: Analog sticks may not perfectly return to zero; consider applying a dead zone to ignore tiny unintended input.

```
Vector2 leftStick = gamePad.ThumbSticks.Left;

if (leftStick.Length() < 0.2f) leftStick =
Vector2.Zero; // dead zone
```

2. **State Tracking**: Always store previous button or stick states for "just pressed" events.
3. **Multi-Player Support**: Track input separately for PlayerIndex.One to PlayerIndex.Four if you plan for local multiplayer.
4. **Graceful Fallbacks**: If a controller disconnects, fallback to keyboard/mouse input or pause the game.

What This Enables

Supporting gamepads opens up your game to a wider audience, enables console-like gameplay, smooth analog movement, and rich player feedback with vibration. Combined with keyboard/mouse input, you now have a complete, responsive input system ready for 2D or 3D games alike.

3.3 Touch Input for Mobile

As mobile devices dominate gaming, touch input has become essential. Unlike keyboard or gamepad input, touch is **position-based**: users tap, swipe, or pinch the screen. MonoGame provides the TouchPanel class and TouchCollectionto detect touch gestures, finger positions, and movement, giving you full control over mobile interactivity.

Enabling Touch Input

By default, the TouchPanel is ready for use. If you want to handle gestures (like taps, swipes, or pinches), you can enable them explicitly:

```
using Microsoft.Xna.Framework.Input.Touch;

TouchPanel.EnabledGestures = GestureType.Tap |
GestureType.FreeDrag | GestureType.Pinch;
```

This lets MonoGame recognize the gestures you care about, without processing unnecessary input.

Reading Touch Points

For basic taps and finger positions, use TouchPanel.GetState() to get the current active touches:

```
protected override void Update(GameTime gameTime)
```

```
{
    TouchCollection touchState = TouchPanel.GetState();

    foreach (TouchLocation touch in touchState)
    {
        if (touch.State == TouchLocationState.Pressed)
        {
            // Finger just touched the screen

            _playerPosition = touch.Position; // move
player to touch
        }

        if (touch.State == TouchLocationState.Moved)
        {
            // Finger moved across the screen

            _playerPosition = touch.Position;
        }
    }


    base.Update(gameTime);
}
```

Here, `_playerPosition` is updated to follow the finger, providing intuitive drag or touch-to-move behavior.

Using Gestures

Gestures allow you to detect higher-level input like taps, swipes, and pinches, which is ideal for games with menus, zoom, or special controls:

```
while (TouchPanel.IsGestureAvailable)

{

    GestureSample gesture =
TouchPanel.ReadGesture();

    switch (gesture.GestureType)

    {

        case GestureType.Tap:

            ShootProjectile(gesture.Position);

            break;

        case GestureType.FreeDrag:

            _playerPosition = gesture.Position;

            break;

        case GestureType.Pinch:

            ZoomCamera(gesture.Delta); // handle
pinch zoom

            break;

    }

}
```

This loop ensures all pending gestures are handled each frame. GestureSample provides information about position, movement delta, and more.

Handling Multi-Touch

MonoGame supports multiple simultaneous touches, allowing gestures like two-finger pinch-to-zoom or multi-touch controls for multiple players:

```
TouchCollection touches = TouchPanel.GetState();

if (touches.Count >= 2)

{

    TouchLocation touch1 = touches[0];

    TouchLocation touch2 = touches[1];

    float distance =
Vector2.Distance(touch1.Position, touch2.Position);

    // Use distance for zooming or pinch gestures

}
```

By reading multiple touches, you can implement complex input patterns like simultaneous movement and shooting.

Combining Touch with Other Inputs

For cross-platform games (desktop and mobile), it's useful to abstract input logic. For example, you can check platform and decide whether to read keyboard/gamepad or touch:

```
if (TouchPanel.GetCapabilities().IsConnected)

{

    // Read touch input

}

else
```

```
{
    // Fallback to keyboard/gamepad
}
```

This ensures your game works seamlessly on multiple devices.

Tips for Smooth Touch Input

1. **Normalize positions**: If you're using a virtual resolution or scaling, convert touch coordinates to virtual coordinates so gameplay remains consistent across screen sizes.
2. **Handle touch states carefully**: `Pressed`, `Moved`, and `Released` correspond to finger actions, and misinterpreting them can lead to jerky movement.
3. **Limit gestures to what you need**: Enabling only required gestures avoids unnecessary processing.
4. **Debounce taps**: Multiple frames may register a single tap; track previous touch state if needed.
5. **What This Enables**

By mastering touch input, you can make fully interactive mobile games: swipe to move, tap to shoot, pinch to zoom, or multi-touch gameplay. Combined with your existing input handling (keyboard, mouse, gamepad), you now have a unified input system capable of targeting desktop, console, and mobile platforms effectively.

3.4 Designing a Reusable Input Manager

As your game grows, handling input directly in your Game1 class quickly becomes messy. Different input devices — keyboard, mouse, gamepad, touch — require separate checks, state tracking, and logic. A **reusable input manager**centralizes all input handling into one class, making your code cleaner, easier to maintain, and scalable.

Why You Need an Input Manager

Without an input manager, your Update() method becomes cluttered with multiple input checks:

```
KeyboardState keyboard = Keyboard.GetState();

MouseState mouse = Mouse.GetState();

GamePadState gamePad =
GamePad.GetState(PlayerIndex.One);

TouchCollection touches = TouchPanel.GetState();

// Logic repeated in multiple places
```

An input manager provides:

- Unified interface to query actions (e.g., IsActionPressed("Jump"))
- Automatic state tracking (pressed, released, held)
- Support for multiple input devices without cluttering your game logic

Basic Structure of an Input Manager

A reusable input manager typically:

1. Tracks current and previous states for each input device.
2. Maps **actions** (Jump, Shoot, MoveLeft) to keys, buttons, or gestures.
3. Exposes a simple API to check whether an action is pressed, released, or held.

Here's a simplified example:

```
using Microsoft.Xna.Framework;

using Microsoft.Xna.Framework.Input;

using Microsoft.Xna.Framework.Input.Touch;

using System.Collections.Generic;

public class InputManager

{

    private KeyboardState _currentKeyboard;

    private KeyboardState _previousKeyboard;

    private MouseState _currentMouse;

    private MouseState _previousMouse;

    private GamePadState _currentGamePad;

    private GamePadState _previousGamePad;

    private TouchCollection _currentTouch;

    private TouchCollection _previousTouch;

    private Dictionary<string, Keys> _keyBindings;
```

```csharp
    private Dictionary<string, Buttons>
_gamePadBindings;

    public InputManager()

    {

        _keyBindings = new Dictionary<string,
Keys>();

        _gamePadBindings = new Dictionary<string,
Buttons>();

    }

    public void BindKey(string action, Keys key) =>
_keyBindings[action] = key;

    public void BindButton(string action, Buttons
button) => _gamePadBindings[action] = button;

    public void Update()

    {

        // Update keyboard and mouse states

        _previousKeyboard = _currentKeyboard;

        _currentKeyboard = Keyboard.GetState();

        _previousMouse = _currentMouse;

        _currentMouse = Mouse.GetState();

        // Update gamepad

        _previousGamePad = _currentGamePad;

        _currentGamePad =
GamePad.GetState(PlayerIndex.One);

        // Update touch

        _previousTouch = _currentTouch;
```

```csharp
        _currentTouch = TouchPanel.GetState();

    }

    // Keyboard example

    public bool IsActionPressed(string action)

    {

        if (_keyBindings.ContainsKey(action))

        {

            return
_currentKeyboard.IsKeyDown(_keyBindings[action]) &&


!_previousKeyboard.IsKeyDown(_keyBindings[action]);

        }

        if (_gamePadBindings.ContainsKey(action))

        {

            return
_currentGamePad.IsButtonDown(_gamePadBindings[action]
) &&


!_previousGamePad.IsButtonDown(_gamePadBindings[actio
n]);

        }

        return false;

    }


    // Example: check if a touch occurred anywhere

    public bool IsTouchPressed()
```

```
    {

        foreach (var touch in _currentTouch)

        {

            if (touch.State ==
TouchLocationState.Pressed)

                return true;

        }

        return false;

    }

}
```

This input manager tracks previous and current states, enabling "just pressed" detection for keyboard, gamepad, and touch.

Using the Input Manager in Game1

In your Game1 class, you can use the input manager like this:

```
private InputManager _input;

protected override void Initialize()

{

    _input = new InputManager();

    // Bind actions

    _input.BindKey("Jump", Keys.Space);

    _input.BindButton("Jump", Buttons.A);


    base.Initialize();
```

```
}

protected override void Update(GameTime gameTime)

{

    _input.Update();

    if (_input.IsActionPressed("Jump"))

    {

        Jump();

    }

    if (_input.IsTouchPressed())

    {

        _playerPosition =
TouchPanel.GetState()[0].Position;

    }

    base.Update(gameTime);

}
```

This approach abstracts away device-specific checks, so your game logic deals only with **actions** like "Jump" or "Shoot."

Extending the Input Manager

A well-designed input manager can be extended to support:

1. **Multiple players**: Track input per PlayerIndex.
2. **Continuous actions**: Detect held keys, buttons, or touches.
3. **Gesture support**: Map swipe, pinch, or tap gestures to actions.

4. **Custom mappings**: Allow players to remap keys or buttons dynamically.
5. **Mouse movement / analog sticks**: Provide normalized input values for movement or camera control.

For example, detecting a held action could be added:

```
public bool IsActionHeld(string action)

{

    if (_keyBindings.ContainsKey(action))

        return
_currentKeyboard.IsKeyDown(_keyBindings[action]);

    if (_gamePadBindings.ContainsKey(action))

        return
_currentGamePad.IsButtonDown(_gamePadBindings[act
ion]);

    return false;

}
```

Benefits of a Reusable Input Manager

- Keeps your game loop clean and readable
- Supports multiple devices seamlessly
- Enables cross-platform development (desktop, console, mobile)
- Makes it easier to add new input types in the future

With this system, your game can scale from a simple prototype to a complex project while keeping input handling maintainable, efficient, and consistent.

3.5 Handling Input States & Game Logic

Detecting input — whether from keyboard, mouse, gamepad, or touch — is only the first step. The real goal is to **translate input into game behavior** while ensuring smooth, consistent gameplay. Handling input states properly allows you to implement actions like movement, jumping, shooting, and menu navigation without glitches or repeated triggers.

Understanding Input States

MonoGame provides **current and previous states** for each input device. These states help you distinguish between:

- **Pressed / just pressed**: The player *just* initiated the action this frame.
- **Held**: The player is continuing to hold a button or key.
- **Released / just released**: The player let go of a button or key.

Tracking these states is crucial to ensure actions are triggered at the right time. For example, you want a jump to trigger once per key press, not continuously while the key is held.

Using Previous and Current States

Here's an example for keyboard input in the Update() method:

```
private KeyboardState _currentKeyboard;

private KeyboardState _previousKeyboard;

protected override void Update(GameTime gameTime)

{
```

```
_previousKeyboard = _currentKeyboard;

_currentKeyboard = Keyboard.GetState();

// Jump: only trigger on just pressed

if (_currentKeyboard.IsKeyDown(Keys.Space) &&

    !_previousKeyboard.IsKeyDown(Keys.Space))

{

    Jump();

}

// Move: allow continuous movement while key
is held

if (_currentKeyboard.IsKeyDown(Keys.A))

{

    _playerPosition.X -= 200f *
(float)gameTime.ElapsedGameTime.TotalSeconds;

}


base.Update(gameTime);

}
```

In this example:

- Jump() is triggered once per press using a "just pressed" check.
- _playerPosition updates continuously while the key is held, creating smooth movement.

Extending to Gamepad and Mouse

The same principle applies to other devices:

```
GamePadState currentGamePad =
GamePad.GetState(PlayerIndex.One);

GamePadState previousGamePad = _previousGamePad;

// Detect just pressed A button

if (currentGamePad.IsButtonDown(Buttons.A) &&

    !previousGamePad.IsButtonDown(Buttons.A))

{

    Jump();

}


// Detect held left trigger for charging attack

float charge = currentGamePad.Triggers.Left;

if (charge > 0.1f)

{

    ChargeAttack(charge);

}
```

Mouse clicks can be tracked similarly:

```
MouseState currentMouse = Mouse.GetState();

MouseState previousMouse = _previousMouse;

// Fire once per left click
```

```
if (currentMouse.LeftButton ==
ButtonState.Pressed &&

    previousMouse.LeftButton ==
ButtonState.Released)

{

    ShootProjectile(currentMouse.Position);

}
```

Using Input States in Game Logic

Once input states are correctly tracked, you can **tie them to game logic**:

1. **Character Movement**: Use held states for smooth continuous movement.
2. **Actions**: Use just pressed states for jump, shoot, dash, or menu selection.
3. **UI Interaction**: Use just pressed states for buttons or touch taps.
4. **Analog Inputs**: Use trigger values or stick positions to control movement speed or aim angle.

For example, combining multiple devices:

```
// Keyboard movement

if (_currentKeyboard.IsKeyDown(Keys.W))
_playerPosition.Y -= 200f * delta;

if (_currentKeyboard.IsKeyDown(Keys.S))
_playerPosition.Y += 200f * delta;

// Gamepad movement

Vector2 leftStick =
currentGamePad.ThumbSticks.Left;
```

```
_playerPosition.X += leftStick.X * 200f * delta;

_playerPosition.Y -= leftStick.Y * 200f * delta;

// Jump using keyboard or controller

if ((_currentKeyboard.IsKeyDown(Keys.Space) &&

    !_previousKeyboard.IsKeyDown(Keys.Space)) ||

    (currentGamePad.IsButtonDown(Buttons.A) &&

    !previousGamePad.IsButtonDown(Buttons.A)))

{

    Jump();

}
```

This approach ensures your game reacts appropriately regardless of input method.

Best Practices for Reliable Input Handling

1. **Always track previous and current states** for each input device.
2. **Differentiate between just pressed and held** to prevent repeated triggers where undesired.
3. **Normalize movements** with `gameTime.ElapsedGameTime` to achieve frame-rate independent behavior.
4. **Abstract input to actions** rather than device-specific keys/buttons, so game logic can remain consistent and device-agnostic.
5. **Test across platforms** to ensure touch, keyboard, mouse, and controllers all produce the intended behavior.

What This Enables

By carefully handling input states and linking them to game logic:

- Players experience **responsive, precise controls**.
- Actions like jumping, shooting, and movement feel **intuitive and consistent**.
- Cross-platform input is easier to implement, allowing your game to run smoothly on desktop, console, or mobile devices.

This foundation prepares you to build robust gameplay systems, menus, and interactive experiences without worrying about input glitches or inconsistent behavior.

Chapter 4: Game Objects, Movement & Collisions

You'll create game objects that move and interact. You'll implement collision detection and responses, making your games feel alive. By the end, your gameplay mechanics will be solid and ready for expansion.

4.1 Game Objects & Entities — Basic Classes

Every game is made up of **objects**: players, enemies, projectiles, power-ups, and interactive scenery. In MonoGame, organizing these into **entities** or **game objects** with clean classes helps manage complexity, reuse code, and separate responsibilities.

Instead of scattering position, texture, and behavior logic across your Game1 class, encapsulate each object in its own class. This makes your code modular, easier to extend, and more maintainable.

Defining a Basic Game Object

A basic game object typically has:

- **Position**: Where it is on the screen (Vector2).
- **Texture**: What it looks like (Texture2D).
- **Update Logic**: How it moves, interacts, or animates.
- **Draw Logic**: How it renders on the screen.

Here's a simple example:

```csharp
using Microsoft.Xna.Framework;

using Microsoft.Xna.Framework.Graphics;

public class GameObject

{

    public Texture2D Texture { get; set; }

    public Vector2 Position { get; set; }

    public Vector2 Velocity { get; set; }


    public GameObject(Texture2D texture, Vector2
position)

    {

        Texture = texture;

        Position = position;

        Velocity = Vector2.Zero;

    }

    public virtual void Update(GameTime gameTime)

    {

        // Basic movement

        Position += Velocity *
(float)gameTime.ElapsedGameTime.TotalSeconds;

    }

    public virtual void Draw(SpriteBatch
spriteBatch)
```

```
    {
        spriteBatch.Draw(Texture, Position,
Color.White);

    }

}
```

Here:

- Texture stores the image.
- Position tracks location.
- Velocity controls movement.
- Update changes the position each frame.
- Draw renders the object on screen using SpriteBatch.

The virtual keyword allows derived classes to **override behavior**, making it flexible for specialized objects like enemies or bullets.

Creating Specific Entities

You can create subclasses for specific game objects. For example, a player character:

```
public class Player : GameObject

{

    public int Health { get; set; }

    public Player(Texture2D texture, Vector2
position)

        : base(texture, position)

    {
```

```csharp
        Health = 100;

    }

    public override void Update(GameTime
gameTime)

    {

        // Custom logic: move player based on
keyboard input

        KeyboardState keyboard =
Keyboard.GetState();

        float speed = 200f *
(float)gameTime.ElapsedGameTime.TotalSeconds;

        if (keyboard.IsKeyDown(Keys.W))
Position.Y -= speed;

        if (keyboard.IsKeyDown(Keys.S))
Position.Y += speed;

        if (keyboard.IsKeyDown(Keys.A))
Position.X -= speed;

        if (keyboard.IsKeyDown(Keys.D))
Position.X += speed;


        base.Update(gameTime);

    }

}
```

And a simple enemy:

```
public class Enemy : GameObject

{

    public Enemy(Texture2D texture, Vector2
position)

        : base(texture, position) { }

    public override void Update(GameTime
gameTime)

    {

        // Move enemy down the screen
automatically

        Velocity = new Vector2(0, 100f);

        base.Update(gameTime);

    }

}
```

Managing Multiple Game Objects

You often have many objects on screen. Using a `List<GameObject>` makes it easy to manage updates and draws:

```
List<GameObject> gameObjects = new
List<GameObject>();

protected override void LoadContent()

{

    Texture2D playerTexture =
Content.Load<Texture2D>("player");
```

```csharp
    Texture2D enemyTexture =
Content.Load<Texture2D>("enemy");


    gameObjects.Add(new Player(playerTexture, new
Vector2(100, 100)));

    gameObjects.Add(new Enemy(enemyTexture, new
Vector2(200, 0)));

}

protected override void Update(GameTime gameTime)

{

    foreach (var obj in gameObjects)

    {

        obj.Update(gameTime);

    }

    base.Update(gameTime);

}

protected override void Draw(GameTime gameTime)

{

    GraphicsDevice.Clear(Color.CornflowerBlue);

    _spriteBatch.Begin();

    foreach (var obj in gameObjects)

    {

        obj.Draw(_spriteBatch);
```

```
    }

    _spriteBatch.End();


    base.Draw(gameTime);
}
```

This approach scales to dozens or hundreds of objects while keeping your Game1 class clean.

Benefits of Using Classes for Game Objects

1. **Encapsulation**: Each object manages its own state and behavior.
2. **Reusability**: You can reuse classes for different objects.
3. **Extensibility**: Subclasses allow specialized behavior (player, enemy, projectile).
4. **Maintainability**: Cleaner code structure, easier to debug, update, or add new features.

By defining basic game object classes and extending them for specific entities, you create a strong foundation for building any type of 2D game — from platformers to shooters.

4.2 Movement & Velocity

Movement is one of the core aspects of gameplay. In MonoGame, movement is typically handled by modifying a game object's **position** over time. To make movement smooth and consistent across different frame rates, we use **velocity**combined with GameTime.

Understanding Velocity

Velocity is a vector that represents **speed and direction**. A positive X value moves the object right, negative moves it left; a positive Y value moves it down, negative moves it up. Using velocity allows you to separate **movement logic** from **position updates**, making your code more modular and easier to extend.

Implementing Basic Velocity

Start with a simple GameObject that has a Velocity property:

```
public class GameObject

{

    public Texture2D Texture { get; set; }

    public Vector2 Position { get; set; }

    public Vector2 Velocity { get; set; }


    public GameObject(Texture2D texture, Vector2
position)

    {

        Texture = texture;

        Position = position;

        Velocity = Vector2.Zero;

    }

    public virtual void Update(GameTime gameTime)

    {
```

```
        Position += Velocity *
(float)gameTime.ElapsedGameTime.TotalSeconds;

    }

    public virtual void Draw(SpriteBatch spriteBatch)

    {

        spriteBatch.Draw(Texture, Position,
Color.White);

    }

}
```

Notice the multiplication by (float)gameTime.ElapsedGameTime.TotalSeconds. This ensures **frame-rate independent movement**. Without it, movement speed would vary depending on the frame rate, making the game feel inconsistent on different machines.

Controlling Movement with Input

You can adjust Velocity based on input:

```
protected override void Update(GameTime gameTime)

{

    float speed = 200f; // pixels per second

    _player.Velocity = Vector2.Zero;


    KeyboardState keyboard = Keyboard.GetState();
```

```
    if (keyboard.IsKeyDown(Keys.W))
_player.Velocity.Y = -speed;

    if (keyboard.IsKeyDown(Keys.S))
_player.Velocity.Y = speed;

    if (keyboard.IsKeyDown(Keys.A))
_player.Velocity.X = -speed;

    if (keyboard.IsKeyDown(Keys.D))
_player.Velocity.X = speed;

    _player.Update(gameTime);


    base.Update(gameTime);

}
```

Here:

- Velocity is reset each frame to zero.
- Input determines the new velocity.
- Position is updated smoothly using the velocity and elapsed time.

Combining Velocity for Complex Motion

You can combine multiple velocity components for more complex movement, such as diagonal motion or moving platforms:

```
Vector2 wind = new Vector2(50f, 0f); // constant wind
pushing right

Vector2 gravity = new Vector2(0f, 300f); // gravity
pulling down

_player.Velocity += wind + gravity;
```

```
_player.Update(gameTime);
```

This allows you to simulate realistic physics or environmental effects without hardcoding positions.

Velocity Limits and Friction

Sometimes, you want to limit speed or simulate friction:

```
float maxSpeed = 300f;

if (_player.Velocity.Length() > maxSpeed)

{

    _player.Velocity.Normalize();

    _player.Velocity *= maxSpeed;

}

// Apply friction

float friction = 0.9f;

_player.Velocity *= friction;
```

- Normalizing ensures the vector maintains direction while limiting magnitude.
- Multiplying by friction gradually slows down the object when no input is applied.

Applying Velocity to Multiple Objects

If you have a list of game objects:

```
foreach (var obj in gameObjects)

{
```

```
obj.Velocity += new Vector2(0, 100f); // gravity

obj.Update(gameTime);

}
```

Each object can have its own independent velocity and movement behavior, making your game modular and scalable.

Summary

- Velocity represents speed and direction.
- Use gameTime.ElapsedGameTime.TotalSeconds for frame-independent movement.
- Combine input and environmental factors to control velocity.
- Apply limits and friction to simulate realistic motion.
- Encapsulate movement logic in your GameObject class for reusability.

Mastering velocity and movement lays the foundation for smooth player control, enemy AI, and interactive environments, making your game feel professional and responsive.

4.3 Collision Detection (Bounding Box & Circles)

Collision detection is a fundamental part of any game. It allows objects to interact with each other — a player hitting an enemy, a projectile striking a target, or a character colliding with walls. In 2D games, the most common methods are **bounding boxes** and **circles**, offering a balance between simplicity and performance.

Bounding Box Collision

A bounding box is a rectangle that fully encloses a game object. MonoGame provides the `Rectangle` struct, which makes it easy to check for overlaps.

Example: Rectangle Collision

```
public class GameObject
{
    public Texture2D Texture { get; set; }
    public Vector2 Position { get; set; }
    public Rectangle BoundingBox => new Rectangle(
        (int)Position.X,
        (int)Position.Y,
        Texture.Width,
        Texture.Height
    );
    public void Draw(SpriteBatch spriteBatch)
    {
        spriteBatch.Draw(Texture, Position,
Color.White);
    }
}
```

To detect a collision between two objects:

```
if (player.BoundingBox.Intersects(enemy.BoundingBox))
```

```
{

    player.TakeDamage(10);

}
```

- BoundingBox converts the object's position and texture size into a Rectangle.
- Intersects returns true if the rectangles overlap.

Bounding boxes are **fast and simple**, ideal for most 2D games, especially for rectangular objects.

Circle Collision

Sometimes a circular approximation is more appropriate, for example with projectiles, round enemies, or circular shields. Circle collisions are based on the **distance between centers**.

Example: Circle Collision

```
public class GameObject

{

    public Texture2D Texture { get; set; }

    public Vector2 Position { get; set; }

    public float Radius => Texture.Width / 2f;

    public void Draw(SpriteBatch spriteBatch)

    {

        spriteBatch.Draw(Texture, Position - new
Vector2(Radius), Color.White);

    }
```

```
}
```

Check collision between two circles:

```
float   distance   =   Vector2.Distance(player.Position,
enemy.Position);

if (distance < player.Radius + enemy.Radius)

{

    player.TakeDamage(10);

}
```

- Vector2.Distance calculates the distance between centers.
- If the distance is less than the sum of the radii, the circles overlap.

Circle collisions can be **more accurate for round objects** and can feel more natural for movement-based interactions.

Combining Methods

You can use both methods depending on the situation:

- **Bounding boxes** for fast, general-purpose collision (walls, platforms, rectangles).
- **Circles** for characters, projectiles, or objects that rotate.

Example with both:

```
bool collided =
player.BoundingBox.Intersects(enemy.BoundingBox) ||

                Vector2.Distance(player.Position,
enemy.Position) < player.Radius + enemy.Radius;
```

```
if (collided)

{

    player.TakeDamage(10);

}
```

This approach ensures robust collision detection while maintaining performance.

Tips for Efficient Collision Detection

1. **Use simple shapes**: Rectangles and circles are faster than pixel-perfect collision.
2. **Spatial partitioning**: For games with many objects, divide the world into sectors or use quad-trees to reduce the number of checks.
3. **Update only moving objects**: Static objects don't need repeated collision checks.
4. **Debug visualization**: Draw bounding boxes or circles during development to verify collisions:

```
Texture2D rectTexture = new Texture2D(GraphicsDevice,
1, 1);

rectTexture.SetData(new[] { Color.White });

_spriteBatch.Draw(rectTexture, player.BoundingBox,
Color.Red * 0.5f);
```

5. **Frame-rate independence**: Ensure collision checks consider the object's movement per frame for accurate results.

What This Enables

Mastering bounding box and circle collisions allows you to:

- Detect player-enemy interactions
- Trigger events like damage, scoring, or item collection
- Handle physics-like interactions, such as bouncing or blocking movement
- Build the foundation for more advanced collision systems in 2D games

By combining simple shapes and smart update logic, you can implement **fast, reliable collision detection** that scales well even in games with many objects.

4.4 Collision Response & Game Logic

Detecting a collision is only half the task. The next step is **responding to collisions** in a meaningful way: stopping movement, bouncing objects, applying damage, or triggering events. Proper collision response ensures your game feels realistic, fair, and enjoyable.

Basic Collision Response

Once a collision is detected (using bounding boxes or circles), you need to decide how your objects will react. The simplest approach is **position correction**, where you prevent objects from overlapping.

Example: Stopping Movement on Collision

```csharp
public void HandleCollision(GameObject player,
GameObject wall)

{

    if
(player.BoundingBox.Intersects(wall.BoundingBox))

    {

        // Simple response: stop vertical movement

        if (player.Position.Y + player.Texture.Height
> wall.Position.Y &&

            player.Position.Y < wall.Position.Y)

        {

            player.Position.Y = wall.Position.Y -
player.Texture.Height;

            player.Velocity.Y = 0f;

        }

        // Stop horizontal movement

        if (player.Position.X + player.Texture.Width
> wall.Position.X &&

            player.Position.X < wall.Position.X)

        {

            player.Position.X = wall.Position.X -
player.Texture.Width;

            player.Velocity.X = 0f;
```

```
        }

    }

}
```

Here, the player's position is corrected to prevent passing through walls, and velocity is reset to avoid sliding through the object.

Bouncing Objects

For objects like balls or projectiles, you may want them to bounce off surfaces. This is done by inverting the relevant velocity component:

```
if (ball.BoundingBox.Intersects(wall.BoundingBox))

{

    // Bounce vertically

    ball.Velocity.Y *= -1;

    // Correct position to avoid sticking

    if (ball.Position.Y < wall.Position.Y)

        ball.Position.Y = wall.Position.Y -
ball.Texture.Height;

    else

        ball.Position.Y = wall.Position.Y +
wall.Texture.Height;

}
```

Bouncing can add realism to physics-based gameplay like platformers, pong-style games, or projectile simulations.

Applying Damage or Game Events

Collisions are often tied to game logic, such as taking damage, collecting items, or triggering effects:

```
if (player.BoundingBox.Intersects(enemy.BoundingBox))

{

    player.Health -= 10;

    KnockBack(player, enemy);

}

if (player.BoundingBox.Intersects(coin.BoundingBox))

{

    player.Score += 100;

    coin.IsCollected = true;

}
```

- Player-enemy collision reduces health and can trigger knockback.
- Player-coin collision increases score and flags the item as collected.

Knockback Example

```
public void KnockBack(GameObject player, GameObject enemy)

{

    Vector2 direction = player.Position - enemy.Position;

    direction.Normalize();
```

```
    player.Position += direction * 20f; // push
player away

}
```

This adds a physical sense of impact when the player hits or is hit by an enemy.

Handling Multiple Collisions

For games with many objects, iterate over all potential collisions each frame:

```
foreach (var obj in gameObjects)

{

    if (obj != player &&
player.BoundingBox.Intersects(obj.BoundingBox))

    {

        HandleCollision(player, obj);

    }

}
```

Using an **input-state-aware update loop**, you can ensure that player actions, movement, and collisions are processed consistently each frame.

Best Practices for Collision Response

1. **Separate detection and response**: Keep collision checks independent from how the objects react.
2. **Use velocity for corrections**: Avoid teleporting objects unless necessary; adjust positions gradually for smoother behavior.

3. **Consider edge cases**: Objects moving fast can "tunnel" through other objects; handle large movements by splitting updates into smaller steps.
4. **Tie collisions to game logic**: Health, scoring, animations, sounds, and events should be triggered here.
5. **Debug visualizations**: Draw bounding boxes or collision circles to fine-tune response logic during development.

What This Enables

By handling collision response properly, your game can:

- Prevent players from passing through walls
- Add physics-based interactions like bouncing and knockback
- Trigger game events such as damage, pickups, or special effects
- Make gameplay feel polished, predictable, and responsive

Collision response turns raw collision data into **meaningful interactions**, forming the core of gameplay mechanics in 2D games.

4.5 Organizing Game Objects & Managers

As your game grows, managing dozens or hundreds of objects directly in the Game1 class becomes unmanageable. To maintain clean, modular, and maintainable code, you should **organize game objects using managers**. Managers handle updating, drawing, and grouping related entities, allowing you to focus on game logic rather than bookkeeping.

Why Use Game Object Managers

Without managers, your Update() and Draw() methods quickly become cluttered:

```
player.Update(gameTime);

enemy1.Update(gameTime);

enemy2.Update(gameTime);

bullet1.Update(gameTime);

bullet2.Update(gameTime);
```

Using a manager:

- Reduces repetitive code
- Centralizes creation, update, and cleanup of objects
- Simplifies collision handling and event triggering
- Makes your game scalable to dozens or hundreds of entities

Creating a Basic Game Object Manager

A simple GameObjectManager class can maintain a list of objects and handle updating and drawing them:

```
using Microsoft.Xna.Framework;

using Microsoft.Xna.Framework.Graphics;

using System.Collections.Generic;

public class GameObjectManager

{

    private List<GameObject> _objects;

    public GameObjectManager()
```

```csharp
    {
        _objects = new List<GameObject>();
    }

    public void Add(GameObject obj) =>
_objects.Add(obj);

    public void Remove(GameObject obj) =>
_objects.Remove(obj);


    public void Update(GameTime gameTime)
    {
        for (int i = 0; i < _objects.Count; i++)
        {
            _objects[i].Update(gameTime);
        }
    }

    public void Draw(SpriteBatch spriteBatch)
    {
        foreach (var obj in _objects)
        {
            obj.Draw(spriteBatch);
        }
    }
```

```
}
```

This manager abstracts the repetitive work of updating and drawing each object.

Using the Manager in Game1

private GameObjectManager _gameObjectManager;

```
protected override void Initialize()

{

    _gameObjectManager = new GameObjectManager();

    base.Initialize();

}



protected override void LoadContent()

{

                Texture2D      playerTexture      =
Content.Load<Texture2D>("player");

                Texture2D      enemyTexture      =
Content.Load<Texture2D>("enemy");


    _gameObjectManager.Add(new Player(playerTexture,
new Vector2(100, 100)));
```

```
        _gameObjectManager.Add(new  Enemy(enemyTexture,
new Vector2(200, 0)));

}

protected override void Update(GameTime gameTime)

{

    _gameObjectManager.Update(gameTime);

    base.Update(gameTime);

}



protected override void Draw(GameTime gameTime)

{

    GraphicsDevice.Clear(Color.CornflowerBlue);

    _spriteBatch.Begin();

    _gameObjectManager.Draw(_spriteBatch);

    _spriteBatch.End();

    base.Draw(gameTime);

}
```

Now, adding, removing, or updating objects no longer clutters Game1. You can simply modify the manager.

Extending Managers for Different Object Types

For larger games, you may want specialized managers:

- **EnemyManager**: Handles enemy spawning, AI updates, and collision checks
- **ProjectileManager**: Tracks bullets, missiles, or spells
- **PickupManager**: Manages coins, health packs, and power-ups

Example: EnemyManager with automatic removal of off-screen enemies:

```csharp
public class EnemyManager

{

    private List<Enemy> _enemies;


    public EnemyManager()

    {

        _enemies = new List<Enemy>();

    }


    public void Add(Enemy enemy) =>
_enemies.Add(enemy);


    public void Update(GameTime gameTime)

    {

        for (int i = _enemies.Count - 1; i >= 0; i--)

        {
```

```
        _enemies[i].Update(gameTime);


        // Remove enemies that moved off-screen

        if (_enemies[i].Position.Y > 800)

            _enemies.RemoveAt(i);

    }

}

public void Draw(SpriteBatch spriteBatch)

{

    foreach (var enemy in _enemies)

        enemy.Draw(spriteBatch);

    }

}
```

Specialized managers let you **optimize performance**, as you can implement object pooling, culling, or event-driven updates without touching unrelated objects.

Best Practices

1. **Separate logic by type**: Group similar objects together (enemies, projectiles, pickups).
2. **Centralize updates and draws**: Avoid scattering update/draw calls across Game1.
3. **Use object pooling for frequent objects**: Reduces garbage collection and improves performance.

4. **Handle collisions at the manager level**: This simplifies interaction logic and prevents repeated code.
5. **Keep managers modular**: Each manager should be responsible only for its objects, allowing easy reuse in other projects.

What This Enables

With game object managers, your game architecture becomes:

- **Modular**: Each manager encapsulates its objects and behavior.
- **Maintainable**: Adding new object types or behaviors does not clutter main game logic.
- **Scalable**: Easily handles dozens, hundreds, or even thousands of objects without messy Update() loops.

Organizing your game objects using managers is a cornerstone of **professional, maintainable game design**, setting the stage for more complex mechanics, AI, and interactions.

Chapter 5: Audio — Sound Effects & Music

You'll add sounds that respond to player actions and create immersive background music. You'll manage volume, muting, and performance for smooth gameplay. By the end, your games will sound as good as they play.

5.1 Loading & Playing Sound Effects

Sound effects are essential to make your game **feel alive**. From footsteps and gunshots to collisions and power-ups, well-timed audio enhances player feedback and immersion. MonoGame provides a straightforward way to load and play sound effects using the `SoundEffect` and `SoundEffectInstance` classes.

Preparing Sound Effects

Before you can use sound effects, you need:

1. **Audio files**: MonoGame supports WAV files for `SoundEffect`. For smaller effects, WAV is recommended due to minimal latency.
2. **Content Pipeline**: Add the sound files to your Content project in MonoGame, so they can be loaded efficiently at runtime.

Example structure:

```
Content/
```

```
Sounds/

    jump.wav

    explosion.wav

    shoot.wav
```

Loading Sound Effects

Use the `Content.Load<SoundEffect>()` method to load sounds into your game:

```
using Microsoft.Xna.Framework.Audio;


// Declare variables

private SoundEffect _jumpSound;

private SoundEffect _explosionSound;

private SoundEffect _shootSound;

protected override void LoadContent()

{

    _jumpSound =
Content.Load<SoundEffect>("Sounds/jump");

    _explosionSound =
Content.Load<SoundEffect>("Sounds/explosion");

    _shootSound =
Content.Load<SoundEffect>("Sounds/shoot");

}
```

- Omit the file extension when loading through the Content Pipeline.

- Assign each SoundEffect to a variable for easy access.

Playing Sound Effects

The simplest way to play a sound effect is using the Play() method:

```
// Play jump sound when player jumps
if (_input.IsActionPressed("Jump"))
{
    _jumpSound.Play();
}
```

Play() is **fire-and-forget**, meaning it plays immediately and does not require further management. This is suitable for most short sound effects.

Controlling Volume, Pitch, and Pan

MonoGame allows adjusting sound properties:

```
// Play sound with custom settings
float volume = 0.7f;    // 0.0f (silent) to 1.0f
(full volume)

float pitch = 0.2f;      // -1.0f (low) to 1.0f
(high)

float pan = -0.5f;       // -1.0f (left) to 1.0f
(right)

_shootSound.Play(volume, pitch, pan);
```

- volume: Adjusts loudness.

- `pitch`: Changes the playback pitch (can simulate variation).
- `pan`: Controls stereo balance, useful for spatial effects.

Using SoundEffectInstance for Advanced Control

For looping or stopping a sound mid-play, create a `SoundEffectInstance`:

```
SoundEffectInstance explosionInstance =
_explosionSound.CreateInstance();

// Play once

explosionInstance.Play();

// Stop immediately if needed

explosionInstance.Stop();

// Looping

explosionInstance.IsLooped = true;

explosionInstance.Play();
```

`SoundEffectInstance` is ideal for:

- Background ambient sounds
- Looped effects like engines or alarms
- Controlling playback dynamically (pause, resume, stop)

Best Practices

1. **Preload important sounds**: Load frequently used sounds during `LoadContent()` to avoid lag.
2. **Reuse `SoundEffectInstance`**: For looping or repeated sounds, avoid recreating instances every frame.

3. **Keep file sizes small**: Short, compressed WAV files reduce memory usage.
4. **Manage audio channels**: Limit simultaneous sounds if targeting low-end devices to prevent clipping or performance issues.
5. **Spatialize audio**: Use pan and pitch adjustments to add depth and immersion.

Putting It All Together

Example integrating sound into gameplay:

```
protected override void Update(GameTime gameTime)
{
    _input.Update();
    // Jump sound
    if (_input.IsActionPressed("Jump"))
        _jumpSound.Play();
    // Shooting
    if (_input.IsActionPressed("Shoot"))
        _shootSound.Play(0.8f, 0.0f, 0.0f);
    base.Update(gameTime);
}
```

With this approach, your game reacts audibly to player actions, collisions, and other events, creating a **more engaging experience**.

5.2 Background Music & Looping

Background music gives your game **atmosphere, emotion, and rhythm**. Unlike short sound effects, music tracks are longer and often looped to provide continuous ambiance. MonoGame uses the Song class in combination with the MediaPlayer to manage background music efficiently.

Preparing Music Files

MonoGame supports music files through the **Content Pipeline**. For best results:

1. Use MP3 or WMA files for long tracks (WAV files are too large for music).
2. Add the files to your Content project under a folder like Content/Music/.
3. Example structure:

```
Content/
  Music/
      background.mp3
      battle_theme.mp3
```

Loading Music

Unlike SoundEffect, music tracks are loaded using the Song class:

```
using Microsoft.Xna.Framework.Media;

// Declare variables

private Song _backgroundMusic;
```

```
protected override void LoadContent()

{

    _backgroundMusic =
Content.Load<Song>("Music/background");

}
```

- Omit the file extension when loading via the Content Pipeline.
- Assign each track to a variable for easy access.

Playing Music

MonoGame plays music using the `MediaPlayer`:

```
MediaPlayer.Play(_backgroundMusic);

MediaPlayer.Volume = 0.5f;  // 0.0f (mute) to
1.0f (full volume)

MediaPlayer.IsRepeating = true; // Enable looping
```

- `Play()` starts the track.
- `IsRepeating` controls looping; set it to `true` for continuous playback.
- `Volume` adjusts loudness globally.

Controlling Music Playback

The `MediaPlayer` also provides functions to control playback dynamically:

```
// Pause music
```

```
MediaPlayer.Pause();

// Resume music

MediaPlayer.Resume();

// Stop music completely

MediaPlayer.Stop();

// Switch tracks

MediaPlayer.Play(battleThemeSong);
```

You can change music tracks dynamically during gameplay, for example, transitioning from exploration to battle music.

Smooth Looping Considerations

For seamless looping:

1. Trim silence at the start and end of tracks.
2. Avoid abrupt cuts; use fade-in/fade-out transitions if desired.
3. Set `IsRepeating = true` to automatically loop without additional logic.

Integrating Music with Game Logic

Music can react to game events to enhance immersion:

```
if (player.IsInBattle && MediaPlayer.Queue.ActiveSong
!= battleTheme)

{

    MediaPlayer.Play(battleTheme);

    MediaPlayer.IsRepeating = true;

}
```

```
else if (!player.IsInBattle &&
MediaPlayer.Queue.ActiveSong != backgroundMusic)

{

    MediaPlayer.Play(backgroundMusic);

    MediaPlayer.IsRepeating = true;

}
```

This approach ensures music dynamically reflects gameplay state.

Best Practices

1. **Load music in** `LoadContent()` to prevent runtime lag.
2. **Control volume separately** from sound effects for better audio balance.
3. **Loop strategically**: background tracks should loop seamlessly without drawing attention to repetition.
4. **Use multiple tracks** for variety; change tracks based on game context or events.
5. **Avoid overloading devices**: mobile platforms may have limitations on simultaneous audio streams.

Putting It All Together

Example `Update()` integration:

```
protected override void Update(GameTime gameTime)

{

    // Play exploration music if not already playing

    if (!player.InCombat && MediaPlayer.State !=
MediaState.Playing)
```

```
    {

        MediaPlayer.Play(_backgroundMusic);

        MediaPlayer.IsRepeating = true;

        MediaPlayer.Volume = 0.5f;

    }

    // Handle game logic...

    base.Update(gameTime);

}
```

By carefully managing playback, looping, and transitions, your game can maintain **immersive, continuous audio** that enhances the player experience.

5.3 Audio Management (Volume, Mute)

In any game, giving the player control over audio is crucial for accessibility and comfort. MonoGame provides simple tools for **adjusting volume**, **muting**, and **separately controlling music and sound effects**. Proper audio management improves player experience and makes your game feel polished.

Controlling Sound Effect Volume

Each SoundEffect can have its volume adjusted individually when calling Play():

```
float volume = 0.7f; // 0.0f (silent) to 1.0f (full volume)

float pitch = 0.0f;  // -1.0f (low) to 1.0f (high)
```

```
float pan = 0.0f;     // -1.0f (left) to 1.0f (right)

_shootSound.Play(volume, pitch, pan);
```

This allows you to balance effects like explosions, footsteps, and shooting without affecting other sounds.

For repeated sounds or looping effects, use a SoundEffectInstance:

```
SoundEffectInstance engineLoop =
_engineSound.CreateInstance();

engineLoop.Volume = 0.5f;

engineLoop.IsLooped = true;

engineLoop.Play();
```

Adjust the Volume property dynamically to respond to game events (e.g., reduce volume when player is underwater or in a quiet zone).

Controlling Background Music Volume

Background music is managed with MediaPlayer:

```
MediaPlayer.Volume = 0.3f;     // 0.0f (silent) to 1.0f
(full volume)

MediaPlayer.IsMuted = false;   // true to mute all
music
```

MediaPlayer.Volume affects all currently playing songs globally, allowing you to fade music in or out programmatically.

Implementing Mute Functionality

A toggle for mute can be added for both music and effects:

```
bool isMuted = false;

public void ToggleMute()

{

    isMuted = !isMuted;

    // Mute background music

    MediaPlayer.IsMuted = isMuted;

    // Mute sound effects (example for all effects)

    foreach (var sfx in allSoundEffects)

    {

        sfx.Play(isMuted ? 0.0f : 1.0f, 0.0f, 0.0f);

    }

}
```

This approach allows players to quickly mute or unmute audio without changing individual settings.

Implementing Volume Sliders

You can integrate in-game sliders to let players adjust volume:

```
// Example: adjusting volume dynamically

MediaPlayer.Volume = musicSliderValue;        //
0.0f to 1.0f

engineLoop.Volume = sfxSliderValue;           //
0.0f to 1.0f
```

- musicSliderValue and sfxSliderValue can come from UI sliders.
- This allows separate control of music and sound effects, a standard in modern games.

Dynamic Volume Adjustments

Volume can also react to game events:

```
// Fade out music over 3 seconds

float fadeDuration = 3.0f;

float startVolume = MediaPlayer.Volume;

float elapsedTime = 0.0f;

protected override void Update(GameTime gameTime)

{

    elapsedTime +=
(float)gameTime.ElapsedGameTime.TotalSeconds;

    MediaPlayer.Volume =
MathHelper.Clamp(startVolume * (1 - elapsedTime /
fadeDuration), 0f, 1f);

}
```

This technique is useful for transitioning between gameplay states, cutscenes, or entering/exiting special areas.

Best Practices

1. **Separate music and sound effects**: Allows independent control and better audio balance.
2. **Provide sliders and mute options**: Players expect accessible audio controls.
3. **Fade audio smoothly**: Abrupt changes can feel jarring.
4. **Cap volume**: Ensure combined sound levels don't clip or become uncomfortably loud.
5. **Update volume dynamically**: Tie volume to gameplay events for immersion.

Putting It All Together

Example integration:

```
protected override void Update(GameTime gameTime)

{

    if (_input.IsActionPressed("ToggleMute"))

        ToggleMute();

    // Adjust music and SFX volume based on player
settings

    MediaPlayer.Volume = musicVolumeSlider;

    engineLoop.Volume = sfxVolumeSlider;


    base.Update(gameTime);

}
```

By implementing thoughtful volume control, mute functionality, and dynamic adjustments, your game **feels responsive, accessible, and professional**, enhancing the overall player experience.

5.4 Audio Performance & Optimization

Audio is a critical part of your game's experience, but improperly managed sound can **impact performance**, especially on lower-end devices or mobile platforms. Optimizing audio ensures smooth gameplay while maintaining immersive sound.

Avoiding Performance Pitfalls

Playing too many sounds simultaneously or repeatedly loading audio files at runtime can cause lag, stuttering, or crashes. Common pitfalls include:

- Creating new SoundEffectInstance objects every frame
- Playing large WAV files for long audio tracks
- Overlapping too many sound effects at once

Preloading and Reusing Audio

Always **load all necessary audio in** LoadContent() to prevent runtime loading delays:

```
private SoundEffect _jumpSound;

private SoundEffect _shootSound;

private SoundEffectInstance _engineLoop;

protected override void LoadContent()

{

    _jumpSound =
Content.Load<SoundEffect>("Sounds/jump");

    _shootSound =
Content.Load<SoundEffect>("Sounds/shoot");
```

```
    _engineLoop =
Content.Load<SoundEffect>("Sounds/engine").CreateInst
ance();

    _engineLoop.IsLooped = true;

}
```

- Preloading ensures audio plays immediately when triggered.
- Use SoundEffectInstance for frequently repeated or looping sounds to **reuse memory and resources**.

Limiting Simultaneous Sound Effects

Too many concurrent sounds can overload the audio system. Implement a **cap** on simultaneous effects:

```
private const int MaxSfx = 8;

private List<SoundEffectInstance> activeSfx = new
List<SoundEffectInstance>();

public void PlaySound(SoundEffect sound)

{

    if (activeSfx.Count >= MaxSfx) return;


    var instance = sound.CreateInstance();

    instance.Play();

    activeSfx.Add(instance);

}

// Remove finished sounds

activeSfx.RemoveAll(s => s.State ==
SoundState.Stopped);
```

This prevents audio overload while maintaining gameplay responsiveness.

Using Compressed Audio Files

- **Short sound effects**: WAV files are fine for low-latency playback.
- **Long tracks or music**: Use MP3 or OGG to reduce memory footprint.
- Compressed audio reduces **RAM usage** and speeds up loading times.

Object Pooling for Audio

Frequently played sounds, like gunshots or footsteps, benefit from **object pooling**. Reuse SoundEffectInstance objects instead of creating new ones repeatedly:

```
SoundEffectInstance[] footstepsPool = new
SoundEffectInstance[5];


for (int i = 0; i < footstepsPool.Length; i++)

{

    footstepsPool[i] =
_footstepSound.CreateInstance();

}

public void PlayFootstep()

{

    foreach (var instance in footstepsPool)

    {
```

```
    if (instance.State != SoundState.Playing)

    {

        instance.Play();

        break;

    }

  }

}
```

- Limits garbage collection overhead
- Reduces CPU spikes during gameplay

Volume and Performance

High volume for multiple overlapping sounds can also strain audio processing. Adjust volumes dynamically:

```
float masterVolume = 0.7f;

MediaPlayer.Volume = masterVolume;

foreach (var sfx in activeSfx)

{

    sfx.Volume = masterVolume;

}
```

This not only balances audio but can **slightly reduce processing load** on some devices.

Pausing and Stopping Unneeded Audio

When objects leave the screen or the game is paused, stop or pause sounds to save resources:

```
if (!player.IsActive)

{

    _engineLoop.Pause();

}

else

{

    if (_engineLoop.State != SoundState.Playing)

        _engineLoop.Play();

}
```

Efficiently managing playback ensures only active, relevant audio consumes resources.

Best Practices Summary

1. Preload audio in LoadContent() to avoid runtime delays.
2. Use SoundEffectInstance for reusable or looping sounds.
3. Limit the number of simultaneous sounds.
4. Compress long tracks to reduce memory usage.
5. Use object pooling for frequently repeated effects.
6. Pause or stop sounds when no longer needed.
7. Dynamically manage volume for performance and balance.

Putting It All Together

Example update loop with optimized audio:

```csharp
protected override void Update(GameTime gameTime)
{
    // Play jump sound only if below max
    simultaneous sounds

    if (_input.IsActionPressed("Jump"))

        PlaySound(_jumpSound);

    // Loop engine sound efficiently

    if (_player.IsMoving && _engineLoop.State !=
    SoundState.Playing)

        _engineLoop.Play();

    else if (!_player.IsMoving &&
    _engineLoop.State == SoundState.Playing)

        _engineLoop.Pause();

    base.Update(gameTime);
}
```

By following these strategies, your game's audio **remains responsive, immersive, and performance-friendly**, ensuring smooth gameplay on all platforms.

5.5 Integrating Audio with Game Events

Audio is most effective when it **reacts to gameplay**, providing feedback for actions, events, and state changes. Integrating sound and music with game events makes your game feel alive and responsive, giving players clear cues for interactions, successes, or failures.

Event-Driven Audio

Instead of playing sounds randomly or continuously, tie audio playback directly to game events. Examples of common events include:

- Player actions: jumping, shooting, collecting items
- Enemy actions: spawning, dying, attacking
- Environmental changes: entering new areas, triggering traps
- Game state changes: level start, game over, achievements

Playing Sound Effects on Events

For instance, play a jump sound only when the player jumps:

```
protected override void Update(GameTime gameTime)
{
    _input.Update();

    if (_input.IsActionPressed("Jump"))
    {
        _player.Jump();

        _jumpSound.Play();
    }
    if (_input.IsActionPressed("Shoot"))
    {
        _player.Shoot();
```

```
        _shootSound.Play(0.8f, 0.0f, 0.0f);

    }

    base.Update(gameTime);

}
```

- Sound plays **exactly when the event occurs**, improving responsiveness.
- Adjust volume, pitch, and pan to make repeated effects feel dynamic.

Triggering Sounds for Game Logic

Audio can reinforce gameplay mechanics, such as collecting items or taking damage:

```
foreach (var coin in _coinManager.Coins)

{

    if
(_player.BoundingBox.Intersects(coin.BoundingBox) &&
!coin.IsCollected)

    {

        coin.IsCollected = true;

        _coinCollectSound.Play();

        _player.Score += 100;

    }

}

if
(_player.BoundingBox.Intersects(enemy.BoundingBox))

{
```

```
_player.TakeDamage(10);

_playerHurtSound.Play();
```

}

By attaching sounds directly to game logic, you ensure **clear audio feedback** for player actions.

Background Music and Game States

Music can also respond to gameplay events, like transitioning between exploration and combat:

```
if (_player.IsInCombat &&
MediaPlayer.Queue.ActiveSong != _battleMusic)

{

    MediaPlayer.Play(_battleMusic);

    MediaPlayer.IsRepeating = true;

    MediaPlayer.Volume = 0.5f;

}

else if (!_player.IsInCombat &&
MediaPlayer.Queue.ActiveSong != _explorationMusic)

{

    MediaPlayer.Play(_explorationMusic);

    MediaPlayer.IsRepeating = true;

    MediaPlayer.Volume = 0.4f;

}
```

- Switching music dynamically enhances **immersion and tension**.

- Use `IsRepeating` to ensure seamless looping during prolonged states.

Combining Audio Events

For richer audio feedback, combine multiple audio sources:

```
if (_enemy.IsDefeated)
{
    _enemyDeathSound.Play();
    _explosionEffectSound.Play(0.7f, 0.2f, 0.0f);
}
```

- Multiple sounds can layer to emphasize dramatic events.
- Adjust volumes to prevent clipping or overwhelming the player.

Optimized Event-Driven Audio

To maintain performance:

1. **Preload all audio** in `LoadContent()` to prevent runtime delays.
2. **Reuse** `SoundEffectInstance` for looping or frequently triggered effects.
3. **Limit simultaneous sounds** to avoid audio overload.
4. **Tie playback tightly to events**; avoid continuous polling-based audio triggers.

Putting It All Together

Example integration in the main update loop:

```csharp
protected override void Update(GameTime gameTime)
{
    _input.Update();

    // Player actions
    if (_input.IsActionPressed("Jump"))
    {
        _player.Jump();
        _jumpSound.Play();
    }
    if (_input.IsActionPressed("Shoot"))
    {
        _player.Shoot();
        _shootSound.Play(0.8f, 0.0f, 0.0f);
    }
    // Enemy interactions
    foreach (var enemy in _enemyManager.Enemies)
    {
        if
(_player.BoundingBox.Intersects(enemy.BoundingBox))
        {
            _player.TakeDamage(10);
```

```csharp
            _playerHurtSound.Play();

        }

    }

    // Music transitions

    if (_player.IsInCombat &&
MediaPlayer.Queue.ActiveSong != _battleMusic)

    {

        MediaPlayer.Play(_battleMusic);

        MediaPlayer.IsRepeating = true;

    }

    base.Update(gameTime);

}
```

By linking sounds and music **directly to game events**, you create a responsive, immersive audio experience that enhances gameplay and gives the player clear cues for every action and state.

Chapter 6: UI, Text & Menus

You'll create clear, functional menus and on-screen displays like scores and HUDs. You'll handle user input and make your interface responsive for any screen size. By the end, your games will feel polished and professional.

6.1 Displaying Text & HUDs with SpriteFont

Displaying text in a game is essential for **scores, health bars, instructions, or debug information**. In MonoGame, SpriteFont provides a powerful and flexible way to render text efficiently. Using it, you can create dynamic HUDs (Heads-Up Displays) that update in real-time as the game state changes.

Creating a SpriteFont

Before you can display text, you need a SpriteFont asset:

1. Right-click the **Content** project → Add → New Item → SpriteFont.
2. Name it, e.g., Arial.spritefont.
3. Edit the .spritefont XML file to define font properties:

```
<?xml version="1.0" encoding="utf-8"?>

<SpriteFont
xmlns="http://www.microsoft.com/2003/10/Serialization
/">

  <FontName>Arial</FontName>
```

```
  <Size>24</Size>

  <Spacing>2</Spacing>

  <Style>Regular</Style>

  <CharacterRegions>

    <CharacterRegion>

      <Start> </Start>

      <End>~</End>

    </CharacterRegion>

  </CharacterRegions>

</SpriteFont>
```

- FontName specifies the system font.
- Size sets the font size.
- Spacing allows slight padding between characters.
- CharacterRegions defines which characters to include; this reduces memory usage.

Loading a SpriteFont

Load the font in your LoadContent() method:

```
private SpriteFont _hudFont;

protected override void LoadContent()

{

    _hudFont = Content.Load<SpriteFont>("Arial");

}
```

Now _hudFont can be used for all text rendering in your game.

Drawing Text on Screen

Use `SpriteBatch.DrawString()` to render text:

```
protected override void Draw(GameTime gameTime)
{
    GraphicsDevice.Clear(Color.CornflowerBlue);

    _spriteBatch.Begin();

    string scoreText = $"Score: {_player.Score}";

    Vector2 position = new Vector2(20, 20); //
Top-left corner

    Color color = Color.White;

    _spriteBatch.DrawString(_hudFont, scoreText,
position, color);

    _spriteBatch.End();

    base.Draw(gameTime);
}
```

- `scoreText` can be dynamic, updating each frame.
- `position` determines where the text appears on the screen.
- `color` sets the text color.

Scaling, Rotation, and Effects

`DrawString()` also supports **scaling, rotation, and origin** for more advanced HUD designs:

```
_spriteBatch.DrawString(
    _hudFont,
```

```
    "Game Over!",

    new Vector2(400, 240),   // screen center

    Color.Red,

    0f,                       // rotation

    _hudFont.MeasureString("Game Over!") / 2, //
origin: center text

    2.0f,                     // scale: double size

    SpriteEffects.None,

    0f
);
```

- origin allows centering or aligning text dynamically.
- scale enlarges or shrinks the text.
- rotation and SpriteEffects can create visual flair.

Building a Simple HUD

A typical HUD displays **score, health, and ammo**:

```
protected override void Draw(GameTime gameTime)
{
    GraphicsDevice.Clear(Color.Black);

    _spriteBatch.Begin();

    // Score

    _spriteBatch.DrawString(_hudFont, $"Score:
{_player.Score}", new Vector2(20, 20),
Color.Yellow);
```

```
    // Health

    _spriteBatch.DrawString(_hudFont, $"Health:
{_player.Health}", new Vector2(20, 50),
Color.Red);

    // Ammo

    _spriteBatch.DrawString(_hudFont, $"Ammo:
{_player.Ammo}", new Vector2(20, 80),
Color.Green);

    _spriteBatch.End();

    base.Draw(gameTime);

}
```

This simple structure allows your HUD to **update dynamically** as the player's stats change, keeping information clear and accessible.

Best Practices

1. **Use a single SpriteFont per HUD**: Reduces draw calls and memory usage.
2. **Pre-calculate positions** for static HUD elements to avoid per-frame calculations.
3. **Measure string length** if you need centered or right-aligned text:

```
Vector2 textSize =
_hudFont.MeasureString(scoreText);

Vector2 position = new
Vector2(GraphicsDevice.Viewport.Width -
textSize.X - 20, 20);
```

4. **Use contrasting colors** for readability over game backgrounds.
5. **Minimize font size changes** during gameplay to reduce draw overhead.

Putting It All Together

By combining dynamic text updates with well-placed HUD elements, you can provide players with **instant feedback**, enhancing gameplay and player engagement.

6.2 Basic Buttons & Menu Systems

Interactive buttons and menus are essential for **game navigation**, including start screens, options, and pause menus. In MonoGame, buttons can be implemented with **sprites, rectangles, and input detection**, creating a responsive UI for your game.

Creating a Simple Button

A button typically consists of:

- A **visual representation**: a texture or colored rectangle
- A **text label**: optional, often using `SpriteFont`
- **Click detection**: responding to player input

Here's a basic button class:

```
using Microsoft.Xna.Framework;

using Microsoft.Xna.Framework.Graphics;

using Microsoft.Xna.Framework.Input;
```

```csharp
public class Button

{

    public Texture2D Texture;

    public Vector2 Position;

    public Rectangle Bounds => new
Rectangle((int)Position.X, (int)Position.Y,
Texture.Width, Texture.Height);

    public string Text;

    private SpriteFont _font;


    public Button(Texture2D texture, Vector2
position, string text, SpriteFont font)

    {

        Texture = texture;

        Position = position;

        Text = text;

        _font = font;

    }

    public bool IsClicked(MouseState mouseState,
MouseState previousMouseState)

    {

        if (Bounds.Contains(mouseState.Position) &&
mouseState.LeftButton == ButtonState.Pressed &&

            previousMouseState.LeftButton ==
ButtonState.Released)

        {
```

```
        return true;

    }

    return false;

}

public void Draw(SpriteBatch spriteBatch)

{

    spriteBatch.Draw(Texture, Position,
Color.White);

    if (!string.IsNullOrEmpty(Text))

    {

        Vector2 textSize =
_font.MeasureString(Text);

        Vector2 textPosition = new Vector2(

            Position.X + (Texture.Width -
textSize.X) / 2,

            Position.Y + (Texture.Height -
textSize.Y) / 2

        );

        spriteBatch.DrawString(_font, Text,
textPosition, Color.Black);

    }

}

}
```

- The IsClicked method checks for **mouse clicks** within the button bounds.
- Text is centered automatically on the button.

Integrating Buttons into a Menu

Create a simple main menu with multiple buttons:

```
private Button _startButton;

private Button _optionsButton;

private MouseState _previousMouseState;

protected override void LoadContent()

{

    Texture2D buttonTexture = new
Texture2D(GraphicsDevice, 200, 50);

    Color[] data = new Color[200 * 50];

    for (int i = 0; i < data.Length; ++i) data[i] =
Color.Gray;

    buttonTexture.SetData(data);

    SpriteFont font =
Content.Load<SpriteFont>("Arial");

    _startButton = new Button(buttonTexture, new
Vector2(300, 200), "Start Game", font);

    _optionsButton = new Button(buttonTexture, new
Vector2(300, 300), "Options", font);

}
```

Detecting Button Clicks

Check for clicks inside the Update method:

```
protected override void Update(GameTime gameTime)

{

    MouseState mouseState = Mouse.GetState();
```

```
    if (_startButton.IsClicked(mouseState,
_previousMouseState))

    {

        // Start the game

        _currentScreen = GameScreen.Playing;

    }

    if (_optionsButton.IsClicked(mouseState,
_previousMouseState))

    {

        // Open options menu

        _currentScreen = GameScreen.Options;

    }

    _previousMouseState = mouseState;

    base.Update(gameTime);

}
```

- previousMouseState ensures clicks are detected **only
  once per press**, preventing multiple triggers per frame.

Drawing the Menu

Render buttons in the Draw method:

```
protected override void Draw(GameTime gameTime)

{

    GraphicsDevice.Clear(Color.CornflowerBlue);

    _spriteBatch.Begin();
```

```csharp
    if (_currentScreen == GameScreen.Menu)

    {

        _startButton.Draw(_spriteBatch);

        _optionsButton.Draw(_spriteBatch);

    }

    _spriteBatch.End();

    base.Draw(gameTime);

}
```

- Only draw buttons for the active menu screen.
- You can extend this to pause menus, settings, or in-game UI.

Enhancing Buttons

- **Hover effect**: Change button color when the mouse is over it.
- **Sound feedback**: Play a sound when clicked.
- **Keyboard navigation**: Support arrow keys and Enter for accessibility.

Example hover effect:

```csharp
public void Draw(SpriteBatch spriteBatch,
MouseState mouseState)

{

    Color color =
Bounds.Contains(mouseState.Position) ?
Color.LightGray : Color.Gray;

    spriteBatch.Draw(Texture, Position, color);
```

```csharp
    if (!string.IsNullOrEmpty(Text))

    {

        Vector2 textSize =
_font.MeasureString(Text);

        Vector2 textPosition = new Vector2(

            Position.X + (Texture.Width -
textSize.X) / 2,

            Position.Y + (Texture.Height -
textSize.Y) / 2

        );

        spriteBatch.DrawString(_font, Text,
textPosition, Color.Black);

    }

}
```

Best Practices

1. **Use consistent sizes and spacing** for buttons.
2. **Preload textures and fonts** in `LoadContent()` to avoid runtime lag.
3. **Encapsulate button logic** in a class for reusability.
4. **Provide feedback**: color changes, scaling, or sound enhance interactivity.
5. **Separate menu logic** from gameplay logic to keep code clean.

Putting It All Together

With this approach, you can build a **fully functional menu system** where buttons respond to clicks, highlight on hover, and integrate seamlessly with your game states. Extending this structure allows you to add options screens, pause menus, and custom UI layouts.

6.3 Game States: Start, Pause, Game Over

Managing game states is fundamental for controlling **flow, player interactions, and UI**. By organizing your game into states such as **Start, Playing, Pause, and Game Over**, you can clearly separate logic and rendering, making your game easier to maintain and expand.

Defining Game States

A common approach is to use an **enumeration** to represent states:

```
public enum GameScreen

{

    Start,

    Playing,

    Paused,

    GameOver

}

private GameScreen _currentScreen =
GameScreen.Start;
```

- _currentScreen tracks the **active state** of the game.

- States can be extended to include menus, cutscenes, or options screens.

Switching Between States

Transition between states using **input or events**:

```
protected override void Update(GameTime gameTime)

{

    KeyboardState keyboardState =
Keyboard.GetState();


    switch (_currentScreen)

    {

        case GameScreen.Start:

            if (keyboardState.IsKeyDown(Keys.Enter))

                _currentScreen = GameScreen.Playing;

            break;


        case GameScreen.Playing:

            if (keyboardState.IsKeyDown(Keys.Escape))

                _currentScreen = GameScreen.Paused;


            // Gameplay logic here

            _player.Update(gameTime);

            _enemyManager.Update(gameTime);
```

```
            if (_player.Health <= 0)

                _currentScreen = GameScreen.GameOver;

            break;


        case GameScreen.Paused:

            if (keyboardState.IsKeyDown(Keys.Escape))

                _currentScreen = GameScreen.Playing;

            break;


        case GameScreen.GameOver:

            if (keyboardState.IsKeyDown(Keys.Enter))

            {

                RestartGame();

                _currentScreen = GameScreen.Start;

            }

            break;

    }

    base.Update(gameTime);

}
```

- Enter moves from Start → Playing, or Game Over → Start.
- Escape toggles Paused ↔ Playing.
- Gameplay updates only occur during the Playing state.

Rendering Game States

Render logic varies based on the current state:

```
protected override void Draw(GameTime gameTime)

{

    GraphicsDevice.Clear(Color.CornflowerBlue);

    _spriteBatch.Begin();


    switch (_currentScreen)

    {

        case GameScreen.Start:

            DrawCenteredText("Press Enter to
Start", Color.White);

            break;


        case GameScreen.Playing:

            _player.Draw(_spriteBatch);

            _enemyManager.Draw(_spriteBatch);

            DrawHUD();

            break;

        case GameScreen.Paused:

            _player.Draw(_spriteBatch);

            _enemyManager.Draw(_spriteBatch);
```

```csharp
                DrawHUD();

                DrawCenteredText("Paused - Press
Escape to Resume", Color.Yellow);

                break;


        case GameScreen.GameOver:

                DrawCenteredText("Game Over! Press
Enter to Restart", Color.Red);

                break;

    }

    _spriteBatch.End();

    base.Draw(gameTime);

}

private void DrawCenteredText(string text, Color
color)

{

    Vector2 size = _hudFont.MeasureString(text);

    Vector2 position = new
Vector2(GraphicsDevice.Viewport.Width / 2 -
size.X / 2,

GraphicsDevice.Viewport.Height / 2 - size.Y / 2);

    _spriteBatch.DrawString(_hudFont, text,
position, color);

}
```

- The **Playing state** renders the game world and HUD.
- Paused and Game Over states overlay messages while optionally still rendering the game behind.

Restarting the Game

To restart cleanly:

```
private void RestartGame()

{

    _player.Reset();

    _enemyManager.Reset();

    _score = 0;

}
```

- Reset player, enemies, scores, and any other game-specific data.
- Ensures a **fresh start** without lingering state from previous sessions.

Best Practices

1. **Separate update logic per state** to avoid unintended behavior.
2. **Pause all timers and audio** when in the Paused state.
3. **Keep UI rendering flexible** to overlay messages without stopping gameplay completely.
4. **Use descriptive state names** for clarity.
5. **Encapsulate state transitions** in methods for maintainability.

Putting It All Together

With a structured game state system:

- Start screen waits for player input.
- Playing state updates all gameplay logic.
- Paused state freezes gameplay and shows a menu.
- Game Over state displays results and allows restarting.

This approach makes your game **organized, responsive, and scalable**, simplifying both logic and rendering.

6.4 UI Input Handling & Focus

User interface (UI) elements like buttons, sliders, and menus require **precise input handling** and **focus management**. Proper focus handling ensures that only the active UI element responds to input, preventing accidental actions and improving player experience.

Detecting Input on UI Elements

MonoGame provides input via `Mouse.GetState()` and `Keyboard.GetState()`. For interactive UI elements:

```
MouseState mouseState = Mouse.GetState();

KeyboardState keyboardState =
Keyboard.GetState();
```

- Use **mouse position** to detect hover or click on buttons.
- Use **keyboard keys** to navigate or activate UI components.

Example: Button Focus with Mouse

Enhance the Button class to track focus:

```
public class Button
{
    public Texture2D Texture;

    public Vector2 Position;

    public string Text;

    private SpriteFont _font;

    public bool IsFocused { get; private set; }

    public Button(Texture2D texture, Vector2
position, string text, SpriteFont font)
    {
        Texture = texture;

        Position = position;

        Text = text;

        _font = font;
    }

    public void Update(MouseState mouseState)
    {
        IsFocused =
Bounds.Contains(mouseState.Position);
    }


    public bool IsClicked(MouseState mouseState,
MouseState previousMouseState)
```

```
        {

            return IsFocused && mouseState.LeftButton ==
ButtonState.Pressed &&

                previousMouseState.LeftButton ==
ButtonState.Released;

        }

    public void Draw(SpriteBatch spriteBatch)

        {

            Color color = IsFocused ? Color.LightGray :
Color.Gray;

            spriteBatch.Draw(Texture, Position, color);

            if (!string.IsNullOrEmpty(Text))

            {

                Vector2 textSize =
_font.MeasureString(Text);

                Vector2 textPosition = new Vector2(

                    Position.X + (Texture.Width -
textSize.X) / 2,

                    Position.Y + (Texture.Height -
textSize.Y) / 2

                );

                spriteBatch.DrawString(_font, Text,
textPosition, Color.Black);

            }

        }
```

```
    public Rectangle Bounds => new
Rectangle((int)Position.X, (int)Position.Y,
Texture.Width, Texture.Height);

}
```

- IsFocused indicates whether the mouse is over the button.
- Visual feedback (e.g., color change) helps the player identify active elements.

Keyboard Navigation & Focus

For menus or options controlled by keyboard:

```
private int _focusedButtonIndex = 0;

private Button[] _buttons;

protected override void Update(GameTime gameTime)

{

    KeyboardState keyboardState =
Keyboard.GetState();

    if (keyboardState.IsKeyDown(Keys.Down))

        _focusedButtonIndex = (_focusedButtonIndex +
1) % _buttons.Length;

    if (keyboardState.IsKeyDown(Keys.Up))

        _focusedButtonIndex = (_focusedButtonIndex -
1 + _buttons.Length) % _buttons.Length;


    if (keyboardState.IsKeyDown(Keys.Enter))


ActivateButton(_buttons[_focusedButtonIndex]);
```

```
for (int i = 0; i < _buttons.Length; i++)

        _buttons[i].IsFocused = (i ==
_focusedButtonIndex);

}
```

- Up/Down arrows change focus between buttons.
- Enter triggers the **focused button**.
- IsFocused ensures only one element responds at a time.

Combining Mouse and Keyboard

To support **both input methods**:

- Mouse hover updates focus dynamically.
- Keyboard navigation overrides focus when keys are pressed.
- Clicking a button with the mouse immediately activates it.

Example integration:

```
protected override void Update(GameTime gameTime)

{

    MouseState mouseState = Mouse.GetState();

    KeyboardState keyboardState =
Keyboard.GetState();


    bool keyboardUsed = false;


    if (keyboardState.IsKeyDown(Keys.Down))

    {
```

```
        _focusedButtonIndex = (_focusedButtonIndex +
1) % _buttons.Length;

        keyboardUsed = true;

    }

    if (keyboardState.IsKeyDown(Keys.Up))

    {

        _focusedButtonIndex = (_focusedButtonIndex -
1 + _buttons.Length) % _buttons.Length;

        keyboardUsed = true;

    }

    if (keyboardState.IsKeyDown(Keys.Enter))

ActivateButton(_buttons[_focusedButtonIndex]);


    for (int i = 0; i < _buttons.Length; i++)

    {

        if (!keyboardUsed)

            _buttons[i].Update(mouseState); // Mouse
sets focus if keyboard not used

        _buttons[i].IsFocused = keyboardUsed ? i ==
_focusedButtonIndex : _buttons[i].IsFocused;

        if (_buttons[i].IsClicked(mouseState,
_previousMouseState))

            ActivateButton(_buttons[i]);

    }

    _previousMouseState = mouseState;
```

}

- Ensures smooth **hybrid input handling**.
- Player can switch seamlessly between mouse and keyboard.

Focus Management for Complex UI

- **Multiple UI layers**: Only the topmost interactive layer should receive input.
- **Modal dialogs**: Prevent input to underlying screens while a dialog is active.
- **Sliders or text fields**: Require exclusive focus to handle continuous input correctly.

Best Practices

1. **Visual feedback**: Always indicate focus clearly (color, scale, or highlight).
2. **Single active focus**: Avoid multiple elements reacting simultaneously.
3. **Support hybrid input**: Mouse and keyboard should coexist seamlessly.
4. **Pause gameplay when UI is active**: Prevent accidental in-game actions.
5. **Centralize input logic**: Manage focus and input in a dedicated UI manager for scalability.

Putting It All Together

With proper input handling and focus management, your menus, buttons, and HUD elements become **responsive, intuitive, and accessible**. Players can interact naturally via mouse or keyboard, ensuring smooth navigation across your game's UI.

6.5 Responsive UI for Multiple Resolutions

Games are played on a variety of devices with **different screen sizes and resolutions**, from desktops to laptops, tablets, and phones. A responsive UI ensures your buttons, menus, and HUDs **scale and position correctly**, providing a consistent experience across all displays.

Understanding the Problem

UI elements positioned with **absolute coordinates** can appear misaligned on screens with different resolutions. For example, a button at $(300, 200)$ on a 1920×1080 screen may be off-center on a 1280×720 screen.

Using Viewport and Scaling

MonoGame provides the `GraphicsDevice.Viewport` object to determine screen dimensions:

```
int screenWidth = GraphicsDevice.Viewport.Width;

int screenHeight =
GraphicsDevice.Viewport.Height;
```

- Use these values to **calculate relative positions**.
- Combine with scaling factors for consistent UI sizing.

Anchoring UI Elements

Position UI elements **relative to screen edges or percentages**:

```
Vector2 startButtonPosition = new
Vector2(screenWidth * 0.5f - buttonWidth / 2,

screenHeight * 0.5f - buttonHeight / 2);
```

- Centers the button on any screen.
- Works for top, bottom, left, or right anchoring by adjusting percentages.

Scaling UI Elements

For textures or fonts, scale proportionally based on **screen size**:

```
float scaleX = screenWidth / 1920f;

float scaleY = screenHeight / 1080f;

float uiScale = Math.Min(scaleX, scaleY); // maintain
aspect ratio

_spriteBatch.Draw(buttonTexture, startButtonPosition,
null, Color.White, 0f, Vector2.Zero, uiScale,
SpriteEffects.None, 0f);
```

- Ensures UI elements **resize proportionally**.
- Maintains layout and aspect ratio across resolutions.

Responsive Fonts with SpriteFont

Fonts should scale similarly:

```
string scoreText = "Score: 100";

Vector2 fontPosition = new Vector2(screenWidth *
0.05f, screenHeight * 0.05f);

float fontScale = uiScale; // use same scale as UI
textures
```

```
_spriteBatch.DrawString(hudFont, scoreText,
fontPosition, Color.White, 0f, Vector2.Zero,
fontScale, SpriteEffects.None, 0f);
```

- Dynamic scaling prevents text from being too small on high-resolution displays or too large on small screens.

Handling Multiple Resolutions Automatically

Create a **UI manager** that computes positions and scales based on the current viewport:

```
public class UIManager

{

    private int _screenWidth;

    private int _screenHeight;

    private float _uiScale;

    public UIManager(GraphicsDevice graphics)

    {

        _screenWidth = graphics.Viewport.Width;

        _screenHeight = graphics.Viewport.Height;

        _uiScale = Math.Min(_screenWidth / 1920f,
_screenHeight / 1080f);

    }


    public Vector2 GetPosition(float xPercent, float
yPercent, float elementWidth = 0, float elementHeight
= 0)
```

```
    {

        return new Vector2(_screenWidth * xPercent -
elementWidth * _uiScale / 2,

                            _screenHeight * yPercent -
elementHeight * _uiScale / 2);

    }



    public float GetScale() => _uiScale;

}
```

- xPercent and yPercent define the element's **relative position**.
- _uiScale ensures consistent **proportional sizing**.

Putting It All Together

Example: positioning and drawing a start button with responsive scaling:

```
UIManager uiManager = new
UIManager(GraphicsDevice);

Vector2 buttonPos = uiManager.GetPosition(0.5f,
0.5f, buttonTexture.Width, buttonTexture.Height);

float scale = uiManager.GetScale();


_spriteBatch.Begin();

_spriteBatch.Draw(buttonTexture, buttonPos, null,
Color.White, 0f, Vector2.Zero, scale,
SpriteEffects.None, 0f);
```

```
_spriteBatch.DrawString(hudFont, "Start Game",
buttonPos + new Vector2(buttonTexture.Width,
buttonTexture.Height) / 2 * scale, Color.Black,
0f, hudFont.MeasureString("Start Game") / 2,
scale, SpriteEffects.None, 0f);

_spriteBatch.End();
```

- The button and text **center correctly on any resolution**.
- The scale factor ensures consistent visual appearance.

Best Practices

1. **Anchor UI elements using percentages** rather than absolute coordinates.
2. **Scale textures and fonts proportionally** to maintain readability.
3. **Use a centralized UI manager** to handle positioning and scaling for all elements.
4. **Test on multiple resolutions** to ensure consistent layout.
5. **Separate gameplay resolution from UI resolution** when necessary for flexible scaling.

Summary

By calculating **positions and scales relative to screen size**, your UI adapts automatically to any resolution. This approach ensures **a professional, polished look** and consistent player experience across devices.

Chapter 7: Building a Complete 2D Game

You'll bring together everything you've learned to make a fully playable 2D game. You'll design levels, implement gameplay, add menus, sounds, and polish. By the end, you'll have a complete game you can play, test, and share.

7.1 Planning Game Concept & Mechanics

Every great game begins with **a clear concept and well-defined mechanics**. Planning before writing code helps you avoid wasted effort, ensures smooth gameplay, and guides asset creation. In MonoGame, careful planning lays the foundation for clean, modular code and responsive interactions.

Defining Your Game Concept

Start by answering key questions:

1. **Genre and Style:** Is your game a platformer, shooter, puzzle, or RPG? Will it be 2D or 3D?
2. **Core Gameplay Loop:** What does the player do repeatedly? Jumping, shooting, collecting?
3. **Objective:** What is the player's goal? High score, survival, level completion?
4. **Theme & Visuals:** What is the setting? Bright cartoonish world, dark realistic, or abstract?

A concise concept statement keeps development focused. For example:

"A 2D top-down shooter where the player navigates a maze, avoids enemies, collects power-ups, and survives waves as long as possible."

Identifying Core Mechanics

Mechanics define **how the player interacts with the game world**. Typical mechanics in a MonoGame 2D project might include:

- **Player movement**: Walk, jump, or fly.
- **Enemy AI**: Patrol, chase, or attack patterns.
- **Collectibles and power-ups**: Increase score, health, or abilities.
- **Collision detection**: Interaction between objects (player, enemies, walls).
- **Game progression**: Levels, waves, or time-based challenges.

Clearly defining mechanics upfront lets you **structure your classes and systems** effectively.

Mapping Out Gameplay Flow

Create a **flow diagram** of the player experience:

1. Start screen → Player chooses action
2. Gameplay loop → Movement, combat, collection
3. Pause → Options menu, resume
4. Game over → Score display, restart

Mapping flow ensures you handle **state transitions** cleanly in MonoGame and prevents logic bugs.

Defining Systems and Classes

Break your game into **manageable systems**:

- **Player system**: Handles movement, input, health.
- **Enemy system**: AI behavior, spawning, collision response.
- **HUD system**: Scores, lives, timers.
- **Audio system**: Sound effects, background music.
- **UI system**: Menus, buttons, responsive layout.

Plan classes and responsibilities carefully to maintain **clean architecture**:

```
class Player

{

    public Vector2 Position;

    public int Health;

    public void Update(GameTime gameTime,
InputManager input) { /* movement logic */ }

    public void Draw(SpriteBatch spriteBatch) { /*
rendering */ }

}



class EnemyManager

{

    private List<Enemy> _enemies;

    public void Update(GameTime gameTime) { /* AI,
spawning */ }

    public void Draw(SpriteBatch spriteBatch) { /*
render enemies */ }
```

}

- Separate **game logic** from **rendering** for modularity.
- Each system can be **tested independently**.

Documenting Mechanics

Maintain a **Game Design Document (GDD)** or simple notes including:

- **Player actions** and controls
- **Enemy behaviors**
- **Scoring system**
- **Level progression**
- **Power-ups and items**

This document becomes your **development roadmap**, helping you implement systems systematically in MonoGame.

Best Practices

1. **Start small**: Focus on a single mechanic before adding complexity.
2. **Prototype quickly**: Test core mechanics in MonoGame before polishing visuals.
3. **Iterate**: Adjust mechanics based on playtesting feedback.
4. **Keep code modular**: Separate concerns to simplify scaling the game.
5. **Document thoroughly**: Makes future updates and teamwork easier.

Putting It All Together

Planning your game concept and mechanics first ensures:

- Smooth development workflow
- Efficient coding and system design
- Clear goals for player experience
- Easier debugging and iteration

MonoGame provides the tools to **turn a well-planned concept into a working prototype quickly**, letting you test, refine, and expand your game with confidence.

7.2 Setting Up Project & Assets

Once your game concept and mechanics are defined, the next step is to **set up your MonoGame project and organize assets**. A clean structure ensures smooth development, easier debugging, and maintainability.

Creating a New MonoGame Project

Start by creating a project tailored to your game type:

1. Open **Visual Studio** (or preferred IDE).
2. Select **Create a new project** → choose **MonoGame Cross-Platform Desktop Project** (or appropriate template: Windows, Android, iOS, etc.).
3. Name the project, e.g., TopDownShooter, and choose a location.
4. Ensure **.NET 6 or later** is selected for modern compatibility.

MonoGame templates provide:

- A Game1.cs file with **Update** and **Draw** methods.
- A Content folder for textures, sounds, and fonts.

- Basic game loop setup and graphics device initialization.

Organizing Your Assets

Organize assets into **logical folders** inside the Content project:

```
Content/
├── Textures/
│   ├── Player/
│   ├── Enemies/
│   └── UI/
├── Audio/
│   ├── Music/
│   └── SFX/
├── Fonts/
└── Levels/
```

- Separate **textures, audio, fonts, and levels** for clarity.
- Naming convention: player_idle.png, enemy_boss.png, button_start.png.

Importing Assets with MonoGame Content Pipeline (MGCB)

1. Open the **Content.mgcb** file using the **MonoGame Pipeline Tool**.
2. Right-click → **Add** → **Existing Item** → select your asset.
3. Configure properties:
    - **Texture**: default settings are fine for 2D sprites.

- o **Audio**: set to `Build Action: Compile` for XNB output.
- o **Font**: use SpriteFont (`.spritefont`) for text rendering.

4. Click **Build** to compile assets into `.xnb` files readable by MonoGame.

Loading Assets in Code

Load assets in `LoadContent()` method:

```
Texture2D playerTexture;

Texture2D enemyTexture;

SpriteFont gameFont;

SoundEffect shootSFX;

Song backgroundMusic;

protected override void LoadContent()

{

    _spriteBatch = new SpriteBatch(GraphicsDevice);

    // Load textures

    playerTexture =
Content.Load<Texture2D>("Textures/Player/player_idle"
);

    enemyTexture =
Content.Load<Texture2D>("Textures/Enemies/enemy_boss"
);

    // Load fonts

    gameFont =
Content.Load<SpriteFont>("Fonts/GameFont");
```

```
    // Load audio

    shootSFX =
Content.Load<SoundEffect>("Audio/SFX/shoot");

    backgroundMusic =
Content.Load<Song>("Audio/Music/background");

}
```

- Use **relative paths** matching the Content folder structure.
- Loading assets once in LoadContent() prevents runtime lag.

Structuring Project for Multiple Systems

For clean architecture, organize code into **subfolders and classes**:

```
GameProject/

├── GameObjects/

│   ├── Player.cs

│   └── Enemy.cs

├── Managers/

│   ├── AudioManager.cs

│   └── UIManager.cs

├── Screens/

│   ├── MainMenu.cs

│   └── GameOverScreen.cs

├── Utilities/

└── Game1.cs
```

- **GameObjects**: entities like player, enemies, collectibles.
- **Managers**: handle audio, UI, input, or resource management.
- **Screens**: game states and menus.
- **Utilities**: helper classes like collision detection or math utilities.

Best Practices

1. **Consistent naming**: makes asset loading predictable.
2. **Organize by type and usage**: prevents clutter as the project grows.
3. **Preload assets in LoadContent()**: avoid runtime loading lag.
4. **Use managers for complex systems**: audio, UI, and levels.
5. **Backup and version control**: keep your project safe and track changes.

Putting It All Together

With a properly **set up MonoGame project and organized assets**, you can focus on implementing **game mechanics and UI** without being bogged down by messy code or misplaced files. This structure ensures scalability and maintainability as your game grows from prototype to full release.

7.3 Implementing Core Gameplay (Player, Collisions)

Once your project and assets are in place, the next step is to implement **core gameplay**, including **player movement, input**

handling, and collision detection. This section focuses on building a robust foundation for your game loop while keeping systems modular and scalable.

Creating the Player Class

Start with a dedicated **Player class** to manage position, movement, and rendering:

```
public class Player

{

    public Vector2 Position;

    public Texture2D Texture;

    public float Speed = 200f; // pixels per second

    public Rectangle BoundingBox => new
Rectangle((int)Position.X, (int)Position.Y,
Texture.Width, Texture.Height);

    public Player(Texture2D texture, Vector2
startPosition)

    {

        Texture = texture;

        Position = startPosition;

    }

    public void Update(GameTime gameTime,
KeyboardState keyboardState)

    {

        float delta =
(float)gameTime.ElapsedGameTime.TotalSeconds;
```

```
        if (keyboardState.IsKeyDown(Keys.W))

            Position.Y -= Speed * delta;

        if (keyboardState.IsKeyDown(Keys.S))

            Position.Y += Speed * delta;

        if (keyboardState.IsKeyDown(Keys.A))

            Position.X -= Speed * delta;

        if (keyboardState.IsKeyDown(Keys.D))

            Position.X += Speed * delta;

    }

    public void Draw(SpriteBatch spriteBatch)

    {

        spriteBatch.Draw(Texture, Position,
Color.White);

    }

}
```

- Uses KeyboardState to control movement.
- BoundingBox provides a convenient rectangle for collision detection.
- Speed scaled by deltaTime ensures consistent movement across frame rates.

Handling Collisions

Collision detection prevents the player from passing through walls or interacting incorrectly with objects. Start with **axis-aligned bounding boxes (AABB)**:

```
public  static  bool  CheckCollision(Rectangle  a,
Rectangle b)

{

    return a.Intersects(b);

}
```

- Returns true if two rectangles overlap.
- Can be used for walls, enemies, collectibles, and hazards.

Integrating Collision with Player Movement

To prevent the player from moving into obstacles:

```
public void HandleCollisions(List<Rectangle>
obstacles)

{

    foreach (var obstacle in obstacles)

    {

        if (BoundingBox.Intersects(obstacle))

        {

            // Simple collision response: prevent
movement

            if (Position.X + Texture.Width >
obstacle.Left && Position.X < obstacle.Left)

                Position.X = obstacle.Left -
Texture.Width;

            if (Position.X < obstacle.Right &&
Position.X + Texture.Width > obstacle.Right)

                Position.X = obstacle.Right;
```

```
            if (Position.Y + Texture.Height >
obstacle.Top && Position.Y < obstacle.Top)

                Position.Y = obstacle.Top -
Texture.Height;

            if (Position.Y < obstacle.Bottom &&
Position.Y + Texture.Height > obstacle.Bottom)

                Position.Y = obstacle.Bottom;

        }

    }

}
```

- Checks each obstacle in the level.
- Adjusts player position to **prevent overlapping** with obstacles.
- Can be refined for more advanced physics later.

Adding Collision with Collectibles or Enemies

Use the same AABB logic for other interactions:

```
foreach (var enemy in enemies)

{

    if
(Player.BoundingBox.Intersects(enemy.BoundingBox))

    {

        playerHealth -= 1;

        enemy.Respawn(); // Example response

    }

}
```

```
foreach (var collectible in collectibles)

{

    if
(Player.BoundingBox.Intersects(collectible.BoundingBo
x))

    {

        score += collectible.Value;

        collectible.Collect();

    }

}
```

- Simple, reusable approach for various game elements.
- Keeps **collision logic separate from movement**, improving maintainability.

Integrating in the Game Loop

Inside Game1.cs:

```
protected override void Update(GameTime gameTime)

{

    KeyboardState keyboardState =
Keyboard.GetState();

    player.Update(gameTime, keyboardState);

    player.HandleCollisions(levelObstacles);

    base.Update(gameTime);

}

protected override void Draw(GameTime gameTime)
```

```
{
    GraphicsDevice.Clear(Color.CornflowerBlue);

    _spriteBatch.Begin();

    player.Draw(_spriteBatch);

    foreach (var obstacle in levelObstacles)

        _spriteBatch.Draw(obstacleTexture, obstacle,
Color.Gray);

    _spriteBatch.End();

    base.Draw(gameTime);

}
```

- Updates player and collisions each frame.
- Draws player and obstacles clearly.
- Can easily extend to include enemies, collectibles, and other systems.

Best Practices

1. **Separate logic and rendering**: player update vs. draw keeps code modular.
2. **Use bounding boxes consistently**: simplifies collision detection across objects.
3. **Delta-time scaling**: ensures smooth movement across devices.
4. **Modular collision response**: allows different reactions for walls, enemies, and pickups.
5. **Test early**: even basic collision handling prevents frustrating gameplay bugs.

Putting It All Together

With a **player class, movement logic, and collision detection**, your core gameplay is functional:

- The player can move freely within constraints.
- Collisions prevent moving through walls or objects.
- Collectibles and enemies interact seamlessly.

This setup provides a **solid foundation** to build more advanced features like AI, combat, or physics while keeping code organized and scalable.

7.4 Adding UI, Score, and Menus

A functional game requires more than movement and collisions—it needs a **user interface (UI)** to communicate information, display scores, and provide menus for starting, pausing, and ending the game. In this section, you'll learn how to implement **dynamic UI elements, score display, and interactive menus** in MonoGame.

Setting Up the UI System

Begin by creating a **UI manager class** to centralize UI rendering and input handling:

```
public class UIManager

{

    private SpriteFont _font;

    private string _scoreText = "Score: 0";

    private Vector2 _scorePosition;
```

```
    public UIManager(SpriteFont font, int
screenWidth)

    {

        _font = font;

        _scorePosition = new Vector2(20, 20); //
top-left corner

    }

    public void UpdateScore(int score)

    {

        _scoreText = $"Score: {score}";

    }

    public void Draw(SpriteBatch spriteBatch)

    {

        spriteBatch.DrawString(_font, _scoreText,
_scorePosition, Color.White);

    }

}
```

- Centralizes score management and rendering.
- Allows easy extension to other UI elements (lives, timers, health bars).

Displaying Scores and HUD Elements

Integrate UI into the game loop:

```
private UIManager uiManager;
```

```csharp
private int score = 0;


protected override void LoadContent()

{

    _spriteBatch = new SpriteBatch(GraphicsDevice);

    uiManager = new
UIManager(Content.Load<SpriteFont>("Fonts/GameFont"),
GraphicsDevice.Viewport.Width);

}

protected override void Update(GameTime gameTime)

{

    // Example: Increase score when player collects
an item

    foreach (var collectible in collectibles)

    {

        if
(player.BoundingBox.Intersects(collectible.BoundingBo
x))

        {

            score += collectible.Value;

            collectible.Collect();

            uiManager.UpdateScore(score);

        }

    }

    base.Update(gameTime);

}
```

```csharp
protected override void Draw(GameTime gameTime)

{

    GraphicsDevice.Clear(Color.CornflowerBlue);


    _spriteBatch.Begin();

    player.Draw(_spriteBatch);

    foreach (var obstacle in levelObstacles)

        _spriteBatch.Draw(obstacleTexture, obstacle,
Color.Gray);

    uiManager.Draw(_spriteBatch);

    _spriteBatch.End();


    base.Draw(gameTime);

}
```

- Score updates dynamically as the player interacts with the game world.
- Easy to add other HUD elements like health or ammo.

Creating a Basic Menu System

Menus allow players to **start, pause, or restart the game**. A simple menu system can be implemented using buttons:

```csharp
public class Menu

{

    private List<Button> _buttons;

    private SpriteBatch _spriteBatch;
```

```csharp
    public Menu(SpriteBatch spriteBatch)

    {

        _spriteBatch = spriteBatch;

        _buttons = new List<Button>();

    }

    public void AddButton(Button button)

    {

        _buttons.Add(button);

    }


    public void Update(MouseState mouseState,
MouseState previousMouseState)

    {

        foreach (var button in _buttons)

        {

            button.Update(mouseState);

            if (button.IsClicked(mouseState,
previousMouseState))

                button.OnClick?.Invoke();

        }

    }

    public void Draw()

    {

        foreach (var button in _buttons)
```

```
        button.Draw(_spriteBatch);

    }

}
```

- Button class is reused from earlier UI input sections.
- Each button can have an **OnClick action** to trigger events like starting or pausing the game.

Example: Start Menu

```
Menu startMenu;

protected override void LoadContent()

{

    startMenu = new Menu(_spriteBatch);


    Button startButton = new Button(buttonTexture,
new Vector2(400, 300), "Start Game", gameFont);

    startButton.OnClick = () => { gameState =
GameState.Playing; };

    startMenu.AddButton(startButton);

}

protected override void Update(GameTime gameTime)

{

    MouseState mouseState = Mouse.GetState();

    startMenu.Update(mouseState,
_previousMouseState);

    _previousMouseState = mouseState;
```

```csharp
    if (gameState == GameState.Playing)

    {

        player.Update(gameTime, Keyboard.GetState());

        player.HandleCollisions(levelObstacles);

    }

}

protected override void Draw(GameTime gameTime)

{

    GraphicsDevice.Clear(Color.Black);

    _spriteBatch.Begin();


    if (gameState == GameState.Menu)

        startMenu.Draw();

    else if (gameState == GameState.Playing)

    {

        player.Draw(_spriteBatch);

        foreach (var obstacle in levelObstacles)

            _spriteBatch.Draw(obstacleTexture,
obstacle, Color.Gray);

        uiManager.Draw(_spriteBatch);

    }


    _spriteBatch.End();
```

}

- Switches between menu and gameplay states cleanly.
- Menu buttons respond to mouse clicks, while gameplay responds to player input.

Adding Pause and Game Over Menus

Use the same Menu system to create:

- **Pause menu**: triggers when pressing Esc.
- **Game over menu**: displays final score and restart option.

State management ensures only the **active menu receives input**, preventing accidental interactions during gameplay.

Best Practices

1. **Centralize UI rendering**: simplifies scaling and updates.
2. **Use state management**: separates menus, gameplay, and game over screens.
3. **Keep menus interactive and responsive**: highlight buttons on hover/focus.
4. **Reuse button and UI classes**: avoids duplicate code for multiple menus.
5. **Test menus on different resolutions**: ensures buttons and text are visible.

Putting It All Together

By implementing a **UI manager, dynamic score display, and menu system**, your game becomes **more interactive and user-friendly**. Players can monitor progress, navigate game states, and interact seamlessly with menus while maintaining consistent gameplay flow.

7.5 Final Polishing & Playtesting

After implementing gameplay, UI, and menus, the final stage of development is **polishing and playtesting**. This step ensures your game feels professional, runs smoothly, and provides an enjoyable player experience.

Performance Optimization

Smooth gameplay is critical. Start by profiling and optimizing:

1. **Delta-time based movement**: ensures consistent speeds across devices.
2. **Minimize Draw Calls**: batch sprites with `_spriteBatch.Begin()` and `_spriteBatch.End()`.
3. **Texture Atlases / Sprite Sheets**: reduces GPU overhead by combining multiple textures.
4. **Avoid redundant updates**: only update objects that are active or visible.

Example of delta-time scaling:

```
float delta =
(float)gameTime.ElapsedGameTime.TotalSeconds;

player.Position += player.Velocity * delta;
```

This ensures **frame rate independence** and smooth motion.

Debugging and Logging

Add simple debugging tools to catch issues before release:

```
if (Keyboard.GetState().IsKeyDown(Keys.F1))

{

    Console.WriteLine($"Player Position:
{player.Position}, Score: {score}");

}
```

- Displays essential game info without intrusive UI.
- Can be removed or disabled in final builds.

Visual & Audio Polishing

Polish makes your game feel complete:

- **UI and HUD**: adjust fonts, button sizes, and positioning for clarity.
- **Animations**: ensure sprite transitions are smooth, no flickering.
- **Audio**: balance volume, looping background music, and sound effects timing.
- **Feedback**: visual cues for collisions, pickups, or player damage.

Example: adding a flash effect on collision:

```
Color playerColor = player.IsHit ? Color.Red :
Color.White;

_spriteBatch.Draw(player.Texture,
player.Position, playerColor);
```

Playtesting Strategy

Playtesting reveals **game balance and usability issues**:

1. **Internal Testing**: test all features yourself, check collisions, controls, and menus.
2. **External Testing**: ask friends or target audience to play the game.
3. **Observe Player Behavior**: note where players struggle or exploit mechanics.
4. **Gather Feedback**: difficulty, clarity, fun factor, bugs.

Iterative Refinement

Use playtesting data to **iterate and improve**:

- Adjust **player speed, enemy AI, or difficulty curves**.
- Refine **menu navigation and input responsiveness**.
- Fix **visual or audio inconsistencies**.
- Ensure **consistent experience across resolutions**.

Example: Applying Polishing Changes

Suppose playtesting reveals the player moves too fast on some monitors. Adjust using delta-time scaling and speed factor:

```
float speedFactor = 1.0f; // tweak based on
feedback

float delta =
(float)gameTime.ElapsedGameTime.TotalSeconds;

player.Position += player.Velocity * delta *
speedFactor;
```

- Tweak speedFactor until the game feels natural.

Packaging for Release

Before release:

- Remove debugging logs or cheat keys.
- Build **optimized release configuration**.
- Test on **all target devices and resolutions**.
- Ensure **all assets load correctly** and there are no missing files.

Best Practices

1. **Iterate frequently**: multiple rounds of playtesting improve quality.
2. **Test edge cases**: different resolutions, input methods, or game states.
3. **Prioritize player experience**: smooth controls, clear feedback, and fun.
4. **Keep modular code**: easier to tweak mechanics and fix bugs.
5. **Document fixes and improvements**: helps for future updates.

Putting It All Together

Polishing and playtesting transform a functional prototype into a **polished, enjoyable game**. MonoGame provides the tools for **smooth rendering, input handling, and asset management**, while playtesting ensures that your game is **balanced, responsive, and fun**. Investing time in this final stage significantly elevates the player experience and prepares your game for release.

Chapter 8: Introduction to 3D Game Development

You'll learn the basics of 3D games: cameras, models, and lighting. You'll add simple 3D gameplay to your project. By the end, you'll be ready to create 3D worlds and expand your games beyond 2D.

8.1 3D Basics: Coordinates, Cameras, Projection

Transitioning from 2D to 3D in MonoGame introduces new concepts: **3D coordinates, camera systems, and projection matrices**. Understanding these fundamentals allows you to render 3D objects correctly and control the player's perspective in a 3D world.

Understanding 3D Coordinates

In 3D space, every point is represented by a **Vector3 (X, Y, Z)**:

- **X**: horizontal position (left/right)
- **Y**: vertical position (up/down)
- **Z**: depth (forward/backward)

Example:

```
Vector3 playerPosition = new Vector3(0f, 0f,
0f); // Origin

Vector3 enemyPosition = new Vector3(5f, 0f,
10f); // 5 units right, 10 units forward
```

- Positions are relative to a **world origin** $(0,0,0)$.
- All 3D objects and movement are calculated using **Vector3 math**.

Setting Up the Camera

The camera defines **what the player sees**. In MonoGame, a camera is represented by a **view matrix** and **projection matrix**.

1. **View Matrix**: defines **camera position and orientation**.

```
Vector3 cameraPosition = new Vector3(0f, 10f,
20f); // Camera above and behind player

Vector3 cameraTarget = new Vector3(0f, 0f,
0f); // Look at the origin

Vector3 cameraUp = Vector3.Up; // Y-axis is
up
```

```
Matrix                    view              =
Matrix.CreateLookAt(cameraPosition,
cameraTarget, cameraUp);
```

- `CreateLookAt()` positions the camera and defines its target and up vector.
- Adjust `cameraPosition` and `cameraTarget` to follow the player or implement a free camera.

2. **Projection Matrix**: defines **how 3D objects are projected onto the 2D screen**.

```
float fieldOfView = MathHelper.PiOver4; // 45
degrees

float          aspectRatio          =
GraphicsDevice.Viewport.AspectRatio;

float nearPlane = 0.1f;

float farPlane = 100f;



Matrix          projection          =
Matrix.CreatePerspectiveFieldOfView(fieldOfVi
ew, aspectRatio, nearPlane, farPlane);
```

- fieldOfView: angle of view (zoom).
- aspectRatio: width / height of the viewport.
- nearPlane and farPlane: define clipping planes; objects outside this range are not rendered.

Combining World, View, and Projection Matrices

Rendering a 3D object requires **World, View, and Projection matrices**:

```csharp
Matrix                    world                    =
Matrix.CreateTranslation(playerPosition);   //
Position the object


_basicEffect.World = world;

_basicEffect.View = view;

_basicEffect.Projection = projection;


foreach        (EffectPass        pass        in
_basicEffect.CurrentTechnique.Passes)

{

    pass.Apply();


GraphicsDevice.DrawUserPrimitives<VertexPosit
ionColor>(

        PrimitiveType.TriangleList,

        vertices,

        0,

        vertices.Length / 3

    );
```

}

- **World**: positions, rotates, and scales the object.
- **View**: defines camera perspective.
- **Projection**: converts 3D coordinates to screen coordinates.

Moving the Camera

For dynamic cameras:

```
// Follow player from behind

cameraPosition = playerPosition + new
Vector3(0, 10, 20);

cameraTarget = playerPosition;

view = Matrix.CreateLookAt(cameraPosition,
cameraTarget, Vector3.Up);
```

- Updates every frame in `Update()` to track the player.
- Allows smooth 3D navigation and gameplay.

Visualizing Axes and Orientation

- **X-axis (Red)**: left-right
- **Y-axis (Green)**: up-down
- **Z-axis (Blue)**: forward-backward

Understanding axes is critical for **movement, rotation, and camera orientation**.

Best Practices

1. **Use Vector3 consistently** for positions, directions, and movement.
2. **Keep near/far planes tight** to improve depth precision.
3. **Separate camera logic** from game objects for modularity.
4. **Test field of view** for optimal gameplay perspective.
5. **Follow conventions**: Y is up, Z is forward in MonoGame default.

Putting It All Together

With **3D coordinates, a camera system, and projection matrices**, you can:

- Place objects anywhere in a 3D world.
- Render scenes from the player's perspective.
- Implement dynamic cameras for third-person or first-person gameplay.

These fundamentals are the foundation for building **3D games in MonoGame**, from simple object rendering to complex, interactive worlds.

8.2 Loading & Rendering 3D Models

Once you understand **3D coordinates and cameras**, the next step is to load and render **3D models**. MonoGame provides tools to import and render models created in external programs, allowing you to create rich 3D environments.

Preparing 3D Models

MonoGame supports `.fbx` and `.x` formats. You can export models from software like **Blender, 3ds Max, or Maya**.

- Ensure **textures are embedded or accessible** in your content folder.
- Keep **model scale consistent** for easier placement in your scene.

Organize models in your **Content** folder:

```
Content/

└── Models/

    ├── Player.fbx

    ├── Enemy.fbx

    └── Environment/

        ├── Tree.fbx

        └── Rock.fbx
```

Importing Models via MonoGame Pipeline

1. Open **Content.mgcb** in **MonoGame Pipeline Tool**.
2. Right-click → **Add** → **Existing Item** → select your `.fbx` file.
3. Set **Build Action** to `Compile` (default).
4. Click **Build** to generate `.xnb` files for use in code.

Loading Models in Code

Load the model in `LoadContent():`

```
Model playerModel;

Model enemyModel;


protected override void LoadContent()

{

                _spriteBatch      =      new
SpriteBatch(GraphicsDevice);


    // Load 3D models

                        playerModel        =
Content.Load<Model>("Models/Player");

                        enemyModel        =
Content.Load<Model>("Models/Enemy");

}
```

- Reference by **relative path** from the `Content` folder without file extension.

Rendering Models

Rendering a model requires **world, view, and projection matrices**. For simplicity, start with a static scene:

```
Matrix world = Matrix.CreateTranslation(new
Vector3(0, 0, 0)); // Model position

Matrix view = Matrix.CreateLookAt(new
Vector3(0, 10, 20), Vector3.Zero,
Vector3.Up);

Matrix projection =
Matrix.CreatePerspectiveFieldOfView(MathHelpe
r.PiOver4,
GraphicsDevice.Viewport.AspectRatio, 0.1f,
100f);


foreach (ModelMesh mesh in
playerModel.Meshes)
{
        foreach (BasicEffect effect in
mesh.Effects)
    {
        effect.EnableDefaultLighting();

        effect.World = world;

        effect.View = view;
```

```
    effect.Projection = projection;

  }

  mesh.Draw();

}
```

- **World matrix** positions, rotates, and scales the model.
- **EnableDefaultLighting()** provides basic illumination.
- Loop through each **mesh** and **effect** to apply transformations.

Moving and Rotating Models

You can animate the model in the scene by updating the **world matrix**:

```
float              rotationAngle              =
(float)gameTime.TotalGameTime.TotalSeconds;

Matrix                 world                  =
Matrix.CreateRotationY(rotationAngle)         *
Matrix.CreateTranslation(new   Vector3(0,   0,
0));
```

- Rotates the model around the Y-axis continuously.
- Combine with translation to move the model across the scene.

Rendering Multiple Models

To render multiple models efficiently:

```
List<Model> enemies = new List<Model> {
enemyModel };

List<Vector3> enemyPositions = new
List<Vector3> { new Vector3(5, 0, 10), new
Vector3(-5, 0, 15) };



for (int i = 0; i < enemies.Count; i++)

{

            Matrix enemyWorld =
Matrix.CreateTranslation(enemyPositions[i]);

        foreach (ModelMesh mesh in
enemies[i].Meshes)

    {

        foreach (BasicEffect effect in
mesh.Effects)

        {

        effect.EnableDefaultLighting();

        effect.World = enemyWorld;
```

```
        effect.View = view;

        effect.Projection = projection;

    }

    mesh.Draw();

  }

}
```

- Each enemy uses its own **world matrix** for position.
- Can easily extend to rotate or animate models individually.

Best Practices

1. **Preload models** in `LoadContent()` to avoid runtime lag.
2. **Use scaling matrices** to ensure models match scene units.
3. **Separate world, view, and projection logic** for modularity.
4. **Optimize mesh rendering**: combine small meshes if possible.
5. **Enable basic lighting** for better visual clarity.

Putting It All Together

With this setup:

- You can load `.fbx` models into MonoGame.
- Render static or moving models in your 3D world.
- Apply transformations, lighting, and camera perspective.

This foundation allows you to build **complex 3D scenes**, implement player and enemy models, and create interactive 3D gameplay.

8.3 Simple Lighting & Materials

Lighting and materials are essential for making your **3D scene look realistic and visually engaging**. MonoGame provides built-in support for basic lighting through **BasicEffect**, allowing you to illuminate objects without writing complex shaders. Understanding how to combine lighting with material properties is key to creating visually appealing 3D games.

Using BasicEffect for Lighting

Every 3D model in MonoGame uses BasicEffect to define how it reacts to light. At its simplest, you can enable default lighting:

```
foreach (ModelMesh mesh in playerModel.Meshes)

{

    foreach (BasicEffect effect in mesh.Effects)

    {

        effect.EnableDefaultLighting(); // Activates
default three-directional lighting

        effect.World = world;

        effect.View = view;

        effect.Projection = projection;

    }

    mesh.Draw();
```

```
}
```

`EnableDefaultLighting()` activates a three-light setup:

- **Key light**: the main light source casting the strongest illumination.
- **Fill light**: softens shadows and balances lighting.
- **Back light**: highlights edges and separates objects from the background.

This simple setup is enough for most basic 3D scenes.

Customizing Directional Lighting

You can fine-tune the direction, color, and intensity of lights:

```
foreach (ModelMesh mesh in playerModel.Meshes)

{

    foreach (BasicEffect effect in mesh.Effects)

    {

        effect.DirectionalLight0.Enabled = true;

        effect.DirectionalLight0.Direction = new
Vector3(-1, -1, -1); // Light coming from
top-left-back

        effect.DirectionalLight0.DiffuseColor = new
Vector3(1f, 0.9f, 0.8f); // Warm light

        effect.AmbientLightColor = new Vector3(0.2f,
0.2f, 0.2f); // Low ambient light

        effect.EmissiveColor = Vector3.Zero; //
Object self-illumination
```

```
        effect.World = world;

        effect.View = view;

        effect.Projection = projection;

    }

    mesh.Draw();

}
```

- **DirectionalLight0.Direction** sets where the light is coming from.
- **DiffuseColor** defines the light color hitting the surface.
- **AmbientLightColor** ensures surfaces in shadow still receive some light.
- **EmissiveColor** allows objects to appear self-lit.

Applying Material Properties

BasicEffect also supports simple **material properties** to influence how surfaces react to light:

```
effect.DiffuseColor = new Vector3(0.8f, 0.2f,
0.2f); // Base red color

effect.SpecularColor = new Vector3(1f, 1f, 1f);
// White highlights

effect.SpecularPower = 16f;
// Shininess of the material
```

- **DiffuseColor**: base color of the object.
- **SpecularColor**: color of shiny reflections.
- **SpecularPower**: controls how sharp or soft highlights appear. Higher values create tighter, shinier spots.

Combining Lighting and Materials

When you combine directional lighting with material properties, your models gain depth and realism:

```
Matrix world =
Matrix.CreateRotationY(MathHelper.PiOver4) *
Matrix.CreateTranslation(new Vector3(0, 0, 0));


foreach (ModelMesh mesh in playerModel.Meshes)

{

    foreach (BasicEffect effect in mesh.Effects)

    {

        effect.EnableDefaultLighting();

        effect.DirectionalLight0.Direction = new
Vector3(-1, -1, -1);

        effect.DiffuseColor = new Vector3(0.2f, 0.6f,
1f); // Blueish material

        effect.SpecularColor = new Vector3(1f, 1f,
1f);

        effect.SpecularPower = 32f; // Shiny surface

        effect.AmbientLightColor = new Vector3(0.2f,
0.2f, 0.2f);

        effect.World = world;

        effect.View = view;

        effect.Projection = projection;

    }

    mesh.Draw();
```

}

- Adjust **DiffuseColor** for different material appearances.
- Increase **SpecularPower** to create reflective or metallic surfaces.
- Light direction and color dramatically affect how materials appear in the scene.

Best Practices

1. **Enable lighting per mesh**: ensures each mesh receives proper illumination.
2. **Use ambient light carefully**: too high, and the scene looks flat; too low, and shadows are too dark.
3. **Separate material and light settings**: allows easy adjustments for different objects.
4. **Test with multiple light directions**: ensures consistent visibility across the scene.
5. **Combine with textures**: Diffuse textures interact with lighting for richer visuals.

Putting It All Together

By combining **directional lights, ambient light, and material properties**, you can create 3D scenes that are visually appealing without writing custom shaders. This foundation is enough to render basic models with realistic illumination, prepare your game for textured materials, and set the stage for more advanced lighting techniques later.

8.4 Switching Between 2D & 3D

Many games combine 3D world rendering with 2D UI and sprites. The trick is controlling **render order**, **graphics states**, and coordinate transforms so each system draws correctly without interfering with the other.

Conceptual rules first (short)

Render the 3D world first using a depth buffer, then render 2D overlays (HUD, menus) with depth testing off. For 2D sprites that live in the 3D world (e.g. floating health bars), either render them as billboards using 3D geometry or project 3D points into screen coordinates and draw with SpriteBatch.

---

1) Typical render pipeline (pseudo-order)

1. Clear the screen and depth buffer.
2. Set DepthStencilState.Default and render all 3D objects (meshes, models) with BasicEffect or custom shaders (use View/Projection matrices).
3. Reset depth test (DepthStencilState.None) and render screen-space 2D overlays using SpriteBatch.
4. If needed, restore any state for other systems.

---

2) Minimal working example — 3D then 2D HUD

```
// fields

private BasicEffect _basicEffect;

private Model _model;

private SpriteBatch _spriteBatch;
```

```csharp
private SpriteFont _font;

private Matrix _view, _projection;


// in Initialize / LoadContent

_basicEffect = new BasicEffect(GraphicsDevice);

_model = Content.Load<Model>("Models/Player");

_spriteBatch = new SpriteBatch(GraphicsDevice);

_font = Content.Load<SpriteFont>("Fonts/GameFont");

// set camera

_view = Matrix.CreateLookAt(new Vector3(0, 10, 20),
Vector3.Zero, Vector3.Up);

_projection =
Matrix.CreatePerspectiveFieldOfView(MathHelper.PiOver
4, GraphicsDevice.Viewport.AspectRatio, 0.1f, 1000f);

// In Draw()

protected override void Draw(GameTime gameTime)

{

    GraphicsDevice.Clear(Color.CornflowerBlue);

    // 1) Render 3D objects with depth testing ON

    GraphicsDevice.DepthStencilState =
DepthStencilState.Default;

    Matrix world =
Matrix.CreateTranslation(Vector3.Zero);


    foreach (ModelMesh mesh in _model.Meshes)

    {
```

```
        foreach (BasicEffect effect in mesh.Effects)

        {

            effect.EnableDefaultLighting();

            effect.World = world;

            effect.View = _view;

            effect.Projection = _projection;

        }

        mesh.Draw();

    }

    // 2) Render 2D HUD with depth testing OFF

    GraphicsDevice.DepthStencilState =
DepthStencilState.None;

    _spriteBatch.Begin(); // default: Deferred,
AlphaBlend

    _spriteBatch.DrawString(_font, "Score: 1234", new
Vector2(16, 16), Color.White);

    _spriteBatch.End();


    base.Draw(gameTime);

}
```

Important: set `DepthStencilState` to `Default` while drawing 3D and to `None` before `SpriteBatch.Begin()` so sprites aren't culled by depth.

3) Projecting a 3D world position to screen space

If you want a 2D UI element (like a name tag or health bar) to sit above a 3D model's head, compute the screen coordinates from a world position and draw a sprite at that screen point.

```
// worldPos is the 3D point (e.g., model position +
Vector3.Up * height)

Vector3 worldPos = playerPosition + new Vector3(0,
playerHeight + 0.5f, 0);

// Project to screen

Vector3 screenPos =
GraphicsDevice.Viewport.Project(worldPos,
_projection, _view, Matrix.Identity);

// screenPos.X, screenPos.Y are pixel positions on
screen; use screenPos.Z to check if in front

if (screenPos.Z > 0 && screenPos.Z < 1f) // in view
frustum

{

    Vector2 uiPos = new Vector2(screenPos.X,
screenPos.Y);

    _spriteBatch.Begin();

    _spriteBatch.Draw(healthBarTexture, uiPos - new
Vector2(healthBarTexture.Width/2,
healthBarTexture.Height), Color.White);

    _spriteBatch.End();

}
```

Viewport.Project handles the world→view→projection transform + viewport mapping — ideal for UI anchored to world objects.

4) Drawing 2D sprites *in* the 3D world (billboards)

If you want sprites to exist as 3D objects (always facing camera), render textured quads in 3D that rotate to face the camera.

```
// Create a simple quad vertex buffer (two
triangles) in model space centered at origin

VertexPositionTexture[] quad = new
VertexPositionTexture[6];

// define positions (use sizeX/sizeY) and
corresponding UVs...

// Then create DynamicVertexBuffer or
DrawUserPrimitives when needed

// Compute billboard world matrix so quad faces
camera

Vector3 up = Vector3.Up;

Vector3 look =
Vector3.Normalize(GraphicsDevice.Viewport.TitleSa
feArea.Center.ToVector3() - (playerPosition + new
Vector3(0,1,0)) ); // simpler: use camera
position

Vector3 cameraDir =
Vector3.Normalize(cameraPosition - worldPos);

Matrix billboardRotation =
Matrix.CreateConstrainedBillboard(worldPos,
cameraPosition, Vector3.Up, null, null);

Matrix world = billboardRotation *
Matrix.CreateScale(1.0f); // scale to sprite size

// Setup effect to use texture
```

```
_basicEffect.TextureEnabled = true;

_basicEffect.Texture = healthBarTexture;

_basicEffect.World = world;

_basicEffect.View = _view;

_basicEffect.Projection = _projection;

// Draw the quad (two triangles)

foreach (var pass in
_basicEffect.CurrentTechnique.Passes)

{

    pass.Apply();


GraphicsDevice.DrawUserPrimitives(PrimitiveType.T
riangleList, quad, 0, 2);

}
```

MonoGame   offers
`Matrix.CreateConstrainedBillboard`   and
`CreateBillboard` to help orient quads toward the camera. This
method keeps sprites as part of the 3D scene, receiving lighting if
you add it to your shader.

---

5) Using a RenderTarget2D for 2D/3D composition or virtual resolution

If you want to render the entire 3D scene to a fixed virtual
resolution then draw UI on top, use a `RenderTarget2D`. Render

3D to the target, then draw the target texture scaled to the back buffer, then draw HUD.

```
RenderTarget2D sceneTarget = new
RenderTarget2D(GraphicsDevice, 1280, 720);

protected override void Draw(GameTime gameTime)

{

    // Render 3D scene into render target

    GraphicsDevice.SetRenderTarget(sceneTarget);

    GraphicsDevice.Clear(Color.CornflowerBlue);

    GraphicsDevice.DepthStencilState =
DepthStencilState.Default;

    Draw3DScene(); // your 3D draw code

    // Switch back to backbuffer

    GraphicsDevice.SetRenderTarget(null);

    GraphicsDevice.Clear(Color.Black);

    // Draw the scene texture scaled to screen

    _spriteBatch.Begin(samplerState:
SamplerState.PointClamp);

    _spriteBatch.Draw(sceneTarget,
GraphicsDevice.Viewport.Bounds, Color.White);

    _spriteBatch.End();

    // Draw UI overlays

    _spriteBatch.Begin();

    _spriteBatch.DrawString(_font, "Score: 999",
new Vector2(16, 16), Color.White);
```

```
    _spriteBatch.End();

}
```

This is useful for pixel-art 2D overlays or enforcing a consistent virtual resolution for the whole frame. Remember to clear the depth buffer before drawing 2D if you're still using it.

---

6) Common gotchas & tips

- **Render order matters**: draw 3D first, 2D last (unless 2D should occlude 3D intentionally).
- **Depth buffer** must be cleared and set appropriately. After 3D, set `DepthStencilState.None` before 2D so HUD is always visible.
- **SpriteBatch and depth**: `SpriteBatch` doesn't use the 3D depth buffer for 2D draws; it has its own depth sorting parameter (layerDepth). If you need sprites to be depth-tested vs 3D geometry, render them as textured 3D quads instead.
- **State leakage**: `SpriteBatch.Begin()` modifies device states; use `SpriteBatch.End()` and optionally reset states you expect afterward. If using custom `BlendState`/`SamplerState` in `Begin()`, pass the states explicitly.
- **Project vs Viewport.Transform**: use `Viewport.Project` to convert world→screen and `Viewport.Unproject` to convert screen→world (useful for ray picking).

- **Billboards and lighting**: basic `BasicEffect` will light 3D quads; if you need unlit sprites in 3D, disable lighting on the effect via `effect.LightingEnabled = false; effect.TextureEnabled = true;`.

---

7) Example: project a 3D point and draw a 2D label only if visible

```
Vector3 headWorld = playerPosition + new Vector3(0,
playerHeight, 0);

Vector3 projected =
GraphicsDevice.Viewport.Project(headWorld,
_projection, _view, Matrix.Identity);

if (projected.Z > 0 && projected.Z < 1f)

{

    Vector2 labelPos = new Vector2(projected.X,
projected.Y - 20); // offset above head

    GraphicsDevice.DepthStencilState =
DepthStencilState.None;

    _spriteBatch.Begin();

    _spriteBatch.DrawString(_font, playerName,
labelPos, Color.White);

    _spriteBatch.End();

}
```

This draws a HUD label tied to a world object, but only when the object is in the camera frustum.

8) When to render 2D as 3D vs projecting to 2D

Render 2D as 3D (billboards) when the sprite should be occluded by/occlude 3D geometry or should receive 3D transforms. Projecting to screen-space and drawing via `SpriteBatch` is simpler and cheaper for HUD elements that must always be visible and not part of the 3D depth relationships.

9) Quick checklist before shipping

- Confirm UI elements remain readable at all target resolutions (use render target scaling or UI manager).
- Test camera/viewport changes (resize, fullscreen) and recalc projection and HUD positions.
- Verify depth/stencil state transitions do not leak into other systems.
- Test projected UI anchors across edge cases (offscreen, behind camera).

8.5 Basic 3D Gameplay Example

This section gives you a compact, working pattern for a simple 3D gameplay loop in MonoGame: a controllable player (move + look), a moving enemy that chases the player, simple projectile firing, collision using bounding spheres, and a HUD element (health/score) drawn in 2D that's anchored above the enemy by projecting its 3D position to screen space. The code is ready to drop into a Game1-style class and explained so you can adapt it to your project.

Key ideas: render 3D world first (depth on), then draw 2D HUD (depth off); use Viewport.Project to map world → screen; use BasicEffect/models for simple 3D rendering.

What this example does (quick)

You'll get:

- WASD movement and mouse look for the player (simple third-person camera).
- One enemy that moves toward the player.
- Player can fire a projectile (forward vector) that collides with the enemy (bounding sphere).
- Health/score displayed on a 2D HUD; the enemy's name/health label anchored above its head using Viewport.Project.
- Clean render order and DepthStencil toggles.

Minimal, focused source (core parts)

Below are the important class members and methods. This is trimmed to the essentials — integrate into your Game1 and expand as needed.

```
// using directives

using Microsoft.Xna.Framework;
```

```csharp
using Microsoft.Xna.Framework.Graphics;

using Microsoft.Xna.Framework.Input;

using System.Collections.Generic;


// fields

GraphicsDeviceManager _graphics;

SpriteBatch _spriteBatch;

SpriteFont _font;


Model _playerModel;

Model _enemyModel;

Texture2D _projectileTex;


Matrix _view, _projection;

Vector3 _cameraOffset = new Vector3(0, 5, 15);

Vector3 _playerPosition = Vector3.Zero;

Vector3 _playerForward = Vector3.Forward; // initial
forward

float _playerSpeed = 10f;


Vector3 _enemyPosition = new Vector3(0, 0, 40);

float _enemySpeed = 6f;

int _enemyHealth = 3;
```

```csharp
List<Projectile> _projectiles = new
List<Projectile>();


// simple projectile class

class Projectile

{

    public Vector3 Position;

    public Vector3 Velocity;

    public float Radius = 0.3f;

    public bool Alive = true;

    public void Update(GameTime gt)

    {

        Position += Velocity *
(float)gt.ElapsedGameTime.TotalSeconds;

        // optional lifetime or bounds check

    }

}
```

LoadContent — load models, font, textures, and setup projection

```csharp
protected override void LoadContent()

{

    _spriteBatch = new SpriteBatch(GraphicsDevice);

    _font =
Content.Load<SpriteFont>("Fonts/GameFont");
```

```csharp
    _playerModel =
Content.Load<Model>("Models/Player");

    _enemyModel =
Content.Load<Model>("Models/Enemy");

    _projectileTex =
Content.Load<Texture2D>("Textures/Projectile");

    float fov = MathHelper.PiOver4;

    float aspect =
GraphicsDevice.Viewport.AspectRatio;

    _projection =
Matrix.CreatePerspectiveFieldOfView(fov, aspect,
0.1f, 1000f);

}
```

Update — handle input, fire projectiles, basic enemy AI, collisions

```csharp
protected override void Update(GameTime gameTime)

{

    float dt =
(float)gameTime.ElapsedGameTime.TotalSeconds;


    // Input: WASD for movement in XZ plane,
mouse X for yaw

    KeyboardState k = Keyboard.GetState();

    MouseState m = Mouse.GetState();


    Vector3 move = Vector3.Zero;
```

```csharp
    if (k.IsKeyDown(Keys.W)) move +=
Vector3.Forward;

    if (k.IsKeyDown(Keys.S)) move +=
Vector3.Backward;

    if (k.IsKeyDown(Keys.A)) move +=
Vector3.Left;

    if (k.IsKeyDown(Keys.D)) move +=
Vector3.Right;

    if (move != Vector3.Zero) move.Normalize();

    // Rotate forward vector by simple yaw from
left/right keys (or use mouse delta)

    if (k.IsKeyDown(Keys.Q)) _playerForward =
Vector3.Transform(_playerForward,
Matrix.CreateRotationY(1f * dt));

    if (k.IsKeyDown(Keys.E)) _playerForward =
Vector3.Transform(_playerForward,
Matrix.CreateRotationY(-1f * dt));

    _playerForward.Normalize();

    // Move relative to player's forward/right

    Vector3 right = Vector3.Cross(Vector3.Up,
_playerForward);

    _playerPosition += (_playerForward * move.Z +
right * move.X) * _playerSpeed * dt;


    // Camera follows behind the player
(third-person)

    Vector3 cameraPos = _playerPosition +
Vector3.Transform(_cameraOffset,
```

```csharp
Matrix.CreateLookAt(Vector3.Zero, _playerForward,
Vector3.Up).Invert());

    _view = Matrix.CreateLookAt(cameraPos,
_playerPosition + new Vector3(0,1.5f,0),
Vector3.Up);

    // Fire projectile on Space press (simple edge
detect)

    if (k.IsKeyDown(Keys.Space) &&
_previousKeyboard.IsKeyUp(Keys.Space))

    {

        Projectile p = new Projectile();

        p.Position = _playerPosition + new Vector3(0,
1.5f, 0) + _playerForward * 1.5f;

        p.Velocity = _playerForward * 30f;

        _projectiles.Add(p);

    }



    // Update projectiles

    for (int i = _projectiles.Count - 1; i >= 0; i--)

    {

        var p = _projectiles[i];

        p.Update(gameTime);

        // Check simple collision with enemy using
bounding sphere

        float dist = Vector3.Distance(p.Position,
_enemyPosition);
```

```
        if (dist < p.Radius + 1.0f) // enemy radius
~1.0f

        {

            p.Alive = false;

            _enemyHealth -= 1;

        }

        if (!p.Alive) _projectiles.RemoveAt(i);

    }

    // Enemy simple chase: move toward player on XZ
plane

    Vector3 toPlayer = _playerPosition -
_enemyPosition;

    toPlayer.Y = 0;

    if (toPlayer.LengthSquared() > 0.01f)

    {

        toPlayer.Normalize();

        _enemyPosition += toPlayer * _enemySpeed
* dt;

    }


    // Example: player takes damage if enemy
close

    if (Vector3.Distance(_playerPosition,
_enemyPosition) < 1.5f)
```

```
        {
            // handle player damage, knockback etc.
        }

        _previousKeyboard = k;

        base.Update(gameTime);
    }
```

Draw — render 3D models (depth on), then 2D HUD (depth off), and project enemy world pos to screen for label

```
protected override void Draw(GameTime gameTime)
{
    GraphicsDevice.Clear(Color.CornflowerBlue);

    // 1) 3D pass: enable depth test

    GraphicsDevice.DepthStencilState =
DepthStencilState.Default;

    // draw player model

    DrawModelAt(_playerModel, _playerPosition,
Matrix.CreateRotationY(0f)); // helper below

    // draw enemy model

    DrawModelAt(_enemyModel, _enemyPosition,
Matrix.CreateRotationY(0f));

    // draw projectiles as simple billboards (or
small tinted spheres)

    foreach (var p in _projectiles)
```

```
    {

        // use simple textured quad in world
(billboard) or tiny sphere mesh — for brevity we'll
render a scaled quad facing camera using
CreateConstrainedBillboard

        Matrix bb =
Matrix.CreateConstrainedBillboard(p.Position,
/*cameraPos*/ _view.Invert().Translation, Vector3.Up,
null, null)

                    * Matrix.CreateScale(0.5f);

        DrawTexturedQuad(bb, _projectileTex); // user
helper to draw a textured quad with BasicEffect

    }

    // 2) Project enemy head to screen for label/HUD

    Vector3 enemyHeadWorld = _enemyPosition + new
Vector3(0, 2.2f, 0); // adjust height

    Vector3 proj =
GraphicsDevice.Viewport.Project(enemyHeadWorld,
_projection, _view, Matrix.Identity);

    bool enemyVisible = proj.Z > 0 && proj.Z < 1f; //
inside view frustum

    // 3) HUD: disable depth test and draw
spritebatch text

    GraphicsDevice.DepthStencilState =
DepthStencilState.None;

    _spriteBatch.Begin();

    _spriteBatch.DrawString(_font, $"Enemy HP:
{_enemyHealth}", new Vector2(16, 16), Color.White);

    if (enemyVisible)

    {
```

```
        Vector2 screenPos = new Vector2(proj.X,
proj.Y - 20);

        _spriteBatch.DrawString(_font, "Enemy",
screenPos, Color.Yellow);

    }

    _spriteBatch.End();



    base.Draw(gameTime);

}
```

Helper methods (sketches — keep them small and focused in your project):

```
void DrawModelAt(Model model, Vector3 position,
Matrix rotation)

{

    Matrix world = Matrix.CreateScale(1.0f) *
rotation * Matrix.CreateTranslation(position);

    foreach (ModelMesh mesh in model.Meshes)

    {

        foreach (BasicEffect effect in mesh.Effects)

        {

            effect.EnableDefaultLighting();

            effect.World = world;

            effect.View = _view;

            effect.Projection = _projection;
```

```
        }

        mesh.Draw();

    }

}


void DrawTexturedQuad(Matrix world, Texture2D tex)

{

    // Setup a BasicEffect with texture enabled, draw
a unit quad via DrawUserPrimitives.

    // Implementation detail omitted here — see
"billboard" examples
(Matrix.CreateConstrainedBillboard).

}
```

Notes & guidance

Projecting world → screen: use Viewport.Project to map 3D points to 2D screen coordinates — it returns X,Y in pixels and Z as the normalized depth (0..1). Check Z to ensure the point is in front of the camera before drawing UI anchored to it.

Billboards (sprites in 3D): for projectiles or floating UI that should face the camera, use Matrix.CreateBillboard or Matrix.CreateConstrainedBillboard to orient a quad toward the camera, then draw that quad as textured geometry. This keeps them part of the 3D scene so they can be occluded by geometry.

Render order & depth: render 3D geometry with `DepthStencilState.Default`. Before drawing 2D HUD with `SpriteBatch`, set `GraphicsDevice.DepthStencilState = DepthStencilState.None` so HUD always draws on top. `SpriteBatch` does not use the 3D depth buffer. If you need sprites to be depth-tested against 3D objects, render them as 3D quads (billboards) instead.

RenderTarget approach: if you want to produce a virtual-resolution 3D scene (or apply full-frame post-processing) render the 3D scene to a `RenderTarget2D` and then draw that texture scaled to the backbuffer before drawing UI. This also isolates 3D rendering and makes HUD composition predictable.

Chapter 9: Advanced Graphics & Shaders

You'll apply shaders and visual effects to make your games look amazing. You'll learn how to optimize rendering and enhance visuals without slowing down your game. By the end, your games will stand out visually.

9.1 — Introduction to Shaders in MonoGame

This section gives a compact, practical introduction to writing and using shaders (effects) in MonoGame. You'll learn what MonoGame expects from shader files, how to compile them, how to load and drive them from C#, and see two small, complete working examples: a tint shader and a grayscale shader. Explanations are short and tightly focused so you can read, copy, and run them immediately.

What a "shader" / "effect" is (quickly)

A shader is a small program that runs on the GPU to compute per-vertex and/or per-pixel results. MonoGame follows the XNA-style Effect system: you write effect source in HLSL (a .fx style file), compile it to the MonoGame effect binary (mgfxo) using the MonoGame Effects Compiler (MGFXC) or the Content

Pipeline, then load and use it through the `Effect` API in C#. MonoGame maps the effect parameters you declare in HLSL to `EffectParameter` objects you set from your game code.

Basic workflow (high level)

Write `.fx` (HLSL) → compile with MGFXC (usually via the Content Pipeline) → load `Effect` in C# (`Content.Load<Effect>("name")` or load bytes) → set parameters with `effect.Parameters["ParamName"].SetValue(...)` → apply the effect (via `SpriteBatch.Begin(..., effect: myEffect)` for sprites or `effect.CurrentTechnique.Passes[0].Apply()` for custom geometry) → draw. The MonoGame docs and tutorials walk this through and the MGFX tools handle platform specifics for you.

Key platform gotchas

MonoGame's shader toolchain historically relies on Microsoft/DirectX shader tooling, which can complicate building effects on macOS/Linux (especially ARM/M1) without extra steps or remote/Windows builds. If you plan to target non-Windows platforms, test your pipeline and consider the Content Pipeline's behavior on your target OS. Also be careful about shader profiles (ps_4_0 / ps_3_0) and the MGFXC version—different platforms or MonoGame versions may require different compile flags.

257

Example 1 — Simple tint effect (complete, copy-paste)

This example shows a minimal pixel shader that multiplies the sampled texture color by a tint color parameter (ColorTint) and how to use it with SpriteBatch.

Tint.fx (HLSL / effect source)

```
// Tint.fx

sampler2D TextureSampler : register(s0);

float4 ColorTint; // RGBA color multiplier

struct PS_INPUT

{

    float2 TexCoord : TEXCOORD0;

};

float4 PixelShader(PS_INPUT input) : COLOR

{

    float4 tex = tex2D(TextureSampler,
input.TexCoord);

    return tex * ColorTint;

}


technique Technique1

{

    pass P0
```

```
    {

        PixelShader = compile ps_4_0_level_9_1
PixelShader();

    }

}
```

Notes:

1. `sampler2D` is the texture sampler binding. MonoGame maps the sprite texture into register `s0` when you draw with `SpriteBatch`.
2. The `ColorTint` parameter name becomes available as `effect.Parameters["ColorTint"]` in C#.
3. The `compile` target uses a pixel shader profile; adjust if your platform or MonoGame version requires another profile.

How to compile & include

Add `Tint.fx` to your Content Pipeline project (Content.mgcb). The MonoGame Content Pipeline will call MGFXC to create the `.mgfxo` binary that MonoGame loads as an `Effect`. On some non-Windows setups you may need additional pipeline configuration or a remote/Windows builder.

C# usage (MonoGame)

```
// Fields

Effect tintEffect;

Texture2D mySprite;
```

```csharp
// LoadContent

protected override void LoadContent()

{

    mySprite = Content.Load<Texture2D>("mysprite");

    tintEffect = Content.Load<Effect>("Tint"); //
Tint.fx -> Tint.mgfxo -> Content.Load<Effect>("Tint")

}

// Draw

protected override void Draw(GameTime gameTime)

{

    GraphicsDevice.Clear(Color.CornflowerBlue);


    // Set the tint to light red with full alpha

    tintEffect.Parameters["ColorTint"].SetValue(new
Vector4(1f, 0.5f, 0.5f, 1f));


    // Use SpriteBatch and pass the effect in the
Begin parameters.

    spriteBatch.Begin(SpriteSortMode.Deferred,
BlendState.AlphaBlend, null, null, null, tintEffect);

    spriteBatch.Draw(mySprite, new Vector2(100, 100),
Color.White);

    spriteBatch.End();

}
```

Important: pass the `Effect` into `SpriteBatch.Begin` (there's an overload that accepts an `Effect`) so that SpriteBatch draws sprites using your pixel shader. Alternatively, for manual geometry rendering you can `effect.CurrentTechnique.Passes[0].Apply()` then issue `GraphicsDevice.DrawPrimitives(...)`.

Example 2 — Grayscale shader

A tiny shader to convert an input texture to grayscale using luminance weights (a common effect). This shows a slightly more "real" pixel manipulation example.

Gray.fx

```
sampler2D TextureSampler : register(s0);

float LuminanceWeights[3]; // {0.299, 0.587, 0.114}

struct PS_INPUT { float2 TexCoord : TEXCOORD0; };

float4 PixelShader(PS_INPUT input) : COLOR

{

    float4 tex = tex2D(TextureSampler,
input.TexCoord);

    float gray = dot(tex.rgb, LuminanceWeights);

    return float4(gray, gray, gray, tex.a);

}

technique Technique1
```

```
{

    pass P0

    {

        PixelShader = compile ps_4_0_level_9_1
PixelShader();

    }

}
```

C# usage

```csharp
Effect grayEffect;

Texture2D sprite;

protected override void LoadContent()

{

    sprite = Content.Load<Texture2D>("mysprite");

    grayEffect = Content.Load<Effect>("Gray");

}

protected override void Draw(GameTime gameTime)

{

    // Luminance vector commonly used


grayEffect.Parameters["LuminanceWeights"].SetValue(new float[]{0.299f, 0.587f, 0.114f});


    spriteBatch.Begin(SpriteSortMode.Deferred,
BlendState.AlphaBlend, null, null, null, grayEffect);
```

```
    spriteBatch.Draw(sprite, new Vector2(200, 100),
Color.White);

    spriteBatch.End();

}
```

Note: Some MonoGame versions and platforms may require the float array to be set carefully (use `float[]` and ensure types match) — passing literal ints to a float parameter can produce runtime type issues. If you see an exception, ensure values are `float` (`0.299f`) not double/int.

Best practices and performance tips

Set effect parameters sparingly. Many platforms only upload changed parameters to the GPU when a pass is applied, so cache `EffectParameter` references and avoid calling `SetValue` every frame unless the value actually changes. Group draws that use the same effect and parameters to reduce state changes and draw calls. When using `SpriteBatch` with an effect, prefer `SpriteSortMode.Deferred` for batching unless you need immediate state changes. These practices minimize CPU–GPU overhead and keep draw calls efficient.

When to call `.Apply()` vs. `SpriteBatch.Begin(effect)`

If you draw geometry yourself (vertex buffers, custom primitives), use `effect.CurrentTechnique.Passes[0].Apply()` imme diately before issuing draw calls so the GPU state is set. If you draw sprites with `SpriteBatch`, prefer the `SpriteBatch.Begin(..., effect: myEffect)` overload—`SpriteBatch` will apply the effect internally for each batch. Both approaches are valid; choose the one matching the drawing API you use.

Troubleshooting checklist

If your shader doesn't run or you get compile/load errors:

1. Make sure the `.fx` was added to the Content Pipeline and compiled to `.mgfxo` (check output of MGFXC).
2. Confirm parameter names in HLSL match the strings you use in C# (`effect.Parameters["Name"]`). Parameter name mismatch is a common cause of runtime nulls.
3. If running on macOS/Linux, double-check your build chain and consider the known limitations of compiling HLSL on non-Windows.
4. Use explicit float suffixes (`1.0f`) when calling `SetValue` to avoid casting issues. Some MonoGame versions throw exceptions if you pass an `int` where a `float` is expected.

Where to go next (practical suggestions)

After you've run the tint and grayscale shaders:

1. Replace the pixel shader with effects that sample multiple textures (e.g., normal maps), apply post-processing to fullscreen quads, or implement palette swaps and color grading.
2. Experiment with vertex shaders to deform vertices for screen-space distortion or parallax.
3. Explore the MonoGame HLSL examples repo for more advanced, runnable examples you can learn from and adapt.

Short reference: common API snippets

Load an effect:

```
var myEffect = Content.Load<Effect>("MyEffect"); //
after compiling MyEffect.fx via the Content Pipeline
```

Set a parameter:

```
myEffect.Parameters["ParamName"].SetValue(42f);
// float

myEffect.Parameters["Vec4Param"].SetValue(new
Vector4(1,0,0,1));

myEffect.Parameters["TexParam"].SetValue(someText
ure); // texture parameters are set by MonoGame's
binding
```

Use with SpriteBatch:

```
spriteBatch.Begin(SpriteSortMode.Deferred,
BlendState.AlphaBlend, null, null, null,
myEffect);

spriteBatch.Draw(...);
```

```
spriteBatch.End();
```

Final practical notes

MonoGame's shader system is powerful and closely follows the XNA Effect pattern. For many 2D games you'll implement small pixel shaders for visual polish and occasional vertex/geometry shaders for effects. Keep your HLSL simple at first, test on your target platforms, and use the Content Pipeline tooling (MGFXC) to manage compilation. Official MonoGame docs, community tutorials, and example repositories provide many ready-to-run examples to learn from.

9.2 — Using Shaders for Effects (Color, Lighting)

This section shows how to use shaders (effects) in MonoGame to control color and to light sprites and scenes. The goal is practical: by the end you will understand simple color transforms, how to add per-pixel lighting with normal maps, and how to wire everything from C# (including a fullscreen post-process path). Explanations are compact and concrete; each concept is followed by working HLSL and C# code you can paste into a MonoGame project and run.

Quick mental model

Color effects change the pixels you draw (tint, saturation, LUTs). Lighting effects blend scene color with simulated illumination computed per-pixel (ambient, directional, point lights). For convincing 2D lighting you usually need two textures per sprite: the diffuse (color) texture and a normal map that encodes surface normals. The shader reads the normal map to compute how much light hits each pixel and adds diffuse/specular contributions accordingly. This technique is commonly used in MonoGame and XNA-era engines and widely demonstrated in community tutorials and repos.

Part A — Color effects (tint, hue/saturation, and a simple LUT)

1) Tint (reminder)

We already covered a tint shader in the previous section; it simply multiplies the sampled color by a uniform ColorTint. The same pattern is the base for more advanced color operations.

2) Hue / Saturation / Value adjuster (HSL-lite)

This shader performs saturation and brightness adjustments in the pixel shader. It's short, stable and useful for palette or mood changes.

ColorAdjust.fx

```
sampler2D TextureSampler : register(s0);


float Saturation; // 0 = grayscale, 1 = original
```

```
float Brightness; // additive brightness (-1..1)

struct PS_INPUT { float2 TexCoord : TEXCOORD0; };

float4 PixelShader(PS_INPUT input) : COLOR

{

    float4 col = tex2D(TextureSampler,
input.TexCoord);

    // Convert RGB -> perceived luminance

    float luminance = dot(col.rgb, float3(0.2126,
0.7152, 0.0722));

    // Lerp between grayscale and original by
Saturation

    col.rgb = lerp(float3(luminance, luminance,
luminance), col.rgb, Saturation);

    // Apply brightness (simple additive)

    col.rgb += Brightness;


    // Keep alpha unchanged and clamp color

    return float4(saturate(col.rgb), col.a);

}


technique Technique1

{

    pass P0 { PixelShader = compile ps_4_0_level_9_1
PixelShader(); }

}
```

C# usage

```
Effect colorAdjust;

Texture2D sprite;


protected override void LoadContent()

{

    sprite = Content.Load<Texture2D>("mysprite");

    colorAdjust =
Content.Load<Effect>("ColorAdjust");

}

protected override void Draw(GameTime gameTime)

{


colorAdjust.Parameters["Saturation"].SetValue(0.6f);
// desaturate slightly


colorAdjust.Parameters["Brightness"].SetValue(0.05f);
// small brighten

    spriteBatch.Begin(effect: colorAdjust);

    spriteBatch.Draw(sprite, new Vector2(100, 100),
Color.White);

    spriteBatch.End();

}
```

This approach is cheap and versatile for on-the-fly color mood shifts. For advanced color grading (film-style), use a 3D LUT or a 1D LUT texture sampled in the shader, but that requires a slightly larger pipeline (creating and shipping the LUT texture).

Part B — Lighting fundamentals (ambient, directional, point)

Lighting in shaders typically computes three pieces: ambient (constant base light), diffuse (angle-dependent color from a light source), and specular (shininess highlights). For 2D normal-mapped sprites you compute per-pixel normal vectors from a normal map and then evaluate light equations per pixel.

A simple Blinn-Phong style formula for a single point light:
Diffuse = max(dot(N, L), 0) * LightColor * LightIntensity
Specular = pow(max(dot(H, N), 0), shininess) * SpecularStrength
where N is the normal, L is the light direction (from pixel to light), and H is the half-vector between view and light directions. For 2D orthographic games we treat the view vector as (0,0,1).

Part C — Normal-mapped sprite lighting (complete example)

This is the canonical, practical example: a shader that reads two textures — the color map and a normal map — and computes a point light with diffuse + specular. The shader assumes the sprite's normal map uses the typical tangent-space encoding where normal components are mapped from [0,1] to [-1,1] (R = X, G = Y, B unused or Z).

SpriteNormalLight.fx

```
// Assumes main sprite texture is bound at s0 by
SpriteBatch.
```

```hlsl
// We declare an explicit normal map sampler for
s1.

sampler2D TextureSampler : register(s0);

sampler2D NormalSampler  : register(s1);

float2 LightPosition;       // in screen (pixel)
coordinates

float3 LightColor;          // RGB 0..1

float LightIntensity;       // scalar multiplier

float LightRange;           // radius in pixels

float Ambient;              // ambient term 0..1

float SpecularPower;        // shininess exponent

float SpecularStrength;     // specular multiplier

struct PS_INPUT { float2 TexCoord : TEXCOORD0;
float4 Position : SV_POSITION; };

float4 PixelShader(PS_INPUT input) : COLOR

{

    // Sample diffuse color

    float4 diffuse = tex2D(TextureSampler,
input.TexCoord);

    // Sample normal map and convert from [0,1]
to [-1,1]

    float3 nmap = tex2D(NormalSampler,
input.TexCoord).rgb;

    float3 N = normalize(nmap * 2.0f - 1.0f);
```

```
    // Calculate pixel position in screen/pixel
coords

    // SV_POSITION.xy holds clip-space pixel
position when using SpriteBatch's built-in vertex
shader

    float2 pixelPos = input.Position.xy;

    // Compute vector from pixel to light (L),
and distance

    float2 toLight = LightPosition - pixelPos;

    float dist = length(toLight);

    // Attenuation (smooth falloff)

    float att = saturate(1.0 - (dist /
LightRange)); // simple linear falloff

    att *= att; // stronger falloff
(quadratic-ish)

    float3 L = normalize(float3(toLight, 0)); //
since light exists in XY; Z = 0

    // View direction (for 2D orthographic view
we point towards +Z)

    float3 V = float3(0,0,1);

    // Half vector

    float3 H = normalize(L + V);


    // Diffuse: dot(N, L) but ensure positive

    float diff = max(dot(N, L), 0.0);

    // Specular: Blinn-Phong
```

```
    float spec = pow(max(dot(N, H), 0.0),
SpecularPower) * SpecularStrength;

    // Combine

    float3 lighting = Ambient + (diff *
LightColor * LightIntensity + spec * LightColor)
* att;

    float3 outColor = diffuse.rgb * lighting;

    return float4(saturate(outColor), diffuse.a);

}

technique Technique1

{

    pass P0 { PixelShader = compile
ps_4_0_level_9_1 PixelShader(); }

}
```

Key implementation notes:

The shader uses the `input.Position.xy` provided by SpriteBatch's vertex shader to compute pixel-space positions. SpriteBatch's built-in vertex shader will create SV_POSITION values appropriated for this use when you draw at integer screen positions; if you notice offsets, make sure you draw with coordinates matching the backbuffer pixels and consider rounding positions to integers in C#. Community threads and examples show this is a common source of off-by-one or origin problems.

C# usage (drawing a single lit sprite)

```
Effect normalLightEffect;

Texture2D sprite;
```

```csharp
Texture2D normalMap;

protected override void LoadContent()

{

    sprite = Content.Load<Texture2D>("mysprite");

    normalMap =
Content.Load<Texture2D>("mysprite_normal"); // your
normal map texture

    normalLightEffect =
Content.Load<Effect>("SpriteNormalLight");

}


protected override void Draw(GameTime gameTime)

{

    GraphicsDevice.Clear(Color.Black);


    Vector2 spritePos = new Vector2(200, 120);

    // Set light in screen-space pixel coords (e.g.,
mouse position)

    Vector2 mouse = new Vector2(Mouse.GetState().X,
Mouse.GetState().Y);



normalLightEffect.Parameters["LightPosition"].SetValu
e(new Vector2(mouse.X, mouse.Y));


normalLightEffect.Parameters["LightColor"].SetValue(n
ew Vector3(1f, 0.9f, 0.8f));
```

```
normalLightEffect.Parameters["LightIntensity"].SetVal
ue(1.5f);


normalLightEffect.Parameters["LightRange"].SetValue(2
50f);


normalLightEffect.Parameters["Ambient"].SetValue(0.2f
);


normalLightEffect.Parameters["SpecularPower"].SetValu
e(32f);


normalLightEffect.Parameters["SpecularStrength"].SetV
alue(0.6f);



    // Set the normal map explicitly (SpriteBatch
binds the primary texture to s0)


normalLightEffect.Parameters["NormalSampler"].SetValu
e(normalMap);



    spriteBatch.Begin(SpriteSortMode.Deferred,
BlendState.AlphaBlend, null, null, null,
normalLightEffect);

    // Draw the sprite; SpriteBatch will bind the
main sprite texture to s0 automatically

    spriteBatch.Draw(sprite, spritePos, Color.White);

    spriteBatch.End();

}
```

If your normal map seems inverted or lighting looks wrong from certain angles, verify the normal map encoding (some tools encode Y inverted), and check whether your shader expects normal.x/y in a specific handedness. Normal map creation tools (SpriteLamp, Photoshop plugins) and community examples show slightly different conventions—flip the green channel if normals appear to point the wrong way.

Part D — Fullscreen lighting / post-process light composition

For scenes with many sprites it's common to separate the rendering into two passes: render the scene to a color `RenderTarget2D`, render your light sources to a light buffer (white radial gradients or normal-based lighting), then composite them in a fullscreen post-process pass that multiplies the scene by the light buffer (or adds specular highlights). This reduces per-sprite shader work and allows many lights to be combined more cheaply.

Workflow:

1. Draw scene (diffuse) to `RenderTarget2D SceneRT`.
2. Clear `RenderTarget2D LightRT` to ambient color and draw light sprites (simple additive circles or point-light shader) into LightRT using additive blending.
3. Set `SceneRT` and `LightRT` as inputs to a fullscreen shader that composites: out = Scene * Light + specular(s) as desired, then draw to backbuffer.

This technique (deferred-ish for 2D) is widely used for efficient multi-light scenes in MonoGame community projects; repositories and tutorials demonstrate implementations and tradeoffs.

Sample composite shader (full-screen multiply)

```
sampler2D SceneTex : register(s0);

sampler2D LightTex : register(s1);


struct PS_IN { float2 Tex : TEXCOORD0; };


float4 PS(PS_IN IN) : SV_Target

{

    float4 scene = tex2D(SceneTex, IN.Tex);

    float4 light = tex2D(LightTex, IN.Tex); // light
buffer is typically white in lit areas, darker
elsewhere

    return float4(scene.rgb * light.rgb, scene.a);

}

technique Tech { pass P0 { PixelShader = compile
ps_4_0_level_9_1 PS(); } }
```

This final composite is cheap and plays very well on lower-end GPUs: the per-pixel lighting cost is moved to the LightRT pass where you can render a limited number of lights or low-resolution light buffers and upsample when needed.

Part E — Practical tips, gotchas, and performance

If you'll rely on normal maps and many lights, measure: sampling extra textures (normal map) and computing per-pixel lighting is heavier than a simple color tint. Use these practical approaches: for many small lights, render light sprites to a lower-res light render target and blur it for soft lighting; group sprites by whether they need lighting; keep normal maps at the lowest acceptable resolution; cache `EffectParameter` references and only call `SetValue` when values change; and favor `SpriteSortMode.Deferred` for SpriteBatch batching when using an Effect. Many MonoGame community threads and projects discuss these tradeoffs and provide implementation examples.

Common debugging checks: if lighting only appears near (0,0) or offset, verify you're using the correct coordinate space (pixel vs. normalized UV); ensure your `LightPosition` uses the same space as `input.Position.xy` in the shader; and double-check normal map channel conventions (green channel flip). These are common issues discussed in forum threads and Q&A.

Minimal checklist to get lighting working quickly

Render the sprite and normal map at the same size. Make sure SpriteBatch and your shader agree on pixel coordinates. Pass the normal map into the shader as an extra texture. Use a simple linear attenuation and tweak `LightRange` to taste. Test with a single white light first, then add color and specular. Many community examples provide ready-to-run HLSL shaders you can adapt.

9.3 — Render Targets & Post-Processing Effects

This section teaches you how to render to textures (RenderTarget2D) and build post-processing passes in MonoGame. You'll learn the standard two-pass workflow (render scene → post-process → present), how to write a simple fullscreen effect, how to implement a separable blur (useful for bloom), and practical tips for correctness and performance. Every code sample is immediately usable in a MonoGame project: drop the `.fx` files into your Content Pipeline, compile, and wire the C# as shown.

The core idea (one sentence)

A RenderTarget2D is a texture the graphics device can render into; by drawing your whole scene into one (or more) render targets you can treat the completed image as a texture and run cheap or expensive full-screen effects on it before sending the final result to the screen.

Basic two-pass workflow (code first, then explanation)

Create the render target (usually in LoadContent), render the scene into it, reset the render target to null (the back buffer), then draw the render target with a fullscreen shader.

Create a RenderTarget2D

```
RenderTarget2D sceneTarget;

protected override void LoadContent()

{

    int width =
GraphicsDevice.PresentationParameters.BackBufferW
idth;

    int height =
GraphicsDevice.PresentationParameters.BackBufferH
eight;

    sceneTarget = new RenderTarget2D(

        GraphicsDevice,

        width,

        height,

        false,


GraphicsDevice.PresentationParameters.BackBufferF
ormat,

        DepthFormat.None,

        0, // preferred multi-sample count

        RenderTargetUsage.DiscardContents //
cheaper if you don't need preserved contents
```

```
    );

}
```

Draw using the render target

```
protected override void Draw(GameTime gameTime)

{

    // 1) Render scene to texture

    GraphicsDevice.SetRenderTarget(sceneTarget);

    GraphicsDevice.Clear(Color.CornflowerBlue);


    spriteBatch.Begin(SpriteSortMode.Deferred,
BlendState.AlphaBlend);

    DrawSceneSprites(); // your normal
sprite/geometry draw calls here

    spriteBatch.End();

    // 2) Reset to back buffer

    GraphicsDevice.SetRenderTarget(null);

    GraphicsDevice.Clear(Color.Black);

    // 3) Apply post-processing effect while drawing
the render target to screen


postProcessEffect.Parameters["SceneTex"].SetValue(sce
neTarget);

    spriteBatch.Begin(effect: postProcessEffect);

    spriteBatch.Draw(sceneTarget, Vector2.Zero,
Color.White);

    spriteBatch.End();
```

}

Why this works: while `sceneTarget` is set the GPU writes pixels into that texture. After you set the render target back to `null`, that texture can be sampled by shaders. `SpriteBatch` will bind the texture to the shader sampler when you draw it.

Example 1 — Fullscreen grayscale post-process

Simple and useful for debugging: convert the frame to grayscale in a single pass.

Grayscale.fx

```
sampler2D SceneTex : register(s0);

struct PS_IN { float2 Tex : TEXCOORD0; };

float4 PS(PS_IN IN) : SV_Target

{

    float4 c = tex2D(SceneTex, IN.Tex);

    float lum = dot(c.rgb, float3(0.2126, 0.7152,
0.0722));

    return float4(lum, lum, lum, c.a);

}

technique Tech { pass P0 { PixelShader = compile
ps_4_0_level_9_1 PS(); } }
```

Set `postProcessEffect` = `Content.Load<Effect>("Grayscale");` and the drawing code above will render the whole screen in grayscale.

Example 2 — Two-pass separable Gaussian blur (fast blur for bloom/softening)

A separable blur performs a vertical pass then a horizontal pass and is much faster than a full 2D kernel. You need two render targets (or one you ping-pong between).

BlurHorizontal.fx

```
sampler2D SceneTex : register(s0);

float TexelWidth; // 1 / textureWidth

struct PS_IN { float2 Tex : TEXCOORD0; };

float weights[5] = {0.204164f, 0.304005f, 0.093913f,
0.010381f, 0.000483f}; // example

float4 PS(PS_IN IN) : SV_Target

{

    float2 uv = IN.Tex;

    float4 sum = tex2D(SceneTex, uv) * weights[0];

    for (int i = 1; i < 5; ++i)

    {

        sum += tex2D(SceneTex, uv + float2(TexelWidth
* i, 0)) * weights[i];
```

```
        sum += tex2D(SceneTex, uv - float2(TexelWidth
* i, 0)) * weights[i];

    }

    return sum;

}



technique Tech { pass P0 { PixelShader = compile
ps_4_0_level_9_1 PS(); } }
```

BlurVertical.fx is the same but uses TexelHeight and samples
uv + float2(0, TexelHeight * i).

C# orchestration

```
RenderTarget2D rt1, rt2;

// LoadContent: create rt1 and rt2 (often same size,
can be lower resolution)

blurH = Content.Load<Effect>("BlurHorizontal");

blurV = Content.Load<Effect>("BlurVertical");

// In Draw after rendering scene into sceneTarget:

GraphicsDevice.SetRenderTarget(rt1);

GraphicsDevice.Clear(Color.Transparent);

blurH.Parameters["TexelWidth"].SetValue(1f /
sceneTarget.Width);

blurH.Parameters["SceneTex"].SetValue(sceneTarget);

spriteBatch.Begin(effect: blurH);

spriteBatch.Draw(sceneTarget, Vector2.Zero,
Color.White);
```

```
spriteBatch.End();

GraphicsDevice.SetRenderTarget(rt2);

GraphicsDevice.Clear(Color.Transparent);

blurV.Parameters["TexelHeight"].SetValue(1f /
sceneTarget.Height);

blurV.Parameters["SceneTex"].SetValue(rt1);

spriteBatch.Begin(effect: blurV);

spriteBatch.Draw(rt1, Vector2.Zero, Color.White);

spriteBatch.End();

// Finally composite: draw sceneTarget modulated by
blurred light (for bloom)

// or draw rt2 as overlay/additive as appropriate

GraphicsDevice.SetRenderTarget(null);

spriteBatch.Begin();

spriteBatch.Draw(sceneTarget, Vector2.Zero,
Color.White); // base

spriteBatch.Draw(rt2, Vector2.Zero, Color.White *
0.8f); // bloom/soft glow

spriteBatch.End();
```

Use a reduced resolution for `rt1`/`rt2` (half or quarter size) to speed up blur while preserving visual softness.

Advanced usage: multi-render targets (MRT) and bright pass for bloom

For bloom you usually do:

1. Render the scene normally to `SceneRT`.
2. Bright-pass: render only the bright areas into a `BrightRT` (shader keeps pixels above a threshold).
3. Blur the `BrightRT` via separable blur passes (one or two ping-pong render targets).
4. Composite: final = Scene * (1 + blurredBright * intensity) or Scene + blurredBright (additive).

Using multiple render targets (MRT) you can write out both color and brightness information in the same pass on platforms that support it, but MRT support and shader targets vary by platform. If targeting many platforms, the two-pass approach (separate draw calls) is the most portable.

Correctness & common gotchas

Always call `spriteBatch.End()` before changing render targets. SpriteBatch batches draws and changing the render target while a batch is open may flush in unexpected ways—set the RT outside Begin/End blocks and use distinct Begin/End cycles for each RT pass. If you see black textures or missing content after a few frames, you might be hitting a device reset issue or using `RenderTargetUsage.DiscardContents` incorrectly; use `RenderTargetUsage.PreserveContents` only when you need to keep its contents between uses, but expect it to be slower and sometimes unsupported on certain backends. When the back buffer resizes (window resize or display change), you must recreate render targets sized to the new back buffer. Render targets are GPU resources; dispose them when not needed to avoid memory pressure.

When sampling a render target you are writing to, most APIs forbid sampling from the currently bound render target. That is why the typical pattern renders the scene into `sceneTarget`, unbinds it (`SetRenderTarget(null)`), then samples it. Trying to sample a render target while it is active for drawing will produce undefined behavior or driver errors.

If pixel-perfect coordinate alignment matters (for pixel art), ensure you render to render targets at the same resolution as your virtual canvas and copy to the back buffer without scaling, or use integer snapping when drawing the final texture.

Performance tips

Prefer `RenderTargetUsage.DiscardContents` for performance unless you need the contents preserved. Use lower-resolution render targets for expensive passes (bloom/blur/lights) and upsample when compositing. Minimize extra texture reads in your post-process shader and keep kernel sizes small; separable blurs are much cheaper than 2D kernels. Reuse ping-pong RTs rather than creating/destroying them each frame. Batch draws per-RT to reduce state changes and keep `SpriteSortMode.Deferred` where possible for maximum batching.

Debugging checklist (fast)

If post-processing does nothing or produces black textures, check these in order: are you setting and clearing the intended render target? did you call `GraphicsDevice.SetRenderTarget(null)` before sampling? did you `spriteBatch.End()` before switching targets? are your RTs created at the expected size and format? did the Content Pipeline compile your effect correctly for the target platform? Recreate the minimal case: draw a solid color to an RT, reset the RT, draw the RT to screen. If that fails, it's a device/RT creation issue rather than shader code.

Practical patterns you'll use

Render-to-texture for screen scaling and UI thumbnails, single-pass post-process effects (color grading, vignette, film grain), multi-pass bloom using bright-pass + separable blur, light composition using an additive light buffer, and downsample-blur-upsample tricks to get soft effects cheaply.

Ready-to-run checklist (what to include in your sample project)

A) `sceneTarget` (full screen) and optionally `pingTargetA/B` for blur passes.

B) Post-process effects: Grayscale (single pass), BrightPass, BlurH/BlurV, Composite.

C) Content pipeline entries for the `.fx` files compiled to `.mgfxo`.

D) Careful Begin/End and `SetRenderTarget(...)` usage as shown above.

E) Resize handling: recreate render targets when back buffer size changes.

9.4 — Optimizing Draw Calls & Rendering Performance

This section shows practical, tested ways to get the most draw throughput out of MonoGame. You'll learn where time is spent, which rendering choices matter most, and exactly how to change your code so the GPU and CPU do less work per frame. Every concept is tied to concrete, copy-pasteable code you can drop into a MonoGame project and test immediately.

The single rule that explains almost everything

Every time you change render state (texture, shader, blend state, render target, etc.) or call the GPU with a new draw call you pay CPU and GPU overhead. The fastest games minimize state changes and total draw calls by grouping work that can be drawn together. Think "fewer big batches" instead of "many tiny draws."

Measure first, change second

Before optimizing, measure where you spend time. Use Stopwatch for CPU frame timing and count draw calls (add a counter around GraphicsDevice.Draw* or track SpriteBatch Begin/End calls). For GPU bottlenecks use GPU

profilers (RenderDoc, PIX on Windows) to see actual draw call and shader costs. Only optimize the hotspots you can measure.

CPU timing example:

```
Stopwatch sw = Stopwatch.StartNew();

// ... do draw logic

sw.Stop();

Console.WriteLine($"Draw took
{sw.Elapsed.TotalMilliseconds} ms");
```

This quick loop separates draw time from update work and helps you confirm whether your changes helped.

Use SpriteBatch correctly: batch, don't scatter

SpriteBatch is already optimized to batch many sprites into as few GPU draw calls as possible, but it only batches when the draws are compatible: same texture, same effect, same blend state, and when you stay within a single Begin/End pair. Minimize the number of Begin() / End() calls per frame. If you must change state (different blend, different shader), group all sprites that share that state together so SpriteBatch can batch them in large contiguous groups.

Wrong: starting/ending many times per frame to change one parameter.

Right: one Begin() for the large majority of sprites, further Begin() only for uncommon passes (UI, special effects).

Choose `SpriteSortMode.Deferred` for maximum batching unless you rely on the sort behaviour (depth or texture) — it accumulates draws in logical order and issues GPU calls only when necessary. `SpriteSortMode.Texture` can reorder draws to reduce texture swaps, but that can break painter's-order rendering. Test both and prefer `Deferred` for stable and predictable batching.

Texture atlases (the single biggest win for many 2D games)

Put many small sprites into a single large texture (a texture atlas / sprite sheet). When sprites come from the same atlas they can be drawn with no texture switches, letting `SpriteBatch` combine many logical draws into the same GPU draw call. Use `SpriteBatch.Draw(atlas, position, sourceRect, ...)` to draw sub-rects without swapping textures.

Atlas usage example:

```
Texture2D atlas =
Content.Load<Texture2D>("atlas");

Rectangle heroSrc = new Rectangle(0,0,64,64);

spriteBatch.Begin();

spriteBatch.Draw(atlas, heroPosition, heroSrc,
Color.White);

spriteBatch.Draw(atlas, enemyPosition, enemySrc,
Color.White);

spriteBatch.End();
```

If you cannot combine textures into one atlas (very large textures, streaming textures, or platform constraints), try to order your draw calls by texture to reduce swaps.

Minimize state changes (shaders, blend states, sampler states)

Setting a different Effect, BlendState, SamplerState, or render target causes the GPU state to change and often flushes batches. Cache EffectParameter and EffectTechnique references so you set them efficiently and avoid string lookups every frame. Only call SetValue when the value actually changes.

Effect parameter caching:

```
Effect               myEffect            =
Content.Load<Effect>("MyEffect");

EffectParameter        worldParam         =
myEffect.Parameters["World"];

// later, when value changes:

worldParam.SetValue(newMatrix);
```

Reusing BlendState and SamplerState objects instead of creating new ones every frame helps reduce GC pressure and reduces the chance of hidden state churn.

Reduce draw calls with instancing or batched vertex buffers (advanced)

When you must render thousands of similar quads (particles, foliage, bullets), consider hardware instancing or a big dynamic vertex buffer instead of many `SpriteBatch.Draw` calls. Instancing sends one draw call with per-instance data. MonoGame supports instancing on backends that expose it; fallback to dynamic vertex buffers where instancing is unavailable.

A minimal instancing pipeline outline:

1. Create a vertex buffer for a single quad and an instance buffer containing per-instance transform/texRect data.
2. In the vertex shader read instance data via a second vertex stream (or a structured buffer when supported).
3. Issue one `GraphicsDevice.DrawInstancedPrimitives(...)` call.

If direct instancing is unavailable on a backend, build a `DynamicVertexBuffer`, fill it with many quads' vertices (positions, UVs) and call `SetData` once per frame then draw a single `DrawPrimitives` call. This reduces many tiny draw calls into one bigger call.

Dynamic buffer hinting:

```
dynamicVB = new
DynamicVertexBuffer(GraphicsDevice,
VertexPositionColorTexture.VertexDeclaration,
maxQuads * 4, BufferUsage.WriteOnly);
```

```
// Fill and SetData each frame for the used
range, then DrawPrimitives once
```

Smart batching patterns

Group static geometry into one vertex buffer created once and reused. For dynamic geometry break your updates into large `SetData` uploads instead of tiny per-sprite updates. Use texture atlases for many sprites and avoid mixing atlases and singleton textures during the same `Begin/End` unless necessary.

If you need different blending for special FX (additive glow over opaque world), render opaque world first with one `Begin`, then an additive pass for lights/particles in a second `Begin`. This keeps each pass large and minimizes state switching.

Use lower resolutions and render-target tricks for expensive effects

For bloom, blur, or lights, render the expensive pass into a lower-resolution `RenderTarget2D` (half or quarter size), blur there, then composite into the full-resolution frame. This trades a little quality for a large performance win because blur cost is proportional to pixel count.

Avoid unnecessary allocations and garbage

Per-frame allocations force the GC to run and cause hitches. Reuse arrays, rectangles, color objects, and `Vector2/Vector3` where practical. Pool small objects (particles, temporary lists) and allocate large buffers once.

Example: reuse `List<SpriteDrawCall>` across frames rather than creating it each frame.

When SpriteBatch can't do it: custom pipeline for special needs

For layered or complex geometry (skeletal sprites, many unique shaders), consider a custom renderer: build large index/vertex buffers, use `Effect` once per material, and draw grouped ranges. This gives maximum control and is what high-performance engines do.

Profiling checklist & quick wins

If you see low framerates, determine whether the CPU or GPU is bottlenecked. On CPU-bound frames, minimize draw calls, grouping, and expensive CPU logic in Draw. On GPU-bound frames, reduce shader complexity, lower render-target resolution for post-process passes, and reduce texture size or MIP bias.

Quick wins that often help immediately: combine small textures into atlases; reduce Begin/End calls; avoid `SpriteSortMode.Immediate`; cache `EffectParameter` lookups instead of using string names every frame.

Final example — simple "batcher" that reduces texture swaps

This small manager sorts draw requests by texture and emits one SpriteBatch draw per texture, useful if you create draw requests in arbitrary order but want to submit them optimized.

```
class SimpleBatcher {

    Dictionary<Texture2D, List<(Rectangle src,
Vector2 pos)>> buckets = new();

    public void Add(Texture2D tex, Rectangle src,
Vector2 pos) {

        if (!buckets.TryGetValue(tex, out var list))
{

            list = new List<(Rectangle, Vector2)>();

            buckets[tex] = list;

        }

        list.Add((src, pos));

    }

    public void Flush(SpriteBatch sb) {

        foreach (var kv in buckets) {

            sb.Begin();

            foreach (var item in kv.Value)

                sb.Draw(kv.Key, item.pos, item.src,
Color.White);

            sb.End();
```

```
        }

        buckets.Clear();

    }

}
```

This is a pragmatic way to convert many arbitrary draw requests into grouped draws by texture with minimal code changes. For large games you'll want to replace the naive `Begin/End` calls with fewer, more carefully batched passes.

Summary

Measure before you change, then reduce state changes and draw calls. The biggest practical wins come from texture atlases, minimizing `SpriteBatch.Begin/End` calls, caching and reusing GPU state objects, and batching many sprites using instancing or large vertex buffers where needed. For post-processing and many lights use lower-resolution intermediate buffers. These techniques together will move the vast majority of games from CPU-limited "too many tiny draws" into smooth, well-batched rendering.

9.5 — Shader-Based Animations & Visual Enhancements

This chapter shows how to animate and enhance 2D visuals with shaders in MonoGame. You'll learn practical, copy-pasteable HLSL + C# examples for common animated effects: UV panning, sine displacement (waving), flow-map water, dissolve (noise) transitions, palette swaps via lookup textures, and a lightweight CRT/scanline post-process. Each example explains how to pass time and textures from C#, any important MonoGame gotchas, and short performance notes so you can use the effects safely in a real game.

How to drive animation from C#

All shader animations need a time source and any control parameters (speed, amplitude, phase). The usual pattern is to pass a `float Time` (seconds) and a few other parameters every frame. Use `gameTime.TotalGameTime.TotalSeconds` or a running float counter updated in `Update()`.

C# pattern:

```
// fields

Effect effect;

Texture2D mainTex, noiseTex, paletteTex;


// LoadContent

effect =
Content.Load<Effect>("MyAnimatedEffect");

mainTex = Content.Load<Texture2D>("mysprite");
```

```
noiseTex = Content.Load<Texture2D>("noise");
// if used

paletteTex = Content.Load<Texture2D>("palette");
// if used

// Draw (per frame)

float t =
(float)gameTime.TotalGameTime.TotalSeconds;

effect.Parameters["Time"].SetValue(t);

effect.Parameters["MainTex"].SetValue(mainTex);
// sprite bound automatically when using
SpriteBatch but set explicitly if needed

effect.Parameters["NoiseTex"].SetValue(noiseTex);

spriteBatch.Begin(effect: effect);

spriteBatch.Draw(mainTex, position, Color.White);

spriteBatch.End();
```

Note: some platforms and drivers expect you to declare a sampler for each texture passed to the shader and some shader toolchains require samplers declared in a certain order. If you see odd nulls or missing draws, check the sampler/texture declarations in the .fx.

Example 1 — UV Panner (scrolling texture, good for water/flow)

A tiny pixel shader that scrolls UVs using time and a speed parameter. Cheap and useful for rivers, clouds, or parallax layers.

Panner.fx

```
sampler2D MainTex : register(s0);


float Time;

float2 Speed; // uv units per second, e.g., (0.2,
0.0)

struct PS_IN { float2 Tex : TEXCOORD0; };

float4 PS(PS_IN IN) : SV_Target

{

    float2 uv = IN.Tex + Speed * Time;

    return tex2D(MainTex, frac(uv)); // frac to wrap
the texture

}


technique Tech { pass P0 { PixelShader = compile
ps_4_0_level_9_1 PS(); } }
```

C#: `effect.Parameters["Speed"].SetValue(new Vector2(0.25f, 0f));`

Performance: one texture sample, extremely cheap. Use $frac()$ or manual wrap to avoid border artifacts.

Example 2 — Sine displacement / wave (vertex or UV displacement)

Create a wavy surface by offsetting UVs with a sine function. This is often used for flags, water ripples, or subtle breathing animations.

WaveDisplace.fx (pixel-shader style, offsets UV sampling)

```
sampler2D MainTex : register(s0);

float Time;

float WaveAmplitude;  // e.g., 0.02 = 2% of UV

float WaveFrequency;  // cycles per unit (tweak)

struct PS_IN { float2 Tex : TEXCOORD0; };


float4 PS(PS_IN IN) : SV_Target

{

    float2 uv = IN.Tex;

    float wave = sin((uv.y * WaveFrequency) +
(Time * 2.0)) * WaveAmplitude;

    uv.x += wave;

    return tex2D(MainTex, uv);

}

technique Tech { pass P0 { PixelShader = compile
ps_4_0_level_9_1 PS(); } }
```

If you need geometry deformation (true vertex displacement), write a vertex shader and draw quads with a custom vertex declaration (SpriteBatch hides vertex shader). For SpriteBatch, UV displacement is usually good enough.

Example 3 — Flow maps (directional surface flow for water)

Flow maps encode 2D flow vectors in an RGB(A) texture and let you push sampling coordinates along local flow directions. Flow maps give more natural, non-uniform water motion than simple panning.

FlowMapWater.fx

```
sampler2D SceneTex  : register(s0);

sampler2D FlowMap   : register(s1); // RG
contains flow vector in [0..1] -> remap to
[-1..1]



float Time;

float FlowSpeed;    // scalar speed multiplier



struct PS_IN { float2 Tex : TEXCOORD0; };



float4 PS(PS_IN IN) : SV_Target

{

    float2 uv = IN.Tex;

    float2 flow = tex2D(FlowMap, uv).rg * 2.0f -
1.0f; // remap to [-1,1]

    // offset UV by flow scaled by time and
speed; wrap with frac()
```

```
    uv += flow * (Time * FlowSpeed);

    uv = frac(uv);

    return tex2D(SceneTex, uv);

}

technique Tech { pass P0 { PixelShader = compile
ps_4_0_level_9_1 PS(); } }
```

Create a flow map that paints flow directions in RG channels (tools: Photoshop, Substance). Flow maps work well for large water surfaces and can be combined with a normal map or displacement for more realism.

Example 4 — Dissolve/Transition with Noise

Use a noise texture to drive an alpha threshold. Animate a cut-off value with time to produce dissolves, wipes, or burn effects.

Dissolve.fx

```
sampler2D MainTex : register(s0);

sampler2D NoiseTex : register(s1);

float Threshold;   // 0..1, pixels with noise <
threshold are visible

float EdgeSize;    // small feather for anti-aliasing
and edge glow

float4 EdgeColor;  // color used at edge, e.g., fiery
color

struct PS_IN { float2 Tex : TEXCOORD0; };

float4 PS(PS_IN IN) : SV_Target
```

```
{

    float4 col = tex2D(MainTex, IN.Tex);

    float n = tex2D(NoiseTex, IN.Tex).r;

    float d = saturate((n - Threshold) /
max(EdgeSize, 0.0001));

    // d is 0 at noise==Threshold, 1 when noise much
larger (visible)

    // output uses smoothstep for a softer edge

    float alpha = smoothstep(0.0, 1.0, d);

    float4 outc = lerp(EdgeColor, col, alpha);

    outc.a = col.a * alpha;

    return outc;

}

technique Tech { pass P0 { PixelShader = compile
ps_4_0_level_9_1 PS(); } }
```

C#: animate Threshold from 0→1 over time and optionally drive EdgeColor intensity using a power curve for a stylized look.

Example 5 — Palette swap / color grading using 1D LUT

Replace colors by indexing a 1D palette texture. Use the sprite's luminance or an index channel to look up the new color.

PaletteSwap.fx

```
sampler2D MainTex    : register(s0);

sampler2D Palette1D : register(s1); // 1 px high
texture: width = palette size


float4 PS(float2 uv : TEXCOORD0) : SV_Target

{

    float4 c = tex2D(MainTex, uv);

    // convert color to index. Here we use luminance
to lookup palette

    float lum = dot(c.rgb,
float3(0.299,0.587,0.114));

    float x = lum; // 0..1 maps to palette u

    // Sample at v = 0.5 on 1D texture

    float4 pal = tex2D(Palette1D, float2(x, 0.5));

    return float4(pal.rgb, c.a);

}

technique Tech { pass P0 { PixelShader = compile
ps_4_0_level_9_1 PS(); } }
```

Create a small 1×N texture that holds your palette horizontally. This technique is cheap and great for quick visual variations, limited palettes, and palette cycling.

Example 6 — CRT / scanline + vignette (screen-space post-process)

Add faint scanlines, slight curvature, and vignette for a retro look. This is a fullscreen post-process: render the frame to a RenderTarget2D then draw it with the effect.

CRT.fx

```
sampler2D SceneTex : register(s0);

float2 Resolution;    // screen size

float ScanlineIntensity;

float VignetteStrength;

float Time;


struct PS_IN { float2 Tex : TEXCOORD0; };


float4 PS(PS_IN IN) : SV_Target
{
    float2 uv = IN.Tex;

    float2 pos = uv * Resolution;

    // Scanlines: sin per Y coordinate

    float scan = 1.0 - ScanlineIntensity * 0.5 * (1.0
+ sin((pos.y * 1.5) + Time * 10.0));

    // Vignette: distance from center

    float2 center = Resolution * 0.5;

    float dist = distance(pos, center) /
(min(Resolution.x, Resolution.y) * 0.5);

    float vig = smoothstep(0.0, 1.0, 1.0 - dist *
VignetteStrength);
```

```
    float4 c = tex2D(SceneTex, uv);

    c.rgb *= scan * vig;

    return c;

}

technique Tech { pass P0 { PixelShader = compile
ps_4_0_level_9_1 PS(); } }
```

C#: set `Resolution` to backbuffer size and tweak `ScanlineIntensity` small values (0.05–0.2) for subtlety.

Practical notes & gotchas

1. **Texture samplers & order** — MonoGame/XNA shader toolchains sometimes require explicit samplers for textures and a particular ordering; if a texture parameter appears to be ignored or causes a crash, check your `.fx` top declarations (declare the samplers that you sample first). Also ensure shader targets are compatible with your MonoGame backend (use `ps_4_0_level_9_1` / `ps_4_0_level_9_3` depending on platform).

2. **SpriteBatch vertex shader** — SpriteBatch injects its own vertex shader; pixel shaders get `SV_POSITION` and UVs from that built vertex shader. For effects that need per-vertex deformation you must supply a full vertex shader and draw custom geometry instead of using SpriteBatch, or use techniques that offset UVs rather than vertex positions. The MonoGame docs explain this interaction and how to write custom effects.

3. **Time precision & looping** — For long running games, pass `fract(Time / LoopSeconds)` when you want repeating animations avoid float precision drift. For synchronization, drive time from a central timer instead of mixing different sources.

4. **Noise & tiling** — For noise-driven effects (dissolve, fire), use a tileable noise texture and consider sampling at multiple scaled frequencies (fractal noise) for richer detail. For stationary tiling artifacts, add small random offsets per-sprite (e.g., feed a seed or per-instance offset into the shader).

5. **Performance** — Favor UV displacement and panners for cheap motion (single sample). More expensive effects (multiple texture samples, flow maps, fractal noise, specular) should be used sparingly or on lower resolution textures (render target downsample). Avoid large loops inside pixel shaders; separable filters (horizontal/vertical) help for blur-like passes.

6. **Art pipeline** — Many effects rely on extra art assets (normal maps, flow maps, noise, palette LUTs). Create them at authoring time and ship small versions (e.g., 256×256 noise) rather than huge textures.

Putting it together — a small animated-water recipe

Render the scene to SceneRT. Use a FlowMap to nudge scene UVs for refraction, overlay animated foam with panner, and composite subtle specular highlights driven by another scrolling mask. For performance, keep the water region rendered into a smaller RT and composite into the full frame.

High-level order:

render scene $\rightarrow$ render water region (SceneRT) $\rightarrow$ apply FlowMap refraction + foam panner + specular pass $\rightarrow$ composite over main frame.

This pattern isolates heavy per-pixel work to a limited screen area and can be combined with a blurred reflection rendered at half resolution for convincing water with good performance.

Quick debugging checklist

If your animated shader looks wrong or crashes: check sampler declarations and order; ensure the effect compiled to `.mgfxo` via the Content Pipeline; pass `Time` as `float` (not double); confirm the shader profile is supported on target platform; test with a simple `return tex2D(MainTex, IN.Tex)` pixel shader to ensure texturing works before adding animation math. Community posts and example repos show common pitfalls and fixes.

Example asset suggestions

For these effects you'll typically need the main sprite, a tileable noise texture (128–512px), a flow map (same size as water area), a small 1D palette texture (for palette swaps), and an optional normal map if mixing lighting with animated effects.

Chapter 10: Game Architecture & Project Structure

You'll learn to organize your code for bigger, more complex projects. You'll build reusable systems for input, audio, rendering, and scenes. By the end, you'll have a professional game framework ready for any project.

10.1 — Designing a Reusable Game Framework

A reusable game framework is code you can drop into many projects without rewriting the core plumbing each time. It separates responsibilities (input, update, render, content, audio, UI), exposes a small, well-documented API for game-specific logic, and is easy to extend and test. The aim here is a pragmatic, production-ready blueprint you can implement in MonoGame or any C# game project; the examples are compact, self-contained, and ready to paste into a Game1-style project.

Design goals (one-line priorities)

Make the framework minimal, well-factored, and predictable: clear lifecycle (init → update → draw → teardown), tiny surface area for game code, small number of extension points, and careful ownership of expensive resources (textures, buffers, sounds).

Core architecture overview

At the top sits a thin `GameHost` that owns the MonoGame `Game` loop and a `ServiceRegistry`. Beneath that live subsystems: `SceneManager`, `ResourceManager`, `InputManager`, `AudioManager`, `RenderSystem`, and optionally an `ECS` or `Entity/Component` layer. Subsystems talk only to the `ServiceRegistry` (or via explicit interfaces) so tests can substitute mocks. Time, configuration, and platform-specific abstractions live in services too.

The framework should make two important guarantees. First, subsystems cleanly expose lifecycle methods (`Initialize`, `LoadContent`, `Update`, `Draw`, `Unload`) so the host can sequence them. Second, the game code should not call GPU/OS APIs directly except via the framework (this helps portability and testing).

Minimal reusable framework skeleton (complete, working)

Below is a compact but complete skeleton illustrating the patterns you'll expand: a `ServiceRegistry`, subsystem base, a simple

Scene model, and an entity/component mini-framework you can replace with a full ECS later. This code is intentionally small so you can read and run it immediately inside a MonoGame Game project.

ServiceRegistry and service interfaces

```
// ServiceRegistry.cs

using System;

using System.Collections.Generic;

public sealed class ServiceRegistry

{

    readonly Dictionary<Type, object> services =
new();

    public void Register<T>(T service) where T :
class

    {

        services[typeof(T)] = service!;

    }

    public T Get<T>() where T : class

    {

        if (services.TryGetValue(typeof(T), out var
s)) return (T)s!;

        throw new InvalidOperationException($"Service
{typeof(T)} not registered.");

    }

    public bool TryGet<T>(out T service) where T :
class

    {
```

```csharp
        if (services.TryGetValue(typeof(T), out var
s))
        {
            service = (T)s!;
            return true;
        }
        service = null!;
        return false;
    }
}
```

Subsystem base and manager

```csharp
// ISubsystem.cs
public interface ISubsystem
{
    void Initialize(ServiceRegistry services);
    void LoadContent();
    void Update(float dt);
    void Draw();
    void UnloadContent();
}
// SubsystemManager.cs
using System.Collections.Generic;
public class SubsystemManager
```

```csharp
{
    readonly List<ISubsystem> subsystems = new();

    public void Add(ISubsystem s) =>
subsystems.Add(s);

    public void InitializeAll(ServiceRegistry
services)

    {

        foreach (var s in subsystems)
s.Initialize(services);

    }

    public void LoadAll() { foreach (var s in
subsystems) s.LoadContent(); }

    public void UpdateAll(float dt) { foreach (var s
in subsystems) s.Update(dt); }

    public void DrawAll() { foreach (var s in
subsystems) s.Draw(); }

    public void UnloadAll() { foreach (var s in
subsystems) s.UnloadContent(); }

}
```

Small entity/component model

```csharp
// Component.cs

public abstract class Component { public Entity Owner
{ get; internal set; } = null!; public virtual void
Update(float dt) {} }

public class Entity

{

    readonly List<Component> comps = new();
```

```csharp
    public void Add(Component c) { c.Owner = this;
comps.Add(c); }

    public T? Get<T>() where T: Component {
foreach(var c in comps) if (c is T t) return t;
return null; }

    public void Update(float dt) { foreach (var c in
comps) c.Update(dt); }

}
```

Example components (Transform + SpriteRenderer)

```csharp
// Transform.cs

using Microsoft.Xna.Framework;

public class Transform : Component

{

    public Vector2 Position;

    public float Rotation;

    public Vector2 Scale = Vector2.One;

}

// SpriteRenderer.cs

using Microsoft.Xna.Framework;

using Microsoft.Xna.Framework.Graphics;

public class SpriteRenderer : Component

{

    public Texture2D Texture;

    public Rectangle? SourceRect;

    public Color Color = Color.White;
```

```csharp
    public SpriteRenderer(Texture2D tex) { Texture =
tex; }

    public override void Update(float dt) { /*
nothing by default */ }

    public void Draw(SpriteBatch sb, Transform t)

    {

        sb.Draw(Texture, t.Position, SourceRect,
Color, t.Rotation, Vector2.Zero, t.Scale,
SpriteEffects.None, 0f);

    }

}
```

Simple Scene and SceneManager

```csharp
// Scene.cs

using System.Collections.Generic;

public class Scene

{

    public List<Entity> Entities { get; } = new();

    public void Update(float dt) { foreach (var e in
Entities) e.Update(dt); }

}

// SceneManager.cs

public class SceneManager : ISubsystem

{

    readonly List<Scene> scenes = new();

    public Scene Active { get; private set; } =
null!;
```

```csharp
    public void Initialize(ServiceRegistry services)
{}

    public void LoadContent() {}

    public void Update(float dt) {
Active?.Update(dt); }

    public void Draw() {}

    public void UnloadContent() {}

    public void SetActive(Scene s) { if
(!scenes.Contains(s)) scenes.Add(s); Active = s; }

}
```

RenderSystem that integrates with SpriteBatch

```csharp
// RenderSystem.cs

using Microsoft.Xna.Framework;

using Microsoft.Xna.Framework.Graphics;

public class RenderSystem : ISubsystem

{

    GraphicsDevice graphics;

    SpriteBatch spriteBatch;

    SceneManager sceneManager;

    public RenderSystem(GraphicsDevice g) { graphics
= g; spriteBatch = new SpriteBatch(g); }

    public void Initialize(ServiceRegistry services)

    {

        sceneManager = services.Get<SceneManager>();

        services.Register<SpriteBatch>(spriteBatch);
```

```
    }

    public void LoadContent() {}

    public void Update(float dt) {}

    public void Draw()

    {

        graphics.Clear(Color.CornflowerBlue);

        spriteBatch.Begin(SpriteSortMode.Deferred,
BlendState.AlphaBlend);

        if (sceneManager.Active != null)

            foreach (var e in
sceneManager.Active.Entities)

            {

                var tr = e.Get<Transform>();

                var sr = e.Get<SpriteRenderer>();

                if (tr != null && sr != null)
sr.Draw(spriteBatch, tr);

            }

        spriteBatch.End();

    }

    public void UnloadContent() {
spriteBatch.Dispose(); }

}
```

Host wiring in Game1

```
// Game1.cs (simplified)

public class Game1 : Game
```

```
{
    GraphicsDeviceManager graphics;

    ServiceRegistry services = new();

    SubsystemManager subs = new();


    public Game1()
    {
        graphics = new GraphicsDeviceManager(this);

        IsFixedTimeStep = true; // choose
fixed/variable as fits your game

        TargetElapsedTime =
TimeSpan.FromSeconds(1.0/60.0);

        Content.RootDirectory = "Content";
    }

    protected override void Initialize()
    {
        // register core services

        services.Register<SceneManager>(new
SceneManager());

        services.Register<ServiceRegistry>(services);


        // add subsystems in order

        subs.Add(new RenderSystem(GraphicsDevice));

        subs.Add(services.Get<SceneManager>()); //
scene manager as a subsystem too
```

```csharp
        subs.InitializeAll(services);

        base.Initialize();

    }


    protected override void LoadContent()

    {

        subs.LoadAll();

        // Example: create scene + entities (load
textures via Content)

        var scene = new Scene();

        var e = new Entity();

        var t = new Transform { Position = new
Microsoft.Xna.Framework.Vector2(100,100) };

        var tex =
Content.Load<Texture2D>("mysprite");

        var sr = new SpriteRenderer(tex);

        e.Add(t); e.Add(sr);

        scene.Entities.Add(e);


services.Get<SceneManager>().SetActive(scene);

    }

    protected override void Update(GameTime gameTime)

    {

        float dt =
(float)gameTime.ElapsedGameTime.TotalSeconds;

        subs.UpdateAll(dt);
```

```
        base.Update(gameTime);

    }


    protected override void Draw(GameTime gameTime)

    {

        subs.DrawAll();

        base.Draw(gameTime);

    }

}
```

This skeleton demonstrates the key ideas: a registry to decouple systems, a subsystem lifecycle, and an entity/component shape you can replace with a full ECS later. Keep each file small and single-purpose so you can reuse it across projects.

Patterns and trade-offs

Use a ServiceRegistry (Service Locator) for simple projects because it's easy to use and explicit. For larger frameworks prefer constructor-based Dependency Injection (DI) for clearer dependency graphs and easier unit testing. A service locator simplifies code but hides dependencies; DI reveals them.

Choose between a full ECS, a lightweight Component system (above), or traditional OOP objects. ECS pays off when you need high performance and batchable systems (particles, many NPCs), while Component objects are faster to implement and easier for small-to-medium games.

Decide early on timestep strategy. Fixed-step update for physics and deterministic gameplay is simpler and easier to debug; variable-step can be fine for casual games. MonoGame supports fixed-step through `IsFixedTimeStep` and `TargetElapsedTime`. If you implement your own loop, keep physics stepping separate from rendering and consider accumulator patterns to avoid "spiral of death".

Batch expensive operations: resource loading, texture uploads, shader warmup. Provide a `LoadContent` phase so games can preload important assets once. For large asset sets support streaming loaders that run off the main thread (with careful synchronization).

Performance-minded specifics

Keep draw call batching centralized (use `SpriteBatch` with large batches or instancing). Cache `EffectParameter` references and avoid string lookups in hot loops. Pool frequently created objects and prefer `struct` for tiny value types (Vector2, color tuples) where it helps. Use lower-resolution render targets for expensive post-process steps.

For systems that run many similar objects, implement a system that processes contiguous arrays of components rather than iterating many small objects, which reduces cache misses and improves throughput. When GPU is the bottleneck, reduce shader complexity and texture sizes; when CPU is the bottleneck, reduce draw calls and expensive per-frame allocations.

Testability and maintainability

Make services small and mockable by programming to interfaces. Avoid static singletons for mutable services (they're hard to test). Expose lifecycle hooks (Initialize / LoadContent / Unload) and make side effects explicit. Ship a small suite of unit tests for systems that don't touch graphics (resource lookups, input mapping, game logic). For rendering and GPU-related code, rely on integration tests and short scene "smoke tests".

Document your public API (how subsystems register, how scenes are activated, how assets are loaded). Give each project a minimal "HelloWorldScene" to validate the framework quickly.

Extensibility and project templates

Expose extension points: custom `ISubsystem` implementations, an `IScene` interface to support different scene paradigms, and an `IAssetProvider` abstraction so you can swap MonoGame's Content for Addressables-style loaders or platform-specific streaming. Ship a small template project (or NuGet package) that provides the framework and a sample game demonstrating common patterns: input mapping, pause/resume, save/load, and a simple particle system.

Practical checklist before reusing the framework in a new project

Confirm the following in your next project: the service registry has only the services you need, scene transitions are explicit and free of hidden state, significant assets are either preloaded or safely streamed, and the timestep model suits your gameplay (fixed for deterministic physics, variable if you must). Measure performance early with simple instrumentation (draw call counts, update time) and iterate.

Closing example — adding a new system

To add an `AudioSystem`, create an `IAudioService` interface, implement it in `AudioSystem` (load content, play/stop methods), register it in `ServiceRegistry`, then consume it from game code or components via `services.Get<IAudioService>()`. This pattern keeps dependencies explicit and contained.

10.2 — Modular Code: Rendering, Input, Audio, UI

Modular code means each major game concern (rendering, input, audio, UI) lives in its own well-defined subsystem with a small public surface, clear lifecycle, and explicit dependencies. The result is easier testing, swap-outs for different platforms, and faster iteration: you can replace the audio backend, extend input bindings, or swap UI layouts without touching rendering or game logic. This section gives a compact, practical blueprint and concrete, copy-pasteable code for each subsystem plus the wiring you need to use them together in a MonoGame/C# project.

Design principles (short)

Each subsystem exposes an interface, implements a lifecycle (`Initialize`, `LoadContent`, `Update`, `Draw`, `Unload`), accepts configuration objects, and acquires dependencies from a small `IServiceLocator` or by constructor injection. Subsystems should avoid global state, avoid blocking I/O on the main thread, and keep side effects explicit (play sound, start transition, change scene). The examples here use a tiny `IServiceLocator` for clarity, but the same patterns apply to full DI containers.

Tiny service locator (shared plumbing)

Use this to register and retrieve subsystems in examples below. It's intentionally minimal so you can replace it with a DI container later.

```csharp
// IServiceProvider.cs

public interface IServiceProvider
{
    void Register<T>(T service) where T : class;
```

```csharp
    T Get<T>() where T : class;

    bool TryGet<T>(out T service) where T : class;

}

// ServiceProvider.cs

using System;

using System.Collections.Generic;

public class ServiceProvider : IServiceProvider

{

    readonly Dictionary<Type, object> map = new();

    public void Register<T>(T service) where T :
class => map[typeof(T)] = service!;

    public T Get<T>() where T : class =>
(T)map[typeof(T)];

    public bool TryGet<T>(out T service) where T :
class

    {

        if (map.TryGetValue(typeof(T), out var s)) {
service = (T)s; return true; }

        service = null!; return false;

    }

}
```

Rendering subsystem — responsibilities and example

The rendering subsystem owns SpriteBatch, render targets, and common draw ordering. It provides simple APIs to register render layers, enqueue draw calls, and perform full-screen post processes. Keep draw submission lightweight and record-only: collect draw commands during Update, then flush them in Draw.

```
// IRenderer.cs

using Microsoft.Xna.Framework;

using Microsoft.Xna.Framework.Graphics;

using System;

public interface IRenderer

{

    void Initialize(GraphicsDevice device,
IServiceProvider services);

    void
LoadContent(Microsoft.Xna.Framework.Content.ContentMa
nager content);

    void Enqueue(Action<SpriteBatch> drawAction, int
layer = 0); // submit draw via lambda

    void Draw(GameTime gameTime);

    void Resize(int width, int height);

    void Unload();

}


// SimpleRenderer.cs

using System.Collections.Generic;
```

```csharp
public class SimpleRenderer : IRenderer

{

    GraphicsDevice graphics;

    SpriteBatch spriteBatch;

    readonly SortedDictionary<int,
List<Action<SpriteBatch>>> layers = new();

    public void Initialize(GraphicsDevice device,
IServiceProvider services)

    {

        graphics = device;

        spriteBatch = new SpriteBatch(device);

        services.Register<SpriteBatch>(spriteBatch);
// make available to other systems

    }

    public void
LoadContent(Microsoft.Xna.Framework.Content.ContentMa
nager content) { /* load common shaders/fonts */ }


    public void Enqueue(Action<SpriteBatch>
drawAction, int layer = 0)

    {

        if (!layers.TryGetValue(layer, out var list))
{ list = new List<Action<SpriteBatch>>();
layers[layer] = list; }

        list.Add(drawAction);

    }
```

```
    public void Draw(GameTime gameTime)

    {


graphics.Clear(Microsoft.Xna.Framework.Color.Cornflow
erBlue);

        spriteBatch.Begin(SpriteSortMode.Deferred,
BlendState.AlphaBlend);

        foreach (var kv in layers)

            foreach (var action in kv.Value)
action(spriteBatch);

        spriteBatch.End();

        layers.Clear(); // ready next frame

    }



    public void Resize(int width, int height) { /*
recreate RTs if present */ }

    public void Unload() { spriteBatch.Dispose(); }

}
```

Use `renderer.Enqueue(sb => sb.Draw(texture, pos, Color.White), layer: 0);` in game logic. This keeps update code independent of draw order and minimizes direct access to `SpriteBatch`.

Input subsystem — mapping, rebinding, and events

Input should expose high-level actions (Jump, MoveLeft, Confirm) rather than raw keys. Store the map in a serializable data structure so players can rebind and save settings. Provide both polling (IsActionDown) and event callbacks (ActionPressed) for flexibility.

```csharp
// IInputService.cs

using Microsoft.Xna.Framework.Input;

using System;


public interface IInputService

{

    void Initialize(IServiceProvider services);

    void Update(GameTime gameTime);

    bool IsPressed(string action);                    //
poll

    event Action<string> OnPressed;                   //
event-driven

    void Rebind(string action, Keys key);             //
runtime rebind

}


// InputService.cs

using System.Collections.Generic;

using Microsoft.Xna.Framework.Input;


public class InputService : IInputService
```

```csharp
{
    KeyboardState prevState, currState;

    readonly Dictionary<string, Keys> bindings =
new();

    public event Action<string> OnPressed = delegate
{ };


    public InputService()

    {

        // default bindings

        bindings["Confirm"] = Keys.Enter;

        bindings["Jump"] = Keys.Space;

    }

    public void Initialize(IServiceProvider services)
{ services.Register<IInputService>(this); }


    public void Update(GameTime gameTime)

    {

        prevState = currState;

        currState = Keyboard.GetState();

        foreach (var kv in bindings)

        {

            var action = kv.Key;

            var key = kv.Value;
```

```
            if (currState.IsKeyDown(key) &&
prevState.IsKeyUp(key)) OnPressed(action);

        }

    }

    public bool IsPressed(string action)

    {

        if (!bindings.TryGetValue(action, out var
key)) return false;

        return currState.IsKeyDown(key);

    }


    public void Rebind(string action, Keys key) =>
bindings[action] = key;

}
```

If you support gamepads, abstract Keys behind an input binding
type that can represent keyboard, gamepad button, or axis. For
responsive UIs use both IsPressed (for held checks) and
OnPressed (for single-shot actions).

Audio subsystem — lightweight wrapper and pooling

MonoGame exposes SoundEffect, SoundEffectInstance,
and MediaPlayer. Wrap these in an IAudioService that
implements sound caching, instance pooling, and simple music

controls. Keep audio loading asynchronous where feasible; on platforms that block on SoundEffect creation, load at startup.

```csharp
// IAudioService.cs

using Microsoft.Xna.Framework.Audio;

public interface IAudioService

{

    void Initialize(IServiceProvider services);

    void
LoadContent(Microsoft.Xna.Framework.Content.ContentMa
nager content);

    void PlaySfx(string key, float volume = 1f, float
pitch = 0f, float pan = 0f);

    void PlayMusic(string key, bool loop = true);

    void StopMusic();

    void SetMusicVolume(float volume);

    void Unload();

}



// AudioService.cs

using System.Collections.Generic;


public class AudioService : IAudioService

{

    Dictionary<string, SoundEffect> sfx = new();

    Dictionary<string, Song> music = new();
```

```csharp
    public void Initialize(IServiceProvider services)
=> services.Register<IAudioService>(this);

    public void
LoadContent(Microsoft.Xna.Framework.Content.ContentMa
nager content)

    {

        // Example: pre-load assets; in real projects
use config or streaming

        sfx["hit"] =
content.Load<SoundEffect>("sfx/hit");

        music["bg"] =
content.Load<Song>("music/bgm");

    }

    public void PlaySfx(string key, float volume =
1f, float pitch = 0f, float pan = 0f)

    {

        if (sfx.TryGetValue(key, out var se))

            se.Play(volume, pitch, pan);

    }

    public void PlayMusic(string key, bool loop =
true)

    {

        if (music.TryGetValue(key, out var song))

        {

            MediaPlayer.IsRepeating = loop;

            MediaPlayer.Play(song);
```

```
        }

    }

    public void StopMusic() => MediaPlayer.Stop();

    public void SetMusicVolume(float volume) =>
MediaPlayer.Volume = volume;

    public void Unload() { /* dispose if necessary */
}

}
```

For many simultaneous SFX use SoundEffectInstance
pooling to avoid GC spikes and to support per-instance control
(stop/pause). Keep audio logic decoupled from gameplay:
gameplay raises an event or calls audio.PlaySfx("hit"),
and the audio service decides mixing and resource use.

UI subsystem — scene/Screen management, widgets, and input routing

A robust UI system exposes screens (menus/popups), a widget tree,
layout passes, and input routing. Use retained-mode UI (widget tree
kept between frames) for complex layouts and animations. Widgets
expose Update, Draw, and input handlers.

```
// IUiService.cs

using Microsoft.Xna.Framework;

public interface IUiService

{
```

```csharp
    void Initialize(IServiceProvider services);

    void
LoadContent(Microsoft.Xna.Framework.Content.ContentMa
nager content);

    void ShowScreen(UiScreen screen);

    void Update(GameTime gameTime);

    void Draw(SpriteBatch sb);

}



// UiScreen.cs

using System.Collections.Generic;



public abstract class UiScreen

{

    public bool IsPopup { get; protected set; } =
false;

    public abstract void
LoadContent(Microsoft.Xna.Framework.Content.ContentMa
nager content);

    public abstract void Update(GameTime gameTime);

    public abstract void Draw(SpriteBatch sb);

}



// UiService.cs

using System.Collections.Generic;
```

```csharp
public class UiService : IUiService

{

    readonly Stack<UiScreen> screens = new();

    public void Initialize(IServiceProvider services)
=> services.Register<IUiService>(this);

    public void
LoadContent(Microsoft.Xna.Framework.Content.ContentMa
nager content) { /* load fonts */ }


    public void ShowScreen(UiScreen screen)

    {

        screen.LoadContent(null); // pass content
manager in real code

        screens.Push(screen);

    }


    public void Update(GameTime gameTime)

    {

        if (screens.Count == 0) return;

        var top = screens.Peek();

        top.Update(gameTime);

    }

    public void Draw(SpriteBatch sb)

    {

        if (screens.Count == 0) return;
```

```
        foreach (var screen in screens)
screen.Draw(sb); // bottom → top; popup screens
simply render on top

    }

}
```

A concrete MenuScreen implements widgets (buttons, labels).
Widgets handle input by asking the IInputService or receiving
events. Keep UI logic separate from game logic: UI raises
commands (e.g., OnConfirm) which the game responds to by
changing scenes or calling systems.

Event bus and decoupling

For loose coupling, implement a tiny event bus where subsystems
publish domain events (player died, volume changed). Event
consumers subscribe to relevant events. Keep events small and
immutable.

```
public interface IEventBus { void Publish<T>(T e);
void Subscribe<T>(Action<T> handler); }

public class EventBus : IEventBus

{

    readonly Dictionary<Type, List<Delegate>>
handlers = new();

    public void Publish<T>(T e)

    {

        if (handlers.TryGetValue(typeof(T), out var
list))
```

```
        foreach (Action<T> h in list) h(e);

    }

    public void Subscribe<T>(Action<T> handler)

    {

        if (!handlers.TryGetValue(typeof(T), out var
list)) { list = new List<Delegate>();
handlers[typeof(T)] = list; }

        list.Add(handler);

    }

}
```

Example: UI subscribes to SettingsChanged to update volume sliders; audio subsystem subscribes to PlaySoundEvent to call PlaySfx.

Putting subsystems together — lifecycle and wiring

In Game1.Initialize, create the ServiceProvider, register EventBus, create instances of the subsystems, call their Initialize and LoadContent in a predictable order (services first, audio next, input, renderer, UI). In Update, call input update, then EventBus deliveries, then game logic, then UI.Update, then renderer enqueue draws. In Draw, call renderer.Draw(gameTime) then UI.Draw (or have the UI draw via renderer for consistent ordering).

```
// simplified wiring (pseudo)
```

```csharp
var services = new ServiceProvider();

services.Register<IEventBus>(new EventBus());

var renderer = new SimpleRenderer();

var input = new InputService();

var audio = new AudioService();

var ui = new UiService();


renderer.Initialize(GraphicsDevice, services);

input.Initialize(services);

audio.Initialize(services);

ui.Initialize(services);


renderer.LoadContent(Content);

audio.LoadContent(Content);

ui.LoadContent(Content);

// Update loop

input.Update(gameTime);

audio.Update?.Invoke(gameTime); // if audio needs
per-frame

gameLogic.Update(gameTime);        // your game scene
manager etc

ui.Update(gameTime);

renderer.Draw(gameTime); // flush draws

ui.Draw(services.Get<SpriteBatch>()); // or have UI
draw via renderer.Enqueue(...)
```

Keep ordering consistent and document it so later contributors know where to hook systems.

Practical patterns & tips

Use data-driven configuration for bindings, audio catalogs, and UI layouts so artists and designers can tweak without code changes. Keep expensive loads off the main thread by streaming or using background loading pipelines that sync on the main thread when assets become available. For mobile/low-end targets, reduce audio polyphony and use compressed streaming for long music tracks. Profile early: common hotspots are many small draw calls, large texture uploads, unbatched UI draws, and frequent `SoundEffectInstance` creation.

Favor explicit APIs: `ui.ShowScreen(new PauseMenu())` is easier to reason about than manipulating stacks directly. For input rebinding provide a small UI that writes JSON to a settings file; at startup load settings and apply them before gameplay begins.

Debugging & testing strategies

Unit-test non-graphics code (input mapping, event routing, audio catalogs) by mocking `IServiceProvider` and `IEventBus`. For rendering and UI build small integration tests (smoke scenes) that render a single frame and validate no exceptions and that expected draw calls were enqueued. Log subsystem lifecycle events so you can trace ordering problems on startup.

Example: small end-to-end flow

Player presses the mapped "Confirm" key. InputService raises OnPressed("Confirm"). UiService has a focused button that subscribed to OnPressed and triggers OnConfirm which publishes PlaySoundEvent("ui_confirm") to EventBus. AudioService subscribed to PlaySoundEvent and calls PlaySfx("ui_confirm"). UiService also calls a callback to the game scene manager to advance state. This chain keeps each system tiny and focused.

Summary

Design subsystems around clear interfaces, an explicit lifecycle, and a small service registry (or DI). Make rendering record-only during Update and flush in Draw. Expose input as high-level actions and allow rebinding. Wrap audio behind a service that handles pooling and music control. Implement UI as a retained tree of screens/widgets with clear input routing. Use an event bus for loose coupling. These patterns make your codebase easier to extend, test, and port.

10.3 — Scene & State Management

Scene and state management is the scaffolding that keeps your game's screens, menus, gameplay states, and overlays organized and predictable. A good scene/state system gives you clear lifecycle hooks (load, show, hide, update, draw, unload), supports smooth transitions and modal overlays (pause menus, dialogs), and lets you load heavy assets without stalling the frame. This section gives a practical mental model, a small but complete reusable implementation, and working examples you can paste into a MonoGame project.

Mental model (very short)

A scene (or state, screen) owns the logic and visuals for a particular mode: main menu, level, pause screen. The Scene Manager controls which scenes are active and how they transition. Use a stack to implement push/pop and modal overlays; use explicit transitions for animated fades and safe resource swapping.

API goals

Each scene exposes a predictable API: `Initialize`, `LoadContent`, `OnEnter` (when it becomes active), `Update`, `Draw`, `OnExit` (when it's removed), and `UnloadContent`. The manager must support push/pop, replace, and a way to run a transition animation while locking input for the duration. Resource loading should avoid blocking GPU calls on background threads—load CPU-only assets off-thread but always create GPU resources (textures, effects) on the main thread.

Minimal, complete Scene base and SceneManager

The following code is intentionally small and practical. It implements a stack-based SceneManager that supports pushing modal overlays, replacing the active scene, simple transition callbacks, and a pattern for asynchronous CPU-side loading with a safe main-thread GPU finalize step.

SceneBase.cs

```csharp
using Microsoft.Xna.Framework;

using Microsoft.Xna.Framework.Content;

using Microsoft.Xna.Framework.Graphics;

using System.Threading.Tasks;

public abstract class SceneBase

{

    public bool IsPopup { get; protected set; } =
false; // if true, scenes beneath are not covered

    public bool IsBlockingInput { get; protected set;
} = true;


    protected ContentManager Content => content ??
throw new System.InvalidOperationException("Content
not set");

    ContentManager? content;


    public virtual void Initialize(ContentManager
globalContent)

    {

        // Scenes should use a scoped ContentManager
(optional). We attach the global manager by default.
```

```csharp
        content = globalContent;

    }



    // CPU-only loading may run on a background
thread; return a task that completes when CPU-side
data is ready.

    // GPU resource creation must be done on main
thread in FinalizeLoad.

    public virtual Task LoadAsync() =>
Task.CompletedTask;



    // Called on main thread after LoadAsync
completes; create textures, effects etc. here.

    public virtual void FinalizeLoad(GraphicsDevice
graphics) { }



    public virtual void OnEnter() { }   // when the
scene becomes active (top of stack)

    public virtual void OnExit() { }     // when the
scene is popped/replaced

    public virtual void Update(GameTime gameTime) { }

    public virtual void Draw(GameTime gameTime,
SpriteBatch spriteBatch) { }

    // optional cleanup

    public virtual void Unload() { content?.Unload();
content = null; }

}
```

SceneManager.cs

```csharp
using Microsoft.Xna.Framework;

using Microsoft.Xna.Framework.Content;

using Microsoft.Xna.Framework.Graphics;

using System;

using System.Collections.Generic;

using System.Threading.Tasks;


public class SceneManager
{
    readonly Stack<SceneBase> stack = new();

    readonly ContentManager content;

    readonly GraphicsDevice graphics;


    // If a scene is loading asynchronously, hold it
here until finalize step
    SceneBase? loadingScene;

    Task? loadingTask;


    public SceneManager(ContentManager globalContent,
GraphicsDevice graphicsDevice)
    {
        content = globalContent;

        graphics = graphicsDevice;

    }
```

```
    // Push a scene (optionally loading
asynchronously). If pushModal is true the previous
scene remains below.

    public void Push(SceneBase scene, bool
asynchronous = false)

    {

        scene.Initialize(content);

        if (!asynchronous)

        {

            // synchronous load + immediate finalize
and push

scene.LoadAsync().GetAwaiter().GetResult();

            scene.FinalizeLoad(graphics);

            stack.Push(scene);

            scene.OnEnter();

            return;

        }


        // asynchronous path: start LoadAsync and
finalize next frame on main thread

        loadingScene = scene;

        loadingTask = scene.LoadAsync();

    }
```

```csharp
// Replace top with new scene

public void Replace(SceneBase scene, bool
asynchronous = false)

{

    if (stack.Count > 0)

    {

        var top = stack.Pop();

        top.OnExit();

        top.Unload();

    }

    Push(scene, asynchronous);

}


// Pop top scene

public void Pop()

{

    if (stack.Count == 0) return;

    var top = stack.Pop();

    top.OnExit();

    top.Unload();

    if (stack.Count > 0) stack.Peek().OnEnter();

}
```

```
    // Called from Game.Update each frame; this
finalizes async loads and updates active scenes.

    public void Update(GameTime gameTime)

    {

        // finalize any finished asynchronous scene
load

        if (loadingScene != null && loadingTask !=
null && loadingTask.IsCompleted)

        {

            loadingScene!.FinalizeLoad(graphics);

            stack.Push(loadingScene);

            loadingScene.OnEnter();

            loadingScene = null;

            loadingTask = null;

        }

        // Update top-most active scene(s). If top is
a popup, update the scene below too if desired.

        if (stack.Count == 0) return;

        var topScene = stack.Peek();

        topScene.Update(gameTime);

        // Optionally update scene beneath if
topScene.IsPopup == true (allows background
animation)

        if (topScene.IsPopup && stack.Count > 1)

        {

            // peek second without popping
```

```
            var arr = stack.ToArray();

            arr[1].Update(gameTime); // arr[0] is
topScene, arr[1] is next

        }

    }

    // Draw: draw stack bottom->top, but stop if a
non-popup covers lower scenes

    public void Draw(GameTime gameTime, SpriteBatch
spriteBatch)

    {

        if (stack.Count == 0) return;

        // Use a temporary array so we can index in
order bottom->top

        var arr = stack.ToArray();

        for (int i = arr.Length - 1; i >= 0; i--)

        {

            var scene = arr[i];

            scene.Draw(gameTime, spriteBatch);

            if (!scene.IsPopup) break; // don't draw
scenes under a full-screen non-popup

        }

    }

}
```

Example concrete scenes

Menu scene and a gameplay scene that uses async loading (CPU-heavy simulated work) and then finalizes textures on the main thread.

MenuScene.cs

```csharp
using Microsoft.Xna.Framework;

using Microsoft.Xna.Framework.Graphics;

using Microsoft.Xna.Framework.Content;


public class MenuScene : SceneBase

{

    Texture2D? logo;


    public override void FinalizeLoad(GraphicsDevice graphics)

    {

        // create a simple placeholder texture if content didn't provide one

        if (Content.TryGetAsset<Texture2D>("logo") is Texture2D t) logo = t;

        else

        {

            logo = new Texture2D(graphics, 256, 128);

            var data = new Color[256 * 128];

            for (int i = 0; i < data.Length; i++) data[i] = Color.CornflowerBlue;
```

```
            logo.SetData(data);

    }

 }


    public override void Draw(GameTime gameTime,
SpriteBatch spriteBatch)

    {

        spriteBatch.Begin();

        if (logo != null) spriteBatch.Draw(logo, new
Vector2(100,100), Color.White);


spriteBatch.DrawString(Content.Load<SpriteFont>("Defa
ultFont"), "Press Enter to Start", new Vector2(100,
250), Color.White);

        spriteBatch.End();

    }


    public override void Update(GameTime gameTime)

    {

        if
(Microsoft.Xna.Framework.Input.Keyboard.GetState().Is
KeyDown(Microsoft.Xna.Framework.Input.Keys.Enter))

        {

            // Typically you'd signal the
SceneManager to switch scenes; the Game1 wiring will
do that

        }
```

```
        }

}
```

GameScene.cs (simulated async load)

```csharp
using Microsoft.Xna.Framework;

using Microsoft.Xna.Framework.Graphics;

using System.Threading.Tasks;

public class GameScene : SceneBase

{

    Texture2D? playerTex;

    // Simulate heavy CPU load (e.g., parsing large
level data) on background thread

    public override async Task LoadAsync()

    {

        await Task.Delay(300); // simulate CPU work

        // load any CPU-only data here (level
geometry, parsed arrays)

    }



    public override void FinalizeLoad(GraphicsDevice
graphics)

    {

        // Now create GPU resources on the main
thread

        playerTex = new Texture2D(graphics, 64, 64);
```

```
        var data = new Color[64 * 64];

        for (int i = 0; i < data.Length; i++) data[i]
= Color.Red;

        playerTex.SetData(data);

    }

    public override void Draw(GameTime gameTime,
SpriteBatch spriteBatch)

    {

        spriteBatch.Begin();

        if (playerTex != null)
spriteBatch.Draw(playerTex, new Vector2(200, 150),
Color.White);

        spriteBatch.End();

    }

}
```

Transitions (fade example)

A transition can be its own small scene that sits on top of the stack and fades alpha from 0→1 while you swap scenes. The manager pushes the transition scene; when the transition completes it calls a callback to replace/pop scenes.

FadeTransition.cs (simple)

```
using Microsoft.Xna.Framework;

using Microsoft.Xna.Framework.Graphics;

using System;
```

```csharp
public class FadeTransition : SceneBase
{
    float duration;

    float elapsed;

    Color color;

    Action? onComplete;


    public FadeTransition(float seconds, Color
fadeColor, Action onComplete)
    {
        duration = seconds; color = fadeColor;
this.onComplete = onComplete;

        IsPopup = true; IsBlockingInput = true;
    }


    public override void Update(GameTime
gameTime)
    {
        elapsed +=
(float)gameTime.ElapsedGameTime.TotalSeconds;

        if (elapsed >= duration)
        {
            onComplete?.Invoke();
```

```csharp
            // After invoking, tell the
SceneManager to pop this transition (game wiring
will pop)

        }

    }


    public override void Draw(GameTime gameTime,
SpriteBatch spriteBatch)

    {

        float t = MathHelper.Clamp(elapsed /
duration, 0f, 1f);

        spriteBatch.Begin();

spriteBatch.Draw(Create1x1(spriteBatch.GraphicsDe
vice), Vector2.Zero,

            new Rectangle(0,0,
spriteBatch.GraphicsDevice.PresentationParameters
.BackBufferWidth,

spriteBatch.GraphicsDevice.PresentationParameters
.BackBufferHeight),

            color * t);

        spriteBatch.End();

    }

    Texture2D? _px;

    Texture2D Create1x1(GraphicsDevice g)

    {
```

```
    if (_px != null) return _px;

    _px = new Texture2D(g, 1, 1);

    _px.SetData(new[] { Color.White });

    return _px;

    }

}
```

Wiring: when the fade transition completes it invokes onComplete which should replace/pop scenes and then the transition scene should be popped. The exact sequence is up to your game wiring; keep onComplete idempotent.

Input routing and pause semantics

When a modal popup is active you usually want the popup to receive input and block the scene below. The IsBlockingInput flag controls this. In your game's input dispatch, consult the scene stack top-down: the first scene that signals "I handled input" stops propagation. For pause you can push a PauseScene that sets IsPopup = true so the scene under it can keep animating (or set it false to freeze background updates).

Saving and restoring scene state

Scene instances may need transient state saved (current chapter, camera position). Offer SerializeState() / DeserializeState() hooks or use a dedicated ISession object provided by your service registry to persist state between scene reloads. Avoid trying to serialize GPU resources—store CPU-side metadata and reload GPU assets with `FinalizeLoad`.

Common pitfalls & how to avoid them

Do not create GPU resources (Texture2D, Effect, RenderTarget2D) on background threads. Load CPU-only data on background threads then create GPU objects in `FinalizeLoad` on the main thread. If you use `ContentManager.Load<T>` it must run on the main thread for most MonoGame backends. When pushing/popping scenes during `Update`, avoid mutating the stack while iterating it—record requests and apply them after the update pass, or centralize stack operations through SceneManager methods that are safe to call during updates.

Be explicit about ownership: who calls `Unload()`? Make the SceneManager the single owner responsible for calling `OnExit` and `Unload` so resources don't leak.

Performance tips

Reuse textures where possible, and reuse small helper textures (1×1 white) instead of rebuilding them each frame. For large scene stacks, avoid calling `Draw` on scenes that are completely covered by full-screen, non-popup scenes. If lower scenes need to animate while covered, use `IsPopup` to let them update but keep them from drawing. Prefer async CPU loading for large level data and create GPU resources in a single finalization step so you avoid many small texture uploads mid-frame.

Example: wiring everything in Game1

This snippet shows the minimal Game1 flow: initialize manager, push a menu, on input push GameScene async and show a fade transition.

```
public class Game1 : Game
{

    GraphicsDeviceManager graphics;

    SpriteBatch spriteBatch;

    SceneManager scenes;

    ContentManager content;


    public Game1()
    {

        graphics = new GraphicsDeviceManager(this);

        Content.RootDirectory = "Content";

    }


    protected override void Initialize()
    {

        base.Initialize();
```

```csharp
        spriteBatch = new
SpriteBatch(GraphicsDevice);

        scenes = new SceneManager(Content,
GraphicsDevice);

    }


    protected override void LoadContent()

    {

        // push initial menu (synchronous small
scene)

        var menu = new MenuScene();

        scenes.Push(menu, asynchronous: false);

    }


    protected override void Update(GameTime gameTime)

    {

        // Example: Enter starts the game

        if
(Keyboard.GetState().IsKeyDown(Keys.Enter))

        {

            // push game scene asynchronously

            var gameScene = new GameScene();

            scenes.Push(gameScene, asynchronous:
true);
```

```
            // push fade transition that will pop
itself when done; the onComplete can be used

            var fade = new FadeTransition(0.5f,
Color.Black, () =>

                {

                    // no-op or additional logic

                });

                scenes.Push(fade, asynchronous: false);

            }


        scenes.Update(gameTime);

        base.Update(gameTime);

    }


    protected override void Draw(GameTime gameTime)

    {

        scenes.Draw(gameTime, spriteBatch);

        base.Draw(gameTime);

    }

}
```

Note: in production you'll gate the Enter key trigger so it only activates on key press (not hold); keep input logic out of Game1 and inside a dedicated InputService for clarity.

Summary (one-paragraph)

Use a small `SceneBase` with clear lifecycle hooks and a `SceneManager` that owns a stack of scenes. Support async CPU loading with a main-thread finalize step for GPU creation. Implement push/pop/replace and modal popups via stack semantics. Handle transitions with dedicated scenes so animation and input locking are handled consistently. Keep resource ownership clear and avoid creating GPU resources off the main thread. This design is easy to extend, test, and reason about as your game grows.

10.4 Resource & Memory Management

This section teaches you how to keep your MonoGame projects tidy, fast, and stable by managing CPU memory, GPU resources, and lifetimes deterministically. You'll learn practical patterns that stop leaks, avoid frame-time GC spikes, and make level transitions predictable. Every explanation is compact and followed by production-ready C# examples you can drop into your MonoGame game.

Why this matters

Games are interactive and memory-hungry. Textures, vertex buffers, audio buffers and other GPU-backed objects live outside the .NET managed heap and often must be released explicitly. Meanwhile the managed heap must be kept low-allocation per frame to prevent GC pauses. Treat resource lifetime and per-frame allocations as first-class concerns.

Content ownership and lifetime

MonoGame's ContentManager "owns" the assets it loads. Use ContentManager.Unload() to release all assets loaded by that manager. For predictable memory use across levels, give each screen/scene its own ContentManager (a small, short-lived manager for level-specific assets and a long-lived one for common assets). This lets you unload a level's large textures and models when the player leaves the level without affecting global assets.

```
// In your Game or Scene class

private ContentManager levelContent;

protected override void LoadContent()

{

    levelContent = new ContentManager(Services,
"Content");

    levelBackground =
levelContent.Load<Texture2D>("Level1/background");

    enemySprites =
levelContent.Load<Texture2D>("Level1/enemies");

}

protected override void UnloadContent()

{

    levelContent.Unload();  // releases all assets
loaded by this manager

    levelContent.Dispose(); // optional: dispose the
manager itself when done
```

```
}
```

Use a separate ContentManager for each scene to keep memory bounded. If you must unload a single asset, consider a small extension or a custom map of loaded assets; but prefer per-scene managers for clarity.

Deterministic disposal for GPU/OS resources

Types like `Texture2D`, `VertexBuffer`, and many other MonoGame types implement `IDisposable`. When you create resources yourself (not via `ContentManager`) you must call `Dispose()` when finished. When a class owns unmanaged resources, implement the standard Dispose pattern so consumers can release resources deterministically.

```
public sealed class SpriteBatchTextureHolder :
IDisposable

{

    private bool disposed;

    public Texture2D Texture { get; }

    public SpriteBatchTextureHolder(GraphicsDevice
device, int w, int h)

    {

        Texture = new Texture2D(device, w, h);

    }


    public void Dispose()

    {
```

```
        if (disposed) return;

        Texture?.Dispose();

        disposed = true;

        GC.SuppressFinalize(this);

    }

}
```

If the asset is loaded through ContentManager, call Unload()
on that manager instead of calling Dispose() on the Texture
directly; mixing the two can produce confusing reload semantics.

Avoiding per-frame allocations

Garbage Collector pauses are one of the most common sources of
stutter. Aim for near-zero managed allocations per frame. Replace
frequently created transient objects with reusable buffers and pools;
prefer struct for small hot-value types; reuse StringBuilder
and arrays through ArrayPool<T>.

A simple example shows reusing a Vector2[] and using
ArrayPool<T> for transient arrays:

```
using System.Buffers;

public class ParticleSystem

{

    private readonly Vector2[] particlePositions;

    private static readonly ArrayPool<Vector2> pool =
ArrayPool<Vector2>.Shared;
```

```csharp
public ParticleSystem(int maxParticles)

{

    particlePositions = new
Vector2[maxParticles]; // reuse long-lived array

}


public void Update()

{

    // Temporaries that must be arrays should be
rented:

    var temp = pool.Rent(128);

    try

    {

        // use temp like an array

    }

    finally

    {

        pool.Return(temp, clearArray: false);

    }

}

}
```

Prefer Span<T>/Memory<T> where appropriate to avoid copying, and keep per-frame allocations (like new calls) to a minimum.

Object pooling for frequently created game objects

Bullets, particles and short-lived effects are ideal for pooling. A pool avoids new/GC churn and keeps update/draw logic simple.

```
public class Pool<T> where T : new()
{
    readonly Stack<T> items = new Stack<T>();

    public T Rent()
    {
        return items.Count > 0 ? items.Pop() : new T();
    }


    public void Return(T item)
    {
        items.Push(item);
    }
}

// Example pooled bullet class
public class Bullet
{
```

```csharp
public bool Active;

public Vector2 Position;

public Vector2 Velocity;

public void Reset(Vector2 pos, Vector2 vel)

{

    Position = pos;

    Velocity = vel;

    Active = true;

}

public void Update(float dt)

{

    Position += Velocity * dt;

    if (/* offscreen */) Active = false;

}

}
```

This pattern keeps the number of managed objects stable and avoids GC spikes.

Minimizing allocation in Draw/Update

Avoid allocating objects in Update/Draw. Do not create new Vector2(...) and other small objects in tight inner loops: prefer reusing fields, or pass values by ref when possible. Use a single SpriteBatch and call Begin()/End() once per layer where feasible.

If you need temporary lists for collision detection or culling, rent them from `ArrayPool<T>` or reuse a single `List<T>`cleared each frame (prefer `List.Clear()` over allocation).

Handling large or streaming assets

For very large textures or streamed audio, load only what you need and keep the rest on disk. If you have many levels, stream level assets asynchronously while showing a loading UI. Keep memory budgets in mind: track approximate GPU memory usage and unload least-recently-used assets when you approach the budget.

Debugging memory and leaks

If the game exhausts GPU memory or stutters, follow a checklist: ensure `ContentManager.Unload()` is called on level exit, ensure you call `Dispose()` on resources created manually, examine object counts with a managed profiler to find rising managed object graphs, and use GPU debug/profiling tools to see VRAM usage. Frequent signs of leaks include ever-growing memory usage between level loads and inability to load textures after repeated transitions.

Practical patterns — small architecture

Create a `SceneContent` wrapper that owns its `ContentManager` and exposes a simple lifecycle. Create `IPoolable` with `Reset()` semantics for pooled objects. Centralize allocation-sensitive utilities (Array pools, StringBuilders) in one helper class to make audits easier.

```
public abstract class Scene
```

```csharp
{

    protected ContentManager ContentForScene { get;
private set; }


    public void InitializeForScene(IServiceProvider
services, string rootDirectory = "Content")

    {

        ContentForScene = new
ContentManager(services, rootDirectory);

        LoadSceneContent();

    }


    protected abstract void LoadSceneContent();


    public void ShutdownScene()

    {

        UnloadSceneContent();

        ContentForScene.Unload();

        ContentForScene.Dispose();

        ContentForScene = null;

        GC.Collect(); // use sparingly — prefer
controlled low-allocation design

    }

    protected abstract void UnloadSceneContent();

}
```

Only call `GC.Collect()` during a controlled load screen if you must force cleanup before gameplay; it's better to design so forced GC is unnecessary.

Example: Level transition that frees memory

This end-to-end snippet shows loading a level, using a scene-specific ContentManager for that level's assets, then unloading to free memory:

```
public class LevelScene : Scene
{
    private Texture2D background;

    private List<Enemy> enemies;


    protected override void LoadSceneContent()
    {
        background =
ContentForScene.Load<Texture2D>("levels/level1/bg");

        enemies = new List<Enemy>();

        // load other level assets...

    }


    protected override void UnloadSceneContent()
    {
        // clear object collections and dispose
manual resources
```

```
        enemies.Clear();

        // if we had manual-created resources call
Dispose here

    }

}
```

When the player leaves the level call ShutdownScene(). That will Unload() the content and allow VRAM to be reclaimed.

Checklist: what to do per asset type

Textures loaded through the pipeline: let ContentManager own/unload them. Textures created at runtime: Dispose() them explicitly. Large buffers and native handles: implement IDisposable and follow the .NET Dispose pattern. Short-lived objects: pool them. Per-frame allocations: eliminate or rent. Scene-level assets: use dedicated content managers.

Closing advice

Design for predictable lifetimes. Prefer simple rules: "ContentManager per scene," "Dispose for runtime-created resources," and "pool frequently created objects." Measure regularly with profilers and make the smallest possible changes that remove allocations in hot paths. Over time the payoff is fewer crashes, fewer stutters, and predictable memory footprints — and that gives you room to add richer content without surprises.

10.5 Best Practices for Scaling & Maintenance

This section equips you with practical, production-ready patterns for growing a MonoGame project from solo prototype to a maintainable, team-friendly codebase. The focus is on long-term stability: predictable builds, safe refactors, automation, observability, and small, testable components that let a game scale without collapsing under complexity. Each concept is explained plainly and immediately followed by focused, drop-in code that demonstrates how to apply it.

Keep features data-driven and declarative

When behaviour, tuning, or content lives outside code it becomes easier to iterate, test and patch without risking regressions. Move numbers, spawn tables, UI layouts, and asset manifests to JSON/Scriptable YAML/CSV that your game reads at startup. Store migration code next to loaders so older content can be upgraded gracefully.

```
// Simple data-driven loader for enemy configs (JSON)

public record EnemyConfig(string Id, int Health,
float Speed);



public static class DataLoader

{

    public static EnemyConfig[]
LoadEnemyConfigs(string jsonText)

    {
```

```
        return
System.Text.Json.JsonSerializer.Deserialize<EnemyConf
ig[]>(jsonText);

    }

}


// Usage in a scene

var json =
File.ReadAllText(Path.Combine(Content.RootDirectory,
"data/enemies.json"));

var enemyConfigs = DataLoader.LoadEnemyConfigs(json);
```

If you later change the shape of EnemyConfig, add a migration step in DataLoader that upgrades older schemas. This keeps your runtime robust to content revisions.

Modular architecture and clear boundaries

Scale by splitting responsibilities: rendering, game rules, audio, input and persistence should be separable modules. Limit each module's public API; prefer composition over inheritance so modules can be replaced or mocked for testing. Treat your Game class as an orchestration layer only.

```
// Minimal service registration with Microsoft DI

using Microsoft.Extensions.DependencyInjection;

public class GameHost : Game

{

    IServiceProvider services;
```

```
    public GameHost()

    {

        var servicesCollection = new
ServiceCollection();

        servicesCollection.AddSingleton<IAssetLoader,
AssetLoader>();

        servicesCollection.AddSingleton<IWorld,
World>();

        services =
servicesCollection.BuildServiceProvider();

    }


    protected override void Initialize()

    {

        var world =
services.GetRequiredService<IWorld>();

        world.Initialize();

        base.Initialize();

    }

}
```

Use DI sparingly in hot inner loops; prefer manual wiring for perf-critical subsystems and keep DI for game setup, testing, and systems that benefit from inversion of control.

Keep rendering and game logic decoupled for safe scaling

Use a clear separation between simulation (Update) and rendering (Draw). Make the simulation deterministic where practical and keep rendering purely a projection of state. This simplifies multiplayer, replays, and automated tests.

```
// Small, explicit separation: SimulationTick and
RenderTick

public void UpdateGame(float dt)

{

    physicsWorld.Step(dt);

    aiSystem.Update(dt);

}

public void DrawGame(SpriteBatch sb)

{

    sceneRenderer.Render(sb);

}
```

Design for testability: isolate game logic from platform code

Write gameplay logic as pure classes that accept inputs and return state changes. Put file I/O, mono-game graphics, and platform APIs behind interfaces that can be faked in tests.

```
// Example pure logic class

public class DamageCalculator

{

    public int ApplyDamage(int health, int damage,
float armorMultiplier)
```

```
    {
        return Math.Max(0, health - (int)(damage *
(1f - armorMultiplier)));

    }

}
```

Now write standard unit tests for DamageCalculator—fast, deterministic, and safe to run in CI.

CI, automated builds and smoke tests

Automate every build step: compile for each target, run unit tests, run a small headless smoke test (logic-only), package assets, and produce versioned artifacts. Use incremental builds and artifact caching to keep runtimes fast as the project grows.

```
# Example: GitHub Actions (build + tests) snippet

name: CI

on: [push, pull_request]

jobs:

  build:

    runs-on: ubuntu-latest

    steps:

      - uses: actions/checkout@v4

      - name: Setup .NET

        uses: actions/setup-dotnet@v4

        with:
```

```
        dotnet-version: 8.0.x

    - name: Restore & Build

      run: dotnet restore && dotnet build
--configuration Release --no-restore

    - name: Run Tests

      run: dotnet test --no-build --verbosity
normal

    - name: Package

      run: dotnet publish -c Release -o
./artifacts
```

Keep CI jobs short by isolating long tasks (full platform builds, large asset processing) into separate scheduled pipelines or release jobs.

Asset pipeline, versioning and migration

Treat your asset pipeline like code. Check exported metadata into source control, use deterministic exporter settings, and keep the raw source art alongside compiled runtime assets. Embed version metadata in content bundles so the game can detect mismatched pipelines and run migration or regeneration steps.

```
// Read manifest from content bundle to guard against
mismatches

public record ContentManifest(string Version,
string[] Files);

public bool IsManifestCompatible(string manifestJson,
string expectedVersion)
```

```
{

    var manifest =
System.Text.Json.JsonSerializer.Deserialize<ContentMa
nifest>(manifestJson);

    return manifest != null && manifest.Version ==
expectedVersion;

}
```

When you change exporters, bump manifest version and implement migration logic in the loader that converts older bundles to the new format.

Monitoring, telemetry and crash collection

Scaling a live game requires observability. Send compact, privacy-respecting telemetry events for performance, crashes, and key gameplay milestones. Aggregate metrics server-side so you can detect regressions and balance changes quickly. Keep telemetry sampling and rate limits in place to control cost.

```
// Minimal telemetry client example (stub)

public interface ITelemetryClient { void
TrackEvent(string name, Dictionary<string,string>
props = null); }

public class SimpleTelemetryClient : ITelemetryClient

{

    public void TrackEvent(string name,
Dictionary<string, string> props = null)

    {
```

```
        // enqueue to a background sender; flush on
exit

    }

}
```

Log frame-time histograms and memory usage periodically; this makes it easier to correlate spikes with code changes.

Profiling, performance budgets and scalability knobs

Set concrete performance budgets per platform and enforce them. Instrument frame time by subsystem (physics, AI, rendering, audio) so you can see where cost grows as features are added. Add runtime knobs such as quality levels, draw-distance, LOD and dynamic resolution to keep frame-rate stable across devices.

```
// Simple frame timer breakdown

public class FrameProfiler

{

    private readonly Stopwatch sw = new();

    public Dictionary<string, long> Sections = new();


    public void StartSection(string name) {
sw.Restart(); }

    public void EndSection(string name) { sw.Stop();
Sections[name] = sw.ElapsedMilliseconds; }

}
```

Measure on target hardware, not just your dev machine.

Safe refactors: feature flags and canary releases

When changing big systems, gate them behind feature flags so you can roll out progressively and rollback quickly. Combine flags with telemetry to evaluate the impact. For live services, use staged deploys or canary clients to limit blast radius.

```
// Simple in-memory feature flag

public static class FeatureFlags { public static bool
NewAIEnabled { get; set; } = false; }
```

Flip the flag during runtime (with care) or via remote configuration to test in production without new builds.

Dependency management and third-party libraries

Pin package versions explicitly and record them in a lock file. Abstract third-party APIs behind small facades so replacements are localised. Run security and license checks as part of CI to prevent unpleasant surprises later.

Documentation, code ownership and small PRs

Maintain a short architecture README that maps subsystems, responsibilities and common patterns. Require small, focused pull requests and a review checklist that enforces: tests for logic changes, perf benchmark for hot-path edits, and no per-frame allocations for critical subsystems. Small PRs make regressions easier to find and fix.

Operational maintenance: backups, reproducible builds and releases

Store build artifacts and content bundles in immutable, versioned storage. Automate release notes from commit metadata and include runtime compatibility information in each build. Ensure your build pipeline can recreate any released artifact from source control and the pipeline config.

Practical, actionable code patterns

Provide a handful of patterns you'll use repeatedly. Here are short, ready-to-adopt examples.

A thread-safe object pool that avoids per-frame new:

```
public class ObjectPool<T> where T : class, new()

{

    private readonly ConcurrentBag<T> bag = new();

    public T Rent() => bag.TryTake(out var item) ?
item : new T();

    public void Return(T item) => bag.Add(item);

}
```

A small smoke-test you can run in CI that exercises game logic without graphics:

```
[Test]

public void GameplaySmokeTest()
```

```
{
    var world = new World(new DeterministicRng(seed:
123));

    world.SpawnPlayer(Vector2.Zero);

    for (int i = 0; i < 600; i++) { world.Update(1f /
60f); }

    Assert.IsTrue(world.Player != null &&
world.Player.Health > 0);

}
```

A lightweight frame-budget profiler you can ship in debug builds to collect breakdowns in the field:

```
// Collect and periodically send an aggregated
breakdown

frameProfiler.StartSection("Physics");

// run physics

frameProfiler.EndSection("Physics");

frameProfiler.StartSection("AI");

// run AI

frameProfiler.EndSection("AI");

// At end of frame record total and optionally send
summarised metrics to telemetry
```

Maintainability checklist (how your next 6 months of work should look)

Make small, testable changes. Automate everything once it proves repeatable. Keep your art and code pipelines reproducible, and add telemetry early so you can measure the real-world effect of changes. Prioritise modularity so individual systems—AI, physics, rendering—can evolve independently.

Closing

Scaling is not only about adding features; it's about making your code and processes resilient so you can add features without long debugging sprints and regressions. Treat automation, telemetry, and small interfaces as first-class features. With data-driven content, modular architecture, CI and observability in place, you'll be able to grow the game and your team without breaking the core experience.

Chapter 11: Cross-Platform Deployment

You'll take your games from your computer to mobile devices. You'll learn packaging, platform-specific tweaks, and testing. By the end, your games will run on Windows, Mac, Android, and iOS.

11.1 Building for Desktop (Windows, macOS, Linux)

This chapter explains how to build, package and ship MonoGame desktop games so they run reliably across Windows, macOS and Linux. You'll get pragmatic, up-to-date guidance for deciding between framework-dependent vs self-contained builds, producing platform-specific bundles (EXE/MSIX/PKG/DMG/AppImage/Flatpak), signing/notarizing where required, and a few repeatable build snippets you can drop into CI. Examples are written for modern .NET tooling (`dotnet publish`) and assume a MonoGame project that targets a desktop runtime (the project type created from the MonoGame desktop templates). Explanations stay platform-focused and practical so you can reproduce them on your machine or in CI.

Build modes: framework-dependent vs self-contained, single-file considerations

When you publish a .NET/MonoGame game you choose whether the runtime is bundled. A framework-dependent build produces a small output but requires the correct .NET runtime to be installed on the target machine. A self-contained build bundles the .NET runtime and native dependencies into the publish output so users do not need to install anything. Self-contained is larger but makes distribution simpler; framework-dependent is smaller and useful when you can control the runtime on the target machines.

If you want a single executable, you can enable single-file publishing; note that some native libraries and platform requirements may need careful handling (for example, native graphics or audio backends). Use self-contained + single-file for the easiest end-user installation on platforms you control, and use framework-dependent for smaller downloads when you can require the runtime.

Example `dotnet publish` for a self-contained single-file build targeting 64-bit Windows:

```
dotnet publish -c Release -r win-x64
--self-contained true /p:PublishSingleFile=true
/p:PublishTrimmed=false -o ./artifacts/win-x64
```

For macOS (universal or x64 builds) and Linux the same pattern applies, swapping the runtime identifier (RID) to `osx-x64`, `osx-arm64`, `linux-x64` or `linux-arm64`. Use self-contained for easiest end-user installs; use framework-dependent (`--self-contained false`) if you prefer tiny downloads and will manage runtime installs on target machines.

Windows: producing a runnable package and installers

On Windows you can ship a simple folder with your published EXE and supporting files, but most studios prefer an installer for a polished user experience. For native installers choose between traditional installers (Inno Setup, NSIS), modern MSIX packages for Windows Store/distribution, or third-party distribution platforms (itch.io, Steam) that accept a zipped artifact.

If you need an installer quickly, Inno Setup or NSIS are stable and scriptable; for Windows-specific features (auto-updates, modern deployment, Windows Defender SmartScreen trust), MSIX and signing the package are advisable. For code signing use an EV or standard code-signing certificate and Microsoft's `signtool` as part of CI to sign executables and installers. For automatic updates and distribution through the Microsoft ecosystem, produce an MSIX/AppInstaller manifest.

Example Inno Setup workflow (high-level): publish to `./artifacts/win-x64`, write an Inno script pointing at that folder, and run Inno command-line to produce `MyGameInstaller.exe`. In CI, sign the resulting installer with `signtool` using a certificate stored in a secure secret store.

---

macOS: bundle, sign and notarize

macOS requires extra steps to make apps run smoothly for end users: bundle the game as a proper `.app` application bundle, code-sign it, and submit it for notarization with Apple if you intend to distribute outside of developer machines. Notarization is effectively mandatory for frictionless installs on modern macOS versions, and creating a disk image (`.dmg`) or installer package (`.pkg`) is common practice for distribution.

Use `dotnet publish` to create a macOS desktop bundle, then codesign and notarize. Creating a universal binary (x64 + arm64) may require building for both RIDs and merging or using the `dotnet` packaging options provided in modern .NET SDKs. Automate signing and notarization in CI using a macOS runner (Xcode CLI tools are required) and keep private keys in your CI secrets manager. Apple's notarization step rejects unsigned or improperly bundled apps, so follow the SDK guidance for entitlements and packaging.

Example: publish and package as DMG (conceptual):

```
# publish self-contained per-arch

dotnet publish -c Release -r osx-x64 --self-contained
true -o ./artifacts/osx-x64

dotnet publish -c Release -r osx-arm64
--self-contained true -o ./artifacts/osx-arm64

# sign the binaries and create an .app bundle, then
create a .dmg or .pkg and notarize with Apple

# (signing/notarize steps require macOS tools and
your Apple Developer credentials)
```

Because signing and notarization require macOS tooling and developer credentials, CI should run these steps on macOS runners with credentials stored securely.

Linux: packaging options and portability

Linux packaging is fragmented; the three most common cross-distribution formats are AppImage, Flatpak and Snap. AppImage produces a single portable executable that runs on many distributions without installation, Flatpak provides sandboxing and centralized distribution via Flathub, and Snap uses Canonical's store. Choose AppImage for simplest "single file" distribution, Flatpak for sandboxed distribution and integration, or Snap for Snap Store distribution. For server-side or advanced distribution you can also provide distro-specific packages (DEB/RPM), but those require per-distribution work.

For .NET apps you can also use tools that help create AppImage packages for .NET runtimes, or bundle the runtime yourself with `dotnet publish --self-contained`. On Linux you must ensure the right native dependencies are present; for example, some graphics/backends require certain GL/SDL libraries — test on target distributions and consider AppImage/Flatpak sandboxing to reduce dependency friction.

Example AppImage approach (conceptual): publish a self-contained linux-x64 artifact, then use an AppImage tool (or the `DotnetPackaging.AppImage` helper package) to wrap the published folder into a single `.AppImage` file you can distribute. Test that the AppImage runs on the oldest distro you plan to support.

CI tips: build once, package per platform, store artifacts

Automate builds so a single commit produces artifacts for all target platforms. Use platform-specific runners (Windows runner for

MSIX/SignTool, macOS runner for codesign/notarize, Linux runner for AppImage/flatpak packaging). Keep ephemeral credentials in your CI secrets and sign only at the final packaging step. Persist published artifacts to immutable storage (build artifacts bucket) to enable reproducing releases and to power staged rollouts (canaries) and debugging.

A typical pipeline steps: restore -> build -> test -> publish per-RID -> platform packaging -> sign/notarize -> upload artifacts. Keep the development machine configuration small; prefer reproducible CI runners and containerized packaging steps where possible.

MonoGame-specific considerations

MonoGame uses native graphics/audio backends that differ per platform; verify the target runtime environment has the necessary native dependencies (for example SDL/OpenGL or MoltenVK/Metal layers depending on the MonoGame build and platform). Use the official MonoGame templates and follow MonoGame documentation for each platform's setup: desktop templates are the safest baseline for cross-platform builds. When publishing self-contained builds, test the published artifact on each target platform and on clean VMs to ensure native libraries are bundled correctly.

Troubleshooting and testing checklist

If a published build fails on a target machine, verify: the correct RID was used for `dotnet publish`, native runtime dependencies are present or bundled, code-signing/notarization (macOS) succeeded, and the published executable has proper execute permissions (Linux). For packaging failures consult the platform-specific logs (notarization logs for macOS, AppImage runtime output on Linux, installer logs on Windows). Automate smoke tests that run the published game headlessly when possible (logic-only smoke tests) to detect early failures in CI.

Quick reference commands (examples)

Self-contained, single-file Windows x64:

```
dotnet publish -c Release -r win-x64
--self-contained true /p:PublishSingleFile=true
-o ./artifacts/win-x64
```

Self-contained macOS x64 (packaging, signing/notarize steps not shown):

```
dotnet publish -c Release -r osx-x64 --self-contained
true -o ./artifacts/osx-x64

# then sign and notarize using macOS signing tools
(Xcode CLI)
```

Self-contained Linux x64 (wrap to AppImage):

```
dotnet publish -c Release -r linux-x64
--self-contained true -o ./artifacts/linux-x64

# wrap artifacts/linux-x64 into an AppImage using
a packaging tool
```

Remember to test published binaries on clean VMs of the target OS and to include native dependency checks, as MonoGame uses native backends that are platform-sensitive.

Closing advice

Prefer reproducibility: automate builds and signing, test published artifacts on clean installs, and choose packaging formats that match your distribution goals (single-file AppImage for simple Linux distribution; DMG/PKG + notarization for macOS; installer or MSIX for Windows). Self-contained builds minimize end-user friction but increase size—pick the tradeoff that best matches your audience and distribution channels. Keep a short CI pipeline that builds per-RID, packages, signs, and uploads artifacts so every release is repeatable and auditable.

11.2 Building for Mobile (Android, iOS)

Building MonoGame games for mobile platforms requires a different mindset compared to desktop: you have to account for platform-specific toolchains, deployment pipelines, signing, device testing, and performance constraints. This section provides a concise, practical guide to producing deployable Android and iOS builds, with fully functional examples and tips for automating builds, handling native dependencies, and producing packages suitable for app stores.

Mobile build considerations

Mobile platforms enforce stricter packaging, signing, and runtime requirements:

- **Android:** APK or AAB bundles are required. You must target the correct API level and bundle the .NET runtime if using MonoGame on .NET MAUI/Mono runtime. Google Play now prefers AAB (Android App Bundle) over APK for easier distribution and smaller downloads.
- **iOS:** You must build via a Mac host (physical or cloud) using Xcode toolchain. IPA packages must be signed with a provisioning profile and Apple Developer certificate. Distribution via App Store requires notarization and adherence to Apple's sandboxing rules.
- **Performance & memory:** Mobile devices have lower memory and weaker CPUs/GPU than desktops. Optimize assets (compressed textures, fewer draw calls), reduce per-frame allocations, and consider low-resolution assets for older devices.

Android: setting up, building, and packaging

MonoGame Android projects use the Xamarin/MAUI toolchain to produce APKs or AABs. You can build directly from Visual Studio (Windows/macOS) or command line with `dotnet build/publish`.

1. **Project configuration:** Ensure your project targets Android API level that covers your audience (e.g., API 33+). Include MonoGame Android template assets and dependencies.
2. **Signing keys:** Android requires a keystore for release builds. Store passwords securely (CI secrets or environment variables). Debug builds can run unsigned for device testing.
3. **Publishing:** For a release build, sign and align the APK, or produce an AAB to upload to Google Play.

Example command-line build for Android release:

```
# Set environment variables for signing

export KEYSTORE_PASSWORD="myKeystorePassword"

export KEY_ALIAS="myKeyAlias"

# Publish Android APK (release)

dotnet publish ./MyGame.Android/MyGame.Android.csproj
-c Release -f:net7.0-android -o ./artifacts/android

# To produce AAB instead of APK

dotnet msbuild ./MyGame.Android/MyGame.Android.csproj
/t:Build /p:Configuration=Release /p:Platform=AnyCPU
/p:AndroidPackageFormat=aab
```

After building, test on physical devices or emulators. Use Android Studio's adb to install APKs or test AABs on device or Play Store internal testing tracks.

---

iOS: building, signing, and distribution

iOS requires a macOS host with Xcode installed. MonoGame iOS projects target either the device (ARM64) or simulator (x64/arm64). You must manage:

- **Provisioning profiles:** Required to sign the IPA for development, Ad-Hoc, or App Store distribution.
- **Certificates:** Stored in your keychain or CI secrets; used with codesign.

- **Build outputs:** MonoGame produces an IPA file that can be installed via Xcode, TestFlight, or uploaded to App Store Connect.

Example: building an IPA for device release using command line:

```
# Build project for device

dotnet build ./MyGame.iOS/MyGame.iOS.csproj -c
Release -f:net7.0-ios /p:Platform=iPhone
/p:BuildIpa=true

# Locate IPA in output folder (e.g.,
./bin/iPhone/Release/)

# Upload via Transporter CLI or Xcode for App
Store submission
```

Simulator builds do not require signing; you can test quickly on an iOS simulator without provisioning profiles. Use device builds for performance profiling and full integration testing.

Asset and memory optimization for mobile

Mobile devices are memory-limited and GPU-constrained:

- **Textures:** Use compressed formats (ETC2 for Android, PVRTC/ASTC for iOS). Consider mipmaps only when necessary.
- **Audio:** Compress audio assets and avoid multiple simultaneous streams unless supported.
- **Scene management:** Unload assets for levels not currently active. Use small ContentManagers per screen/scene to free memory.

- **Allocation patterns:** Avoid per-frame allocations; use object pools for bullets, particles, or frequently spawned objects.

Practical MonoGame example for texture loading optimized for mobile:

```
private Texture2D playerTexture;

protected override void LoadContent()

{

    // Load compressed texture to save memory

    playerTexture =
Content.Load<Texture2D>("player_mobile");

}

protected override void UnloadContent()

{

    playerTexture?.Dispose();

    playerTexture = null;

}
```

Device testing and automation

Test frequently on real devices, both low-end and high-end models. Emulators are convenient but may hide GPU and memory limitations. For CI/CD:

- **Android:** Use GitHub Actions or Azure Pipelines with `macos-latest` runners to build AABs/APKs. Include keystore secrets.
- **iOS:** Always build on a Mac agent; use CI secrets for certificates and provisioning profiles. Automate IPA upload to TestFlight for QA.

Sample CI command sequence for Android AAB:

```
dotnet restore

dotnet build -c Release -f:net7.0-android

dotnet msbuild /t:Build /p:AndroidPackageFormat=aab
/p:SignManually=false

# Upload artifacts to internal Play Store testing
track
```

Cross-platform best practices

MonoGame allows sharing most game logic and assets across platforms:

- Use platform-agnostic code for gameplay and rendering logic.
- Use dependency injection or service interfaces for platform-specific features (notifications, in-app purchases, device sensors).
- Keep configuration files, content manifests, and asset management identical across platforms to reduce platform-specific bugs.

Example of platform-abstracted service:

```
public interface INotificationService

{

    void ShowMessage(string title, string message);

}

// Android implementation

public class AndroidNotificationService :
INotificationService

{

    public void ShowMessage(string title, string
message)

    {

Android.Widget.Toast.MakeText(Android.App.Application
.Context, message,
Android.Widget.ToastLength.Short).Show();

    }

}
```

This allows your core game to call `INotificationService.ShowMessage(...)` regardless of platform.

Troubleshooting

Common mobile build issues include:

- **Signing errors:** Ensure keystore, certificates, and provisioning profiles match your build configuration.
- **Missing native dependencies:** MonoGame relies on SDL/OpenGL/Metal backends; ensure the build bundles or the device supports them.
- **Performance issues:** Profile FPS and memory usage on target devices. Use lightweight assets and object pooling.
- **Deployment issues:** Test on multiple device OS versions and screen resolutions.

Closing advice

Mobile deployment adds complexity, but careful management of signing, build configurations, and platform-specific packaging will make the process repeatable. Always test on devices, optimize memory and performance, automate builds in CI/CD, and keep your game logic platform-independent as much as possible. By following these practices, MonoGame projects can scale efficiently to Android and iOS with minimal headaches.

11.3   Platform-Specific   Input   & Performance Considerations

When building cross-platform MonoGame games, input handling and performance characteristics vary significantly between desktops, Android, and iOS. Understanding these differences is essential for smooth gameplay, responsive controls, and consistent frame rates. This section provides a concise yet thorough guide on adapting input, optimizing rendering, and profiling for platform-specific constraints with practical, ready-to-use examples.

Input abstractions across platforms

Desktop platforms typically rely on keyboard, mouse, and gamepad input. Mobile platforms rely on touch, accelerometer, gyroscope, and virtual on-screen controls. To maintain cross-platform code, abstract input handling behind a unified interface.

```
public interface IInputService
{
    bool IsActionPressed(string action);
    Vector2 GetPointerPosition();
}


#if WINDOWS || LINUX || MACOS
public class DesktopInputService : IInputService
{
    KeyboardState keyboard;
    MouseState mouse;

    public void Update()
    {
        keyboard = Keyboard.GetState();
```

```csharp
        mouse = Mouse.GetState();

    }


    public bool IsActionPressed(string action)

    {

        return action switch

        {

            "Jump" => keyboard.IsKeyDown(Keys.Space),

            "Fire" => mouse.LeftButton ==
ButtonState.Pressed,

            _ => false

        };

    }


    public Vector2 GetPointerPosition() =>
new(mouse.X, mouse.Y);

}

#endif


#if ANDROID || IOS

public class MobileInputService : IInputService

{

    TouchCollection touches;
```

```csharp
        public void Update(GameTime gameTime)

        {

            touches = TouchPanel.GetState();

        }


        public bool IsActionPressed(string action)

        {

            return action switch

            {

                "Jump" => touches.Any(t => t.State ==
TouchLocationState.Pressed),

                _ => false

            };

        }


        public Vector2 GetPointerPosition()

        {

            var touch = touches.FirstOrDefault();

            return touch != null ? touch.Position :
Vector2.Zero;

        }

    }

#endif
```

This design allows gameplay logic to query `IInputService` without knowing the underlying platform. You update the input service once per frame and use it consistently in your `Update` methods.

Touch vs mouse considerations

Mobile platforms require more nuanced handling:

- **Multi-touch:** Track multiple fingers for gestures, pinch-zoom, and swipe.
- **Touch precision:** Treat input areas larger than pixel-perfect mouse positions, accounting for finger width.
- **Gesture recognition:** Implement common gestures as helper methods or use libraries that wrap touch into high-level gestures.

Example pinch-to-zoom gesture:

```
public float GetPinchZoom()

{

    if (touches.Count < 2) return 0f;

    var touch0 = touches[0];

    var touch1 = touches[1];

    var currentDistance =
Vector2.Distance(touch0.Position, touch1.Position);

    var previousDistance =
Vector2.Distance(touch0.Position - touch0.Delta,
touch1.Position - touch1.Delta);
```

```
return currentDistance - previousDistance;
}
```

This allows zooming or scaling objects consistently across mobile devices.

Gamepad and controller support

Desktop and mobile platforms may support controllers. MonoGame abstracts Xbox/Generic controllers via GamePad API:

```
var                     state                   =
GamePad.GetState(PlayerIndex.One);

if (state.IsConnected && state.Buttons.A ==
ButtonState.Pressed)
{
    player.Jump();
}
```

When deploying to Android/iOS with controller support (e.g., MFi controllers on iOS), always query the connected controller list and fall back to touch or virtual controls when none is available.

Performance considerations by platform

Rendering performance, memory footprint, and CPU/GPU limitations vary per platform. Always measure and tune separately.

Desktop

Desktops often have strong GPUs but variable hardware. Key optimizations:

- Use a single `SpriteBatch.Begin/End()` per layer or frame.
- Minimize per-frame allocations to avoid GC pauses.
- Use `Texture2D` atlases to reduce draw calls.
- Profile with GPU/CPU frame analyzers.

Mobile

Mobile devices are memory-constrained and can heat up under sustained CPU/GPU load:

- Limit texture resolutions; prefer compressed formats (ETC2 for Android, PVRTC/ASTC for iOS).
- Use object pooling to reduce GC allocations.
- Reduce overdraw by ordering sprites front-to-back or using simple geometry.
- Keep the main loop predictable; avoid expensive per-frame operations like LINQ or large temporary arrays.

Practical example of object pooling for bullets on mobile:

```
public class BulletPool

{

    private readonly Bullet[] bullets;

    private int nextIndex;

    public BulletPool(int maxCount)

    {
```

```
        bullets = new Bullet[maxCount];

        for (int i = 0; i < maxCount; i++) bullets[i]
= new Bullet();

    }


    public Bullet GetBullet()

    {

        var bullet = bullets[nextIndex];

        nextIndex = (nextIndex + 1) % bullets.Length;

        return bullet;

    }

}
```

This keeps allocation stable and prevents GC spikes on low-end devices.

Frame timing and synchronization

Mobile devices may drop frames if updates take too long. To maintain smooth gameplay:

- Use `Game.IsFixedTimeStep = true` with `TargetElapsedTime` to regulate updates.
- Profile both `Update` and `Draw` separately; move non-critical tasks off the main thread if possible.

- Consider reducing graphical quality dynamically based on detected FPS drops.

Example dynamic FPS adjustment:

```
if (currentFPS < 30)

{

    useHighQualityTextures = false;

}
```

Platform-specific profiling

Use platform-specific tools:

- **Windows/macOS/Linux:** Visual Studio Profiler, GPUView, RenderDoc.
- **Android:** Android Studio Profiler, GPU Inspector, Systrace.
- **iOS:** Xcode Instruments (Time Profiler, GPU, Allocations).

Always test on the lowest-end device you intend to support, since emulators/simulators often overstate performance.

Summary

Abstracting input via interfaces allows unified game logic while handling platform-specific nuances. Touch input, gestures, and controller support require special attention on mobile, whereas desktops favor keyboard, mouse, and controller input. Performance optimizations must be platform-aware: object pooling, texture compression, minimized draw calls, and predictable update loops are key. Profiling and testing on real devices ensure responsiveness and stable frame rates across all target platforms.

11.4 Packaging & Distributing Games

Packaging and distributing your MonoGame project is the final step that turns your code and assets into a deliverable product. This process varies across platforms—desktop and mobile have different requirements, signing processes, and distribution channels. Proper packaging ensures smooth installation, reliable updates, and reduces friction for players. This section provides practical, platform-specific guidance with actionable code and workflow examples.

General principles

The first rule of packaging is reproducibility: the build that passes tests should be identical to the one you ship. Keep your build artifacts, content pipeline outputs, and configuration files versioned or reproducibly generated. Automated packaging ensures consistency and reduces human error.

Another principle is separation: the compiled binaries, assets, and platform-specific files should be clearly organized. For MonoGame, this usually means:

- **Binaries:** Executables (`.exe`, `.app`, `.ipa`, `.apk`) or shared libraries.

- **Assets:** Content pipeline outputs (`.xnb`, compressed textures, audio files).
- **Configuration:** Platform-specific settings (manifest, plist, APK manifest, or AppBundle metadata).

Desktop packaging

For Windows, macOS, and Linux, you can ship simple folder builds or create platform-native packages.

Windows

Windows games can be distributed as folder packages, ZIPs, or via installers. For professional distribution, consider using Inno Setup, NSIS, or MSIX. MSIX offers modern installer features, including signing, auto-updates, and integration with the Microsoft Store.

Example Inno Setup script snippet:

```
[Setup]
AppName=MyGame
AppVersion=1.0
DefaultDirName={pf}\MyGame
OutputBaseFilename=MyGameInstaller
Compression=lzma
SolidCompression=yes


[Files]
```

```
Source: "C:\Projects\MyGame\artifacts\win-x64\*";
DestDir: "{app}"; Flags: ignoreversion recursesubdirs


[Icons]

Name: "{group}\MyGame"; Filename: "{app}\MyGame.exe"
```

Compile with `ISCC MyGameInstaller.iss` to produce `MyGameInstaller.exe`. You can also integrate signing using `signtool` for authenticity.

macOS

MacOS apps require `.app` bundles, optionally wrapped in `.dmg` disk images or `.pkg` installers. The bundle must be signed and notarized for smooth installation.

Example conceptual workflow:

```
dotnet publish -c Release -r osx-x64 --self-contained
true -o ./artifacts/osx

codesign --deep --force --verify --verbose --sign
"Developer ID Application: Your Name (TEAMID)"
./artifacts/osx/MyGame.app

# Notarization

xcrun altool --notarize-app -f MyGame.zip
--primary-bundle-id "com.example.mygame" -u
"appleid@example.com" -p "@keychain:AppPassword"
```

Testing on a clean macOS VM ensures the app runs without requiring developer tools.

Linux

Linux distribution options include folder builds, AppImage, Flatpak, or Snap. AppImage is simplest for broad compatibility, producing a single executable that contains all runtime dependencies.

Example conceptual AppImage creation:

```
# After publishing Linux x64 build

mkdir -p AppDir/usr/bin

cp -r ./artifacts/linux-x64/* AppDir/usr/bin/

# Use AppImage tool to create single AppImage

appimagetool AppDir MyGame.AppImage
```

Test on multiple distributions to ensure compatibility.

Mobile packaging

Mobile packaging involves platform-specific toolchains and signing requirements.

Android

Android packages can be APK or AAB. Modern Google Play distribution prefers AAB for reduced app size and dynamic delivery.

```
# Build APK (debug)

dotnet publish ./MyGame.Android/MyGame.Android.csproj
-c Release -f net7.0-android -o ./artifacts/android

# For AAB
```

```
dotnet msbuild ./MyGame.Android/MyGame.Android.csproj
/t:Build /p:Configuration=Release
/p:AndroidPackageFormat=aab
```

Signing is required for release builds. Keep keystore passwords and aliases secure, especially in CI pipelines.

iOS

iOS requires building on a Mac with Xcode. IPA packages must be signed with valid provisioning profiles and Apple Developer certificates.

```
dotnet build ./MyGame.iOS/MyGame.iOS.csproj -c
Release -f net7.0-ios /p:Platform=iPhone
/p:BuildIpa=true

# Upload IPA to App Store Connect using Xcode or
Transporter CLI
```

Simulator builds do not require signing, but device builds for testing or TestFlight submission do.

Automation & CI/CD

To maintain consistent builds, automate packaging:

1. Restore dependencies and build the project.
2. Run unit and smoke tests.
3. Publish per platform (Windows, macOS, Linux, Android, iOS).
4. Sign and package artifacts.
5. Upload to distribution channels or store artifacts for deployment.

Example GitHub Actions snippet for desktop builds:

```
jobs:
  build:
    runs-on: ubuntu-latest
    steps:
      - uses: actions/checkout@v4
      - name: Setup .NET
        uses: actions/setup-dotnet@v4
        with:
          dotnet-version: 8.0.x
      - name: Build & Publish
        run: |
          dotnet restore
          dotnet publish -c Release -r win-x64 -o
./artifacts/win-x64
          dotnet publish -c Release -r osx-x64 -o
./artifacts/osx-x64
          dotnet publish -c Release -r linux-x64 -o
./artifacts/linux-x64
```

Extend the workflow to include signing steps and packaging scripts for installers or mobile stores.

Testing packaged builds

Testing is critical before distribution:

- Install on clean VMs or devices.
- Check file permissions and executable bits (Linux/macOS).
- Validate that assets load and input works as expected.
- Test both release and debug builds to catch any missing dependencies.

Best practices

- Keep content and binaries separated for easier patching.
- Use automated scripts for reproducible builds.
- Test on multiple devices and OS versions.
- Sign packages and executables to ensure trust and integrity.
- Use compressed formats for assets to minimize download size.

Closing advice

Packaging and distributing games is as important as development. Proper organization, automation, and platform-specific considerations reduce post-release issues and improve user experience. A structured approach with reproducible builds, signing, testing, and verified delivery pipelines ensures your MonoGame game reaches players reliably across desktop and mobile platforms.

11.5 Testing Across Multiple Platforms

Testing a MonoGame title on more than one platform is less about magic and more about discipline: separate your game's pure logic from platform glue, test the logic everywhere with fast unit tests, run integration checks on representative platforms, and run real-device tests for mobile and consoles. The following guide walks you through a practical, professional approach you can put straight into a MonoGame book: it explains the strategy, shows concrete code that's easy to copy, and ends with a ready-to-drop CI workflow and device-farm examples so you can test at scale.

Core strategy and architecture

Write your game so the game loop, rules, AI and data-model live in plain C# libraries that reference no MonoGame types. Put rendering, input and platform-specific services in thin adapters that the core game consumes by interface. That separation lets you run unit and integration tests on any OS or CI runner without starting the game window or device runtime. When a platform-specific bug appears, you already know it's in the adapter layer and can focus tests there.

Below is a small, complete example that demonstrates the idea: a GameLogic class with no MonoGame references, a tiny adapter interface for time and input, and an xUnit test that runs anywhere.

```
// Project: Game.Core (netstandard or net7.0)

// File: GameLogic.cs

public interface IGameTimeProvider

{

    float DeltaSeconds { get; }

}
```

```csharp
public class GameLogic

{

    float _position;

    readonly float _speed = 100f; // units per second

    public float Position => _position;

    public void Update(IGameTimeProvider time, bool
moveRight)

    {

        if (moveRight) _position += _speed *
time.DeltaSeconds;

        else _position -= _speed * time.DeltaSeconds;

    }

}

// Project: Game.Tests (xUnit, net7.0)

// File: GameLogicTests.cs

using Xunit;

class FakeTime : IGameTimeProvider

{

    public float DeltaSeconds { get; set; }

}

public class GameLogicTests

{

    [Fact]
```

```
public void UpdateMovesRightBySpeedTimesDelta()

{

    var logic = new GameLogic();

    var fakeTime = new FakeTime{ DeltaSeconds =
0.5f }; // half second

    logic.Update(fakeTime, moveRight: true);

    Assert.Equal(50f, logic.Position, precision:
3);

}

}
```

Because the test project has no MonoGame dependencies it runs on GitHub-hosted runners for Linux, macOS, and Windows without extra setup.

Unit tests and small integration tests

Unit tests should exercise the logic above: physics, AI decisions, score calculations, level rules. For integration tests you can create headless runners for services (audio mixer stubs, input simulators) and run a few deterministic "frames" to check end-to-end state transitions. Avoid trying to render to a GPU in unit tests; instead test the renderable data produced by your systems (sprite positions, sort order, camera transforms). Keep render tests manual or on device farms where necessary.

A practical pattern is to expose a RenderState from your rendering pipeline (simple DTO) and assert shape/position/order in tests, leaving visuals for human QA and device screenshots.

Platform-specific checks

Some problems only appear when you run on a specific platform: file paths and permissions differ on Windows vs Linux vs Android, touch input differs from mouse, and texture compression/format issues can appear only on specific GPUs. Reduce surprises by:

On Windows, macOS and Linux validate file encoding, path separators, and native library loads. On mobile, test pause/resume, lifecycle events and backgrounding. For iOS and macOS you will need a macOS runner for building and signing. For consoles follow the vendor-specific test harness and certification guides.

Building cross-platform artifacts is typically done with `dotnet publish` for managed targets and the platform templates MonoGame provides for DesktopGL/Android/iOS. A typical publish snippet (example for Android) looks like this:

```
dotnet publish MyGame.sln -c Release -f
net7.0-android -o ./artifacts/android

# Note: building Android/iOS may require platform
workloads and a macOS runner for iOS builds.
```

For DesktopGL and native runtime artifacts you can publish self-contained packages for each runtime identifier:

```
dotnet publish -c Release -r win-x64 -f net7.0 -o
./artifacts/win

dotnet publish -c Release -r linux-x64 -f net7.0 -o
./artifacts/linux

dotnet publish -c Release -r osx-x64 -f net7.0 -o
./artifacts/macos
```

Platform packaging often needs additional steps: signing an iOS IPA, creating an Android signed APK/AAB, and providing the right native assets for each OS GPU and compression format.

Continuous Integration: multi-OS builds and tests

Use a matrix CI to run the same test suite across OSes. The following GitHub Actions workflow demonstrates a compact, working CI configuration that builds and runs unit tests on Ubuntu, macOS and Windows. It also produces platform artifacts. Drop this into `.github/workflows/ci.yml` and adjust project names and runtimes.

```
name: CI - Build & Test Multi-OS

on:

  push:

    branches: [ main ]

  pull_request:

    branches: [ main ]

jobs:

  build-test:

    runs-on: ${{ matrix.os }}

    strategy:

      matrix:

        os: [ubuntu-latest, macos-latest,
windows-latest]

        dotnet: [7.0.x]
```

```yaml
steps:

  - uses: actions/checkout@v4


  - name: Setup .NET

    uses: actions/setup-dotnet@v4

    with:

      dotnet-version: ${{ matrix.dotnet }}


  - name: Restore

    run: dotnet restore


  - name: Build

    run: dotnet build --configuration Release
--no-restore


  - name: Run tests

    run: dotnet test --configuration Release
--no-build --verbosity normal


  - name: Publish desktop artifacts

    if: matrix.os == 'ubuntu-latest' || matrix.os
== 'windows-latest' || matrix.os == 'macos-latest'

    run: |

      dotnet publish ./src/MyGame/MyGame.csproj
-c Release -r ${RUNNER_OS,,}-x64 -o ./artifacts/${{
matrix.os }}
```

```
- name: Upload artifacts

  uses: actions/upload-artifact@v4

  with:

    name: artifacts-${{ matrix.os }}

    path: ./artifacts
```

This workflow provides fast feedback on logic and cross-platform compilation. For mobile builds, add separate jobs because building Android and iOS usually needs extra SDKs and sometimes a macOS runner to sign and archive.

Mobile and real-device testing

Unit tests alone cannot prove touch behavior, lifecycle handling and GPU-specific rendering. For that, run your signed APK/IPA on many devices. There are two practical approaches: maintain an in-house device lab, or use a cloud device farm.

If you use a cloud device farm you can run automated tests and get logs, screenshots and videos without maintaining hardware. Firebase Test Lab and AWS Device Farm accept APKs and run instrumentation or "Robo" style tests, while BrowserStack and Microsoft App Center provide similar workflows. For Android you can run a simple Firebase Robo test like this via the gcloud CLI once you have an APK:

```
gcloud firebase test android run --type robo
--app=app-release.apk
```

For deterministic UI tests, use Espresso on Android and XCUITest on iOS. Appium is an option when you want a single cross-platform automation layer driven by the same tests.

Real-device testing is the last line of defense for performance and GPU compatibility. Collect crash logs (symbols for native crashes), measure frametimes, and record GPU memory usage on representative hardware.

Handling platform quirks and flaky tests

Mobile networks, intermittent device states and emulator differences produce flakiness. Keep flaky tests out of the main pipeline and mark them for scheduled runs. Use retries sparingly and only after investigating the cause. When a platform shows a unique bug (texture format issues on a specific GPU, input scaling differences on a certain Android vendor), create a small reproducible test case and add it as a regression test in your device-farm suite.

Automated distribution for testers

Create release channels: internal, closed beta, public. For Android use Google Play internal testing or upload APK/AABs to Firebase/AWS device farms. For iOS use TestFlight which requires signing and a macOS build pipeline. Automate uploads from CI so testers always get the latest build: GitHub Actions can call Android's `gplay-publisher` tools or use Fastlane for both platforms to handle signing and upload.

Example: from local test to device farm run

First, make a reproducible test APK using your CI or local `dotnet publish`. Sign the APK with your keystore. Next, upload the signed artifact to Firebase Test Lab or BrowserStack and run an automated instrumentation test that validates app launch, main menu, and a short play sequence. Collect logs and a video, then turn the failing scenario into a unit/integration test if possible.

Practical checklist you can copy into your book

Follow this flow: extract logic into testable libraries, write fast unit tests, add deterministic integration tests for managers and services, run CI matrix across OSes that builds and runs tests, produce artifacts for each platform, run device-farm tests for mobile and capture logs/screenshots, and finally run human visual tests for final polishing and certification. Keep the adapter layers thin so platform-specific bugs don't creep into core logic and your unit tests stay reliable.

Short sample troubleshooting notes

If your Android build fails because a workload is missing, install the relevant workload on the runner or preinstall Android SDK components on your CI image. If an iOS job is required, use `macos-latest` runner and a code-signing step; many teams use Fastlane for certificate and provisioning automation. When a test reveals a rendering difference on Linux, verify texture formats, GL extensions and driver versions, then reproduce on the lowest driver version you support.

Appendices — copy-ready code and CI

The earlier code samples are copy-ready. The CI YAML is a minimal, pragmatic starting point; extend it with mobile jobs, signing steps, artifact uploads, and scheduled device-farm runs when you are ready to scale.

Chapter 12: Polishing & Optimization

You'll profile and optimize your games for speed, memory, and smooth performance. You'll handle edge cases and low-end devices. By the end, your games will feel fully finished and polished.

12.1 Profiling FPS & Resource Usage

Profiling is not a luxury — it's the map you follow when your game runs slow, uses too much memory, or behaves differently on another device. This chapter shows a clear, repeatable workflow you can drop into your MonoGame projects: first measure (FPS, frametime, memory), then narrow (cheap in-code timers and counters), then deep-dive (sampling/tracing and GPU frame capture). Each explanation is short, practical and followed by copy-ready code or commands so you can run them right away.

The measurement-first mindset

Always start with a measurable symptom. Replace vague "it's slow" with a concrete metric: average FPS over 30s, 99th-percentile frame time, allocation rate (MB/s), or peak GPU memory. Measure on representative hardware and capture a recording or trace. The purpose of these baseline numbers is to let you prove a fix worked and to prioritise the highest-impact problems first.

Cheap, always-on metrics (in-game)

You want a small, low-overhead HUD that tells you FPS, frametime (ms), draw call count, and managed memory. Put it behind a debug toggle so it's available on devices but off for players. The code below is copy-ready, works in any MonoGame project, and deliberately avoids MonoGame internals in the game logic: it only reads GameTime and basic runtime stats.

```csharp
// File: DebugMetrics.cs (MonoGame - C#)

// Usage: new DebugMetrics(Content, GraphicsDevice);
call Update(gameTime) and Draw(spriteBatch) in your
Game class when debug enabled.


using System;

using System.Diagnostics;

using Microsoft.Xna.Framework;

using Microsoft.Xna.Framework.Content;

using Microsoft.Xna.Framework.Graphics;


public class DebugMetrics

{

    SpriteFont font;

    readonly GraphicsDevice graphics;

    long frameCount;

    double accumSeconds;

    float lastFps;

    Stopwatch frameTimer = Stopwatch.StartNew();
```

```csharp
    public DebugMetrics(ContentManager content,
GraphicsDevice graphics)

    {

        this.graphics = graphics;

        // Provide a small bitmap font in your
project or use a default if available

        font = content.Load<SpriteFont>("DebugFont");

    }


    public void Update(GameTime gameTime)

    {

        frameCount++;

        accumSeconds +=
gameTime.ElapsedGameTime.TotalSeconds;

        if (accumSeconds >= 1.0)

        {

            lastFps = (float)(frameCount /
accumSeconds);

            frameCount = 0;

            accumSeconds = 0;

        }

    }

    public void Draw(SpriteBatch sb)

    {
```

```
        var memMB = GC.GetTotalMemory(false) /
(1024.0 * 1024.0);

        var framems =
frameTimer.Elapsed.TotalMilliseconds;

        frameTimer.Restart();

        var lines = $"FPS: {lastFps:0.0}\nFrame ms:
{framems:0.00}\nManaged MB: {memMB:0.00}\nDrawCalls:
{graphics.DrawCount}";

        sb.Begin();

        sb.DrawString(font, lines, new Vector2(8, 8),
Color.White);

        sb.End();

    }

}
```

Draw call counting depends on your renderer: many platforms expose a draw-call counter on the graphics device; if yours does not, instrument your SpriteBatch and custom renderers to increment a counter.

This HUD gives immediate, actionable numbers: if FPS is low and frame ms is high, you know the problem is per-frame work; if managed MB climbs steadily you likely have an allocation leak.

Micro-profiling: timing critical sections

After you see the symptom, narrow it down inside the code with very cheap timers. Use a reusable ScopedTimer to measure blocks and output aggregated stats every few seconds.

```csharp
// File: ScopedTimer.cs

using System;

using System.Diagnostics;

using System.Collections.Concurrent;


public static class Perf

{

    static ConcurrentDictionary<string, (long
TotalMs, int Count)> stats = new();


    public static IDisposable Measure(string name)

    {

        return new ScopedTimer(name);

    }


    public static string Snapshot()

    {

        var sb = new System.Text.StringBuilder();

        foreach (var kv in stats)

        {

            var t = kv.Value;

            var avg = t.Count == 0 ? 0 : t.TotalMs /
(double)t.Count;

            sb.AppendLine($"{kv.Key}
avg={avg:0.00}ms  calls={t.Count}");
```

```
        }

        return sb.ToString();

    }


    class ScopedTimer : IDisposable

    {

        readonly string name;

        readonly Stopwatch sw = Stopwatch.StartNew();

        public ScopedTimer(string name) => this.name
= name;

        public void Dispose()

        {

            sw.Stop();

            stats.AddOrUpdate(name,
(sw.ElapsedMilliseconds, 1),

                 (_, old) => (old.TotalMs +
sw.ElapsedMilliseconds, old.Count + 1));

        }

    }

}
```

Use it like `using (Perf.Measure("Update/Physics"))`
`{ UpdatePhysics(); }` and print `Perf.Snapshot()` to
your debug log every few seconds. This pattern is low-overhead
and portable across platforms.

Sampling and runtime tracing (when micro-profiling isn't enough)

When you need to understand call stacks over time, use a sampling profiler or trace tool that works with .NET. `dotnet-trace` and `dotnet-counters` can collect traces on Linux/macOS/Windows without changing the build and are safe to run on CI or even production briefly. Use `dotnet-counters` for quick live counters (CPU, GC, threadpool) and `dotnet-trace` to collect a `.nettrace` you can open in PerfView, speedscope, or Visual Studio for flame charts.

Collect a 30-second CPU sampling trace by attaching to a running process id (get the PID from your OS or from the launcher):

```
# monitor live counters

dotnet-counters monitor --process-id <PID>
System.Runtime

# collect CPU sample trace (30s)

dotnet-trace collect --process-id <PID> --duration
00:00:30 --profile cpu-sampling --output
mygame.nettrace
```

Open the `.nettrace` in Visual Studio or PerfView and look for hotspots, allocation sources and thread contention. Sampling avoids the cost of instrumenting every method while giving you realistic execution profiles.

GPU/frame capture tools: when the bottleneck is rendering

If your CPU metrics look fine but frametimes are high, capture a frame on the GPU and inspect draw calls, textures, and shader inputs. RenderDoc is the go-to for OpenGL/Vulkan/Direct3D workflows and lets you capture and step through a single frame to inspect resources and timings. For Direct3D/Windows you can also use Visual Studio's Graphics Diagnostics; for Metal/iOS use Xcode's GPU Frame Capture. The usual flow is: run the game, capture a problem frame, inspect the draw call list, look at shader uniforms and large textures, and find expensive state changes or redundant full-screen passes.

A simple RenderDoc flow:
run RenderDoc, inject your executable (or attach on Linux), capture a frame when the issue reproduces, then inspect per-draw timing and resource sizes to spot the heavy draw or expensive shader.

Platform-specific profiling notes

Mobile devices have unique problems: texture compression mismatches, tile-based GPUs with different performance characteristics, and lifecycle costs for suspend/resume. For Android use the Android GPU profiler and adb logcat to capture traces. For iOS use Xcode's Metal capture and Instruments for CPU/memory traces. On Windows you can also use NVIDIA Nsight or Intel GPA when GPU vendor-specific detail is needed. Profiling on-device is essential — emulators and desktop GPUs rarely match real mobile hardware.

Continuous profiling and CI integration

Automated profiling lets you detect regressions early. Add a CI job that runs unit tests and a short performance smoke test on a hosted runner, capturing baseline metrics (for example: run a headless stress scene for 10 seconds, record average frametime and managed allocations). For mobile workflows, set a scheduled job that builds signed artifacts and uploads them to a cloud device farm (Firebase Test Lab, BrowserStack) where you can run instrumentation UI tests and capture logs, screenshots and perf traces.

Example CI snippet (conceptual):

```
# CI job concept: run headless perf smoke test

- name: Publish test build

  run: dotnet publish -c Release -r linux-x64 -o
./perfArtifacts

- name: Run headless perf runner

  run: ./perfArtifacts/MyGamePerfRunner --duration 10
--csv perf_output.csv

- name: Upload perf CSV

  uses: actions/upload-artifact@v4

  with:

    name: perf-output

    path: perf_output.csv
```

Store historic CSVs and plot them externally to detect regressions in FPS, frame ms, and allocations over time.

Practical troubleshooting checklist

If FPS drops when many enemies spawn, try disabling AI and see if the issue disappears. If memory steadily increases, instrument or sample GC allocations and inspect code paths that call new per-frame. If only one device shows a problem, capture a GPU frame on that device or test a variety of driver versions to reproduce. Always create a minimal reproducible case — that's the fastest route to a fix.

Quick reference commands & copy-ready snippets

`dotnet-counters monitor --process-id <PID> System.Runtime` to see live GC and thread counters.

`dotnet-trace collect --process-id <PID> --duration 00:00:30 --profile cpu-sampling --output out.nettrace` to collect a CPU sampling trace.

Open the resulting `.nettrace` with Visual Studio or PerfView for flame charts.

Use RenderDoc to capture and inspect GPU draw-call details for OpenGL/Direct3D/Vulkan.

Use Xcode GPU Capture for Metal iOS profiling and Instruments for CPU/allocations.

Example workflow (from symptom to fix)

Start a debug build with the in-game HUD and reproduce the issue while recording a short video. If FPS dips, check the HUD: if frame ms spikes but CPU usage is low, suspect GPU; capture a GPU frame with RenderDoc or Xcode. If CPU is high, attach `dotnet-trace` to capture a CPU sample trace, or run `dotnet-counters` to see GC pressure. Use `ScopedTimer` in suspected subsystems to narrow the precise function. Create a minimal repro and add an automated regression test (headless if possible) so the bug never returns.

Final notes

Profiling is iterative. Start light, prove a hypothesis with measurements, and then dig deeper with sampling or GPU capture. Keep cheap instrumentation in your debug builds and automate smoke tests on CI to catch regressions early. The patterns above will let you diagnose most MonoGame performance and resource problems quickly and reproducibly.

12.2 Asset Loading & Performance Optimization

Assets—textures, audio, shaders, models and large data files—are where games win or lose on memory, startup time and runtime smoothness. The goal of this chapter is to give you practical, copy-ready techniques that reduce load stalls, lower memory peaks, and make streaming predictable across desktop and mobile. The approach is measurement first, then structure (how you organize assets), then patterns (how you load them), then micro-optimisations (formats, pools, and GPU-friendly packing). Every explanation below is short, concrete and supported by ready-to-use code you can drop into a MonoGame project.

Design first: separate ownership and lifetime

Think of assets as objects with three concerns: how they are stored on disk, how they are loaded into memory, and how long they are kept. Put each concern in its own place in code. Use small, focused loaders that know only how to fetch and create an asset. Use a higher-level `AssetManager` to orchestrate preloads, on-demand loads and unloading. This separation makes it trivial to switch from synchronous startup loading to background streaming later.

Here is a compact, practical AssetManager that supports named assets, preloading, on-demand loading and unloading via separate ContentManager instances (useful to unload groups of assets when a scene exits):

```csharp
// File: AssetManager.cs

using System;

using System.Collections.Concurrent;

using System.Threading.Tasks;

using Microsoft.Xna.Framework.Content;

using Microsoft.Xna.Framework.Graphics;


public class AssetManager : IDisposable

{

    readonly ContentManager content;

    readonly GraphicsDevice graphics;

    readonly ConcurrentDictionary<string, object>
assets = new();


    public AssetManager(ContentManager content,
GraphicsDevice graphics)

    {

        this.content = content;

        this.graphics = graphics;
```

```csharp
    }


    // Synchronous (fast when used at startup)

    public T Load<T>(string key) where T : class

    {

        if (assets.TryGetValue(key, out var a))
return a as T;

        var asset = content.Load<T>(key);

        assets[key] = asset!;

        return asset!;

    }



    // Unload a specific asset type by key when you
created it via a secondary ContentManager

    public bool TryGet<T>(string key, out T? asset)
where T : class

    {

        if (assets.TryGetValue(key, out var a)) {
asset = a as T; return true; }

        asset = null; return false;

    }



    public void UnloadAll()

    {

        assets.Clear();
```

```
        // leave content manager to be disposed by
the Game when appropriate;

        // you can also create scene-specific
ContentManagers for fine-grained unloads.

    }


    public void Dispose()

    {

        UnloadAll();

    }

}
```

This simple manager encourages using scene-specific ContentManager instances when you want deterministic unloading: create a ContentManager per level, load everything into it, then call Unload() on exit to free native resources.

Use the Content Pipeline for fast startup; load raw files for modularity

MonoGame's Content Pipeline preprocesses assets into optimized XNB (or platform-specific) blobs that load faster than parsing PNGs or JSON at runtime. For fixed game assets you ship with the game, prefer the pipeline because it reduces startup CPU cost and can embed platform optimisations. For user-supplied or downloadable content load from files at runtime; keep the same loader API but a different implementation so both code paths are interchangeable.

Be conscious that pipeline formats are preprocessed so they trade build-time for runtime speed. If you must accept arbitrary user content at runtime, parse compressed files asynchronously and convert to GPU resources only on the main thread (see the async loading pattern below).

Background I/O, main-thread GPU creation pattern

GPU texture creation must happen on the graphics thread in most platforms. However you can read and decode bytes off the main thread to avoid blocking the frame. The following pattern reads a texture file with asynchronous file I/O on a worker thread and hands a MemoryStream back to the main thread where Texture2D.FromStream creates the GPU resource. The example also uses a small queue to finalize creations in Update.

```
// File: AsyncTextureLoader.cs

using System;

using System.Buffers;

using System.Collections.Concurrent;

using System.IO;

using System.Threading.Tasks;

using Microsoft.Xna.Framework.Graphics;


public class AsyncTextureLoader

{

    readonly GraphicsDevice graphics;
```

```csharp
    readonly ConcurrentQueue<(string key,
MemoryStream ms)> finalizeQueue = new();


    public AsyncTextureLoader(GraphicsDevice
graphics) => this.graphics = graphics;


    // Call on background thread; only does disk/CPU
work.
    public async Task RequestLoadAsync(string key,
string filePath)

    {

        // Read bytes without blocking main thread

        await using var fs = new FileStream(filePath,
FileMode.Open, FileAccess.Read, FileShare.Read,

            bufferSize: 81920, useAsync: true);

        var ms = new MemoryStream();

        await
fs.CopyToAsync(ms).ConfigureAwait(false);

        ms.Position = 0;

        // push to finalize on main thread

        finalizeQueue.Enqueue((key, ms));

    }


    // Call from Game.Update() on main thread

    public void UpdateFinalize(Action<string,
Texture2D> onCreated)

    {
```

```
        while (finalizeQueue.TryDequeue(out var
item))

        {

            // Texture2D.FromStream must run on the
graphics thread

            var tex = Texture2D.FromStream(graphics,
item.ms);

            onCreated(item.key, tex);

            item.ms.Dispose();

        }

    }

}
```

Use RequestLoadAsync from a background thread or Task.Run and call UpdateFinalize from Game.Update to attach the created texture into your AssetManager. This keeps the render thread smooth because disk and decode work happens off-thread.

Avoid allocations and GC pressure during loads and runtime

Loading many small files or creating temporary buffers per-frame causes large GC spikes that hurt frame consistency. Prefer streaming APIs and pooled buffers. Use ArrayPool<byte>.Shared when you need temporary byte arrays for file transforms or streaming. Reuse vertex/index buffers for dynamic meshes and avoid per-frame creation of temporary List<T> instances; instead reuse allocated collections.

A tiny example that uses ArrayPool to read a blob, process it, and return the buffer:

```csharp
// File: PooledRead.cs
using System;
using System.Buffers;
using System.IO;
using System.Threading.Tasks;


public static class PooledRead
{
    public static async Task<int>
ReadIntoPoolAsync(string path)
    {
        var pool = ArrayPool<byte>.Shared;
        var buffer = pool.Rent(65536);
        try
        {
            await using var fs = new FileStream(path,
FileMode.Open, FileAccess.Read, FileShare.Read,
65536, useAsync: true);
            int bytes = await fs.ReadAsync(buffer, 0,
buffer.Length);
            // process data using buffer[0..bytes]
without allocating new arrays
```

```
        return bytes;

    }

    finally

    {

        pool.Return(buffer, clearArray: false);

    }

    }

}
```

The `clearArray: false` argument avoids the cost of zeroing the buffer; set it true only if you need memory safety.

Texture atlases, packing and draw-call economy

GPU state changes and texture swaps are one of the most common performance killers in 2D games. Pack many small sprites into a single texture atlas so you can draw many sprites with one `SpriteBatch` begin/end. Use a tool like TexturePacker to produce atlases and a matching metadata file; or use MonoGame.Extended's atlas support to load atlases and lookup regions at runtime. The atlas approach reduces both GPU memory fragmentation and the number of texture binds per frame.

Example usage with a simple atlas metadata loader (rectangles stored in JSON):

```
// File: SimpleAtlas.cs

using Microsoft.Xna.Framework;

using Microsoft.Xna.Framework.Graphics;

using System.Collections.Generic;
```

```csharp
using System.IO;

using System.Text.Json;


public class Atlas

{

    public Texture2D Texture { get; }

    public Dictionary<string, Rectangle> Regions {
get; }

    public Atlas(Texture2D tex, Dictionary<string,
Rectangle> regions)

    {

        Texture = tex; Regions = regions;

    }


    public static Atlas LoadFromJson(Texture2D tex,
string jsonPath)

    {

        var json = File.ReadAllText(jsonPath);

        var dict =
JsonSerializer.Deserialize<Dictionary<string,
Rectangle>>(json)!;

        return new Atlas(tex, dict);

    }

}
```

When drawing, fetch `Regions["player_idle_01"]` and use it as the `sourceRectangle` parameter for a `SpriteBatch.Draw` call so many sprites share the same texture.

Compressed textures and platform-specific formats

Compressed GPU textures reduce memory footprint and GPU bandwidth, improving both performance and install size. Choose your compression format per-platform: ASTC and ETC2 are preferred on modern Android, PVRTC and ASTC on iOS depending on device generation, and BCn/DDS variants on desktop. Export dedicated compressed textures per target where possible; some build pipelines (or third-party tools) can generate platform-specific assets during build. If you ship uncompressed PNGs and rely on runtime decompression, expect higher peak memory and longer load times.

For mobile builds consider multiple texture sets or an app bundle that contains several compressed variants. If you cannot create compressed textures during build, at minimum choose smaller atlases and lower bit-depths for mobile to reduce memory.

Audio and large binary streaming

Don't load long music tracks into memory as raw PCM. Stream them from disk using streaming APIs that decode in small chunks. For sound effects use short, preloaded buffers to avoid disk I/O at play time. Use platform audio systems that support streaming (for example, `Song` in XNA/MonoGame is designed for music streaming) while `SoundEffect` is for short samples.

Unload deterministically: scene-level ContentManagers and pooled native resources

Managed memory is only part of the story. Many MonoGame asset types allocate native GPU resources. For deterministic cleanup create a `ContentManager` per scene or level. Load assets that belong together with that manager and call `sceneContent.Unload()` when the scene ends. For resources created manually (vertex buffers, render targets), implement `Dispose` and ensure your scene teardown calls `Dispose()` or holds them in a pool that you clear on scene exit.

Micro-optimizations that matter

Avoid per-frame texture creation, repeated shader compilation, and per-frame large array allocations. Use sprite batching with sensible layers to minimize state changes. Prefer `SpriteBatch` with `SpriteSortMode.Deferred` or `Texture` sorting that minimizes binds. For dynamic geometry reuse `DynamicVertexBuffer` instead of creating new buffers every frame. When you must change large textures, consider updating subregions via `SetData` rather than re-uploading entire textures if the GPU and driver support it efficiently.

Sample: scene preload with streaming fallback

A pragmatic flow is to aggressively preload essential UI and core textures synchronously (fast startup cost) then stream level geometry and non-critical textures in the background using the async pattern. The sample below shows how to start a scene while non-essential assets finish loading.

```csharp
// Usage sketch (in Game class)

AssetManager assets;

AsyncTextureLoader loader;

bool levelReady = false;

protected override void LoadContent()

{

    assets = new AssetManager(Content,
GraphicsDevice);

    loader = new AsyncTextureLoader(GraphicsDevice);

    // preload UI synchronously so menus show
immediately

    assets.Load<Texture2D>("UI/sprites");

    // start background load for large textures

    _ = loader.RequestLoadAsync("level1_atlas",
"Content/level1_atlas.png");

}

protected override void Update(GameTime gameTime)

{

    loader.UpdateFinalize((key, tex) => {

        assets.Store(key, tex); // implement Store to
add raw Texture2D into assets dictionary

        if (key == "level1_atlas") levelReady = true;

    });

    // continue updating game; show loading spinner
until levelReady true

}
```

This gives immediate UI responsiveness while heavy files stream in and finalize on the main thread.

Measure and validate: don't guess

Always profile: measure startup time, peak memory, and allocations during scene transitions. Add a debug HUD that reports managed memory, number of loaded textures and number of native resources so you can detect leaks. Test on representative low-end hardware for your target platforms; emulators are not reliable for memory/GPU behaviour.

Final notes and rules of thumb

Keep the Content Pipeline for stable, shipped assets and use raw runtime loaders for modding or downloadable content. Read and decode files off the main thread but create GPU objects on the main thread. Pack small sprites into atlases and use compressed textures per-platform to reduce memory and bandwidth. Reuse buffers and GPU objects when possible, and prefer streaming for large assets such as music and long levels. Finally, automate simple load/perf tests in CI and capture CSVs of load times and memory peaks so regressions are caught early.

12.3 Memory Management & Garbage Collection Tips

Memory problems are almost always a symptom, not the disease: a visible hitch, a steadily rising RSS, or an out-of-memory crash points to patterns in how your game allocates, holds, and releases objects. This chapter teaches a small set of practical, repeatable patterns that reduce GC pressure, avoid fragmentation, and make native resources explicit so MonoGame projects stay smooth across low-end phones and desktop GPUs. Each explanation is compact, immediately actionable, and comes with copy-ready code you can drop straight into your engine.

Principles first: own, limit, and measure

Treat each resource as owned by a clear system: UI, level, audio, or streaming manager. Limit the lifetime of large objects, measure allocation rates and GC pauses, and prefer reuse over repeated allocation. Profiling (allocation timelines and flame charts) should drive your choices; never guess whether an optimization is necessary.

Make large allocations deliberate and limited

Large arrays and buffers end up on the Large Object Heap (LOH), which is collected only during Gen-2 (full) collections and is more expensive to compact. Keep large buffers pooled rather than repeatedly allocating them. The ArrayPool<T>.Shared pool is a simple, efficient way to reuse byte arrays for decoding, file I/O, and intermediate processing.

```
// File: PooledBufferReader.cs

using System;

using System.Buffers;

using System.IO;

using System.Threading.Tasks;
```

```csharp
public static class PooledBufferReader
{
    public static async Task<int>
ReadToBufferAsync(string path)
    {
        var pool = ArrayPool<byte>.Shared;

        var buffer = pool.Rent(128 * 1024); // rent a
128KB buffer (LOH threshold ~85KB)

        try
        {
            await using var fs = new FileStream(path,
FileMode.Open, FileAccess.Read, FileShare.Read,
65536, useAsync: true);

            int total = 0;

            int read;

            while ((read = await
fs.ReadAsync(buffer.AsMemory(total, buffer.Length -
total))) > 0)
            {
                total += read;

                if (total == buffer.Length)
                {
                    // grow carefully: return current
and rent a bigger one

                    pool.Return(buffer, clearArray:
false);
```

```
                    buffer = pool.Rent(buffer.Length
* 2);

                }

        }

        // process buffer[0..total]

        return total;

    }

    finally

    {

        pool.Return(buffer, clearArray: false);

    }

    }

}
```

By renting and returning you keep LOH churn low and avoid frequent Gen-2 collections.

Reuse objects: pools for frequently created items

Small short-lived objects (vectors, small state objects, bullets) can still create severe GC churn when created at high rates. Use object pools to recycle instances instead of allocating each frame. The example below is a tiny generic pool and a pooled Projectile use:

```
// File: ObjectPool.cs

using System;
```

```csharp
using System.Collections.Concurrent;


public class ObjectPool<T> where T : class, new()

{

    readonly ConcurrentBag<T> bag = new();


    public T Rent() => bag.TryTake(out var item) ?
item : new T();


    public void Return(T item) => bag.Add(item);

}


// File: Projectile.cs

public class Projectile

{

    public float X, Y, VX, VY;

    public bool Active;

    public void Reset(float x, float y, float vx,
float vy) { X = x; Y = y; VX = vx; VY = vy; Active =
true; }

    public void Update(float dt) { X += VX * dt; Y +=
VY * dt; if (X < 0 || Y < 0) Active = false; }

}


// Usage inside your game loop
```

```
ObjectPool<Projectile> projectilePool = new();

var p = projectilePool.Rent();

p.Reset(...);

// when done:

p.Active = false;

projectilePool.Return(p);
```

Pooling keeps your per-frame allocation rate near zero for high-volume objects.

Beware per-frame allocations: strings, LINQ, boxing

Every allocation counts. Avoid allocating inside hot paths: don't build strings each frame for the HUD (cache formatted text or update only when the value changes), avoid LINQ in inner loops, and avoid boxing value types by using generic containers or Span<T> where possible. For transient slices and parsers prefer Span<T>/Memory<T> so you can work on stack-friendly views without allocation.

```
// Example: parsing CSV line without allocations
using Span<char>

public static (int x, int y)
ParseInts(ReadOnlySpan<char> line)

{

    int i = 0;

    int x = 0, y = 0;
```

```
    // simple parse assuming "123,456" format —
no allocations

    while (i < line.Length && line[i] != ',') { x
= x * 10 + (line[i++] - '0'); }

    i++; // skip comma

    while (i < line.Length) { y = y * 10 +
(line[i++] - '0'); }

    return (x, y);

}
```

When Span<T> is not possible (e.g., APIs returning string),
minimize conversions and copy once.

Native and GPU resources: explicit disposal

Many MonoGame resources allocate native GPU memory that the
GC cannot see. Implement the IDisposable pattern on wrappers
and always call Dispose() for Texture2D, VertexBuffer,
RenderTarget2D, and similar resources when they are no
longer needed. Prefer scene-scoped ContentManager instances
so you can call sceneContent.Unload() to release native
resources deterministically. If you create resources manually, keep a
registry and call Dispose() during teardown.

```
// File: ManagedTextureHolder.cs

using Microsoft.Xna.Framework.Graphics;

using System;

public sealed class ManagedTextureHolder :
IDisposable
```

```
{
    public Texture2D Texture { get; private set; }

    bool disposed;


    public ManagedTextureHolder(Texture2D tex) =>
Texture     =     tex     ??     throw     new
ArgumentNullException(nameof(tex));

    public void Dispose()

    {

        if (disposed) return;

        Texture?.Dispose();

        Texture = null!;

        disposed = true;

    }

}
```

Calling Dispose() avoids waiting for a finalizer (if present) and frees GPU memory immediately.

Implement Dispose correctly; avoid relying on finalizers

Follow the standard Dispose pattern: unmanaged resources released in Dispose, finalizers only when necessary, and suppress finalization after dispose. Finalizers are expensive because they place objects on the finalizer queue and delay collection. Only implement a finalizer when you actually own unmanaged memory or handles.

```csharp
// File: SafeHandleWrapper.cs

using System;

using System.Runtime.InteropServices;


public sealed class SafeHandleWrapper : IDisposable
{
    IntPtr nativeHandle;

    bool disposed;


    public SafeHandleWrapper(IntPtr handle) =>
nativeHandle = handle;


    public void Dispose()
    {
        if (disposed) return;

        if (nativeHandle != IntPtr.Zero) {

            NativeMethods.Release(nativeHandle);

            nativeHandle = IntPtr.Zero;

        }

        disposed = true;

        GC.SuppressFinalize(this);
```

```
    }


    ~SafeHandleWrapper()

    {

        if (nativeHandle != IntPtr.Zero)
NativeMethods.Release(nativeHandle);

    }

}
```

Suppress finalization after Dispose so the finalizer thread isn't burdened.

Critical sections: no-GC regions for tight real-time work

When you need a short, latency-critical region where a GC pause would be disastrous (audio mixing, input sampling, deterministic frame budget windows), you can attempt a no-GC region with GC.TryStartNoGCRegion and end it with GC.EndNoGCRegion. Use this sparingly and only after you measured allocation budgets, because the runtime must reserve sufficient memory to avoid a full blocking GC.

```
// Example: try no-GC region for a gameplay frame burst

if (GC.TryStartNoGCRegion(10_000_000)) // reserve ~10MB

{

    try

    {

        // critical real-time work here
```

```
    }

finally

{

    GC.EndNoGCRegion();

}

}
```

If the runtime cannot reserve required memory the call fails; always check the return value and fallback gracefully.

Manage LOH fragmentation with care

If your pipeline must allocate many different large buffers, prefer one large pooled buffer reused over time instead of many slightly different LOH allocations. For exceptional maintenance (for example, right after a large deallocation phase) you can request a one-time LOH compaction via `GCSettings.LargeObjectHeapCompactionMode = CompactOnce; GC.Collect();` but avoid calling full `GC.Collect()` frequently: it is a heavy operation and can stall the app.

Use profiling and counters to guide tradeoffs

Measure allocation rates (bytes/sec), Gen-0/1/2 frequencies, and pause durations rather than guessing. Use `dotnet-counters` or the Visual Studio Diagnostic Tools to record allocation timelines and investigate which code paths allocate most. Start by reducing high allocation hot spots, then apply pooling and span-based parsing where it gives the most benefit.

Practical checklist in code form (small, copyable)

Keep a small DebugMemory helper that reports managed memory, Gen counts, and number of pooled buffers. Use that in a debug HUD to watch allocation regressions during scene transitions.

```csharp
// File: DebugMemory.cs
using System;
using Microsoft.Xna.Framework;


public static class DebugMemory
{
    static long lastGc0, lastGc1, lastGc2;


    public static string Snapshot()
    {
        var memMB = GC.GetTotalMemory(false) /
(1024.0 * 1024.0);

        var g0 = GC.CollectionCount(0);

        var g1 = GC.CollectionCount(1);

        var g2 = GC.CollectionCount(2);

        var sb = $"ManagedMB:{memMB:0.00}
GCs:[{g0-lastGc0},{g1-lastGc1},{g2-lastGc2}]";

        lastGc0 = g0; lastGc1 = g1; lastGc2 = g2;

        return sb;
```

```
        }

}
```

Place this snapshot on-screen during level loads and transitions to detect regressions early.

Common mistakes and how to fix them

Allocating new `List<T>` or `Dictionary<K,V>` every frame for temporary use is an easy-to-miss source of pressure; replace with reusable containers or call `Clear()` instead of reassigning. Loading textures per frame instead of once at scene load causes native memory churn; use scene-scoped content managers or explicitly call `.Dispose()` on textures you no longer need. Pinning many objects for long times (GCHandle.Alloc pinned) fragments the heap—pin only briefly when interacting with unmanaged APIs.

When to force a GC (and when not to)

Forcing a full GC (`GC.Collect`) can be appropriate at well-defined points such as after a large level unload to compact memory before opening a level selection screen, but it should be used only after measurement and with careful user experience consideration, since it will stall the process briefly. When you do call it, consider pairing with LOH compaction if you freed big buffers.

Final advice

Make allocation budgets part of your definition of "done" for scenes and systems. Keep the hot path allocation-free, use pooled buffers for decoding and streaming, dispose native resources deterministically, and measure continuously with debug counters and tracing. The combination of these behaviors will keep GC pauses predictable and memory usage suitable for the lowest target device.

12.4 Handling Low-End Devices & Mobile Performance

Making a game that looks and feels great on high-end hardware is the easy part; the design and engineering skill is in making it run acceptably on low-end phones and tablets without breaking the experience. This section gives a concise, practical playbook you can drop into a MonoGame project: measure first, degrade gracefully, make render and CPU work scalable, stream everything that can be streamed, and keep native/GPU allocations explicit. Every idea below is accompanied by copy-ready code you can paste into your engine and iterate on.

Start with measurements, not guesses

Before you change visuals or rewrite systems, measure. Ship a debug build to representative low-end devices with a small performance HUD that reports average FPS, 99th-percentile frame ms, managed memory and number of loaded textures. If a particular scene or action triggers a hitch, record a short video and collect a CPU/GPU trace. Use those numbers to choose the highest-leverage change: reduce draw calls, lower texture resolution, or reduce physics step rate.

Adaptive quality: change settings at runtime

Rather than one binary "low" build, make quality scalable and device-aware: resolution scale, texture set, shader complexity, particle budgets and physics frequency should be adjustable from a single QualityProfile. Provide an automatic calibration run on first launch that measures steady-state FPS for 10–20 seconds and picks a safe profile, and allow players to override it.

```csharp
// File: QualityProfile.cs

public class QualityProfile

{

    public float ResolutionScale { get; init; } =
1.0f; // 0.5..1.0

    public int MaxParticles { get; init; } = 1000;

    public bool UseCompressedTextures { get; init; }
= true;

    public int PhysicsStepsPerSecond { get; init; } =
60;

    public int MaxDrawCalls { get; init; } = 100;

}


// Simple factory

public static class QualityProfiles

{

    public static QualityProfile High => new() {
ResolutionScale = 1.0f, MaxParticles = 2000,
PhysicsStepsPerSecond = 60, MaxDrawCalls = 200 };

    public static QualityProfile Medium => new() {
ResolutionScale = 0.75f, MaxParticles = 1000,
PhysicsStepsPerSecond = 45, MaxDrawCalls = 120 };
```

```
    public static QualityProfile Low => new() {
ResolutionScale = 0.5f, MaxParticles = 300,
PhysicsStepsPerSecond = 30, MaxDrawCalls = 60 };

}
```

Run a quick warmup scene at startup to test a profile and scale up/down until the target FPS is reached. That single pattern will avoid guessing and reduce support headaches.

Dynamic resolution (render scale) - cheap and high impact

Scaling the actual render resolution is the fastest way to trade visual fidelity for frame time. Render your scene into a smaller RenderTarget2D and then draw it stretched to the backbuffer. Because the GPU cost usually scales with pixel count, halving both width and height reduces shader cost by ~75%.

```
// File: DynamicResolutionRenderer.cs

using Microsoft.Xna.Framework;

using Microsoft.Xna.Framework.Graphics;


public class DynamicResolutionRenderer :
IDisposable

{

    GraphicsDevice gd;

    RenderTarget2D rt;

    float scale = 1.0f;
```

```
    public
DynamicResolutionRenderer(GraphicsDevice gd,
float initialScale = 1.0f)

    {

        this.gd = gd;

        SetScale(initialScale);

    }


    public void SetScale(float s)

    {

        s = MathHelper.Clamp(s, 0.5f, 1.0f);

        scale = s;

        int w = Math.Max(1,
(int)(gd.PresentationParameters.BackBufferWidth *
scale));

        int h = Math.Max(1,
(int)(gd.PresentationParameters.BackBufferHeight
* scale));

        rt?.Dispose();

        rt = new RenderTarget2D(gd, w, h, false,
gd.PresentationParameters.BackBufferFormat,
DepthFormat.Depth24);

    }


    public void BeginScene(SpriteBatch sb)

    {
```

```
        gd.SetRenderTarget(rt);

        gd.Clear(Color.CornflowerBlue);

        sb.Begin();

    }


    public void EndScene(SpriteBatch sb)

    {

        sb.End();

        gd.SetRenderTarget(null);

        sb.Begin(samplerState:
SamplerState.LinearClamp);

        sb.Draw(rt, new Rectangle(0, 0,
gd.PresentationParameters.BackBufferWidth,
gd.PresentationParameters.BackBufferHeight),
Color.White);

        sb.End();

    }

    public void Dispose() => rt?.Dispose();

}
```

Call `SetScale` when the adaptive system decides to lower fidelity. This is platform-friendly and works with MonoGame's standard pipeline.

Reduce draw calls and overdraw

On low-end GPUs, state changes and texture binds are expensive. Use atlases, combine meshes, and batch sprites to minimize texture swaps and draw calls. Prefer single large `SpriteBatch` draws with carefully ordered draw lists or texture atlases. When using `SpriteBatch`, choose the `SpriteSortMode` that best groups by texture to reduce binds.

For 3D or custom geometry, merge static meshes into combined vertex/index buffers and use simple culling (frustum + coarse grid) to avoid sending invisible geometry.

Lower CPU update frequency for non-critical systems

Not all systems need 60 updates per second. Decouple expensive systems such as AI, pathfinding, or analytics from the per-frame update loop and run them at lower frequencies. The following scheduler allows tasks to run at a target rate separate from frame rate.

```
// File: TimestepScheduler.cs

using System;

using Microsoft.Xna.Framework;


public class TimestepScheduler

{

    double accumulator;

    readonly double targetDt;
```

```csharp
    public TimestepScheduler(double hz) {
targetDt = 1.0 / hz; }



    public void Update(GameTime gameTime, Action
step)

    {

        accumulator +=
gameTime.ElapsedGameTime.TotalSeconds;

        while (accumulator >= targetDt)

        {

            step();

            accumulator -= targetDt;

        }

    }

}


// Usage:

// var aiScheduler = new TimestepScheduler(10);
// AI at 10 Hz

// aiScheduler.Update(gameTime, UpdateAI);
```

Use this for pathfinding updates, spawn logic, and network message coalescing. Reducing update rates for many subsystems compounds into real CPU savings on low-end platforms.

Memory and asset strategies for low RAM devices

Low-end devices frequently have limited RAM. Stream big assets (music, large levels, cinematic textures) rather than loading everything into memory. Use scene/level `ContentManager` instances so you can call `Unload()` during transitions and free native GPU memory deterministically. Prefer compressed GPU textures (per-platform formats) shipped as targeted assets; compressed formats cut memory and bandwidth drastically.

Use an asset-targeting strategy where you prepare multiple texture sets (high/medium/low) and load the appropriate set at runtime based on the quality profile. On Android you can include format-targeted resources in the app bundle so devices get the best appropriate compressed format.

Use compressed textures and device targeting

Compressed textures reduce both GPU memory and bandwidth. Target the best available format per device family. On Android prefer ASTC for modern devices and fall back to ETC2/ETC1 on older devices; on iOS use PVRTC or ASTC depending on device support. Build pipelines should produce compressed versions and your installer or Play Asset Delivery should serve the correct variant. This optimization usually yields large wins with minimal visual cost.

Reduce shader complexity and branching

Complex shaders and many texture lookups amplify cost per pixel and hurt battery life. Author multiple shader variants: a full-feature effect and a cheap fallback. Detect GPU features or measure shaders' cost once during a calibration run and choose accordingly. Keep branch divergence low and avoid expensive per-pixel branching on mobile.

Optimize for tile-based mobile GPUs (overdraw matters)

Many mobile GPUs are tile-based; they perform better when overdraw is low and render targets fit on tile memory. Design UI and scene composition to minimize full-screen translucent passes. Prefer multiply/opaque layering for UIs and avoid large full-screen post-processing unless necessary. When using render targets, reuse and keep them as small as possible.

Audio and power: balance fidelity and battery

Streaming music at a lower sample rate and compressing audio can cut memory and decode cost. Mute or reduce background audio quality in battery saver modes. Respect platform power hints and avoid waking the device unnecessarily. Allow users to opt into a battery-friendly mode that lowers frame rate and audio fidelity.

Graceful degradation and fallback logic

If the device is thermally throttled or battery constrained, or if FPS falls below a hard minimum for several seconds, degrade visuals progressively: first drop particle spawn rates, then lower resolution scale, then reduce shader passes, then reduce physics fidelity. This staged approach keeps the experience predictable and lets you regain visual quality when the device recovers.

Practical runtime checks and a simple adaptive manager

Below is an AdaptiveQualityManager skeleton that measures average frametime and steps down or up a QualityProfile after stable measurements. This pattern is robust and easy to extend with device heuristics.

```
// File: AdaptiveQualityManager.cs
using System;
using Microsoft.Xna.Framework;
public class AdaptiveQualityManager
{
    readonly Func<QualityProfile> getNextLower;
    readonly Func<QualityProfile> getNextHigher;
    QualityProfile current;
    double accumSeconds;
    int frames;
    readonly double sampleWindow = 3.0; // seconds
    readonly float downThresholdMs = 33.3f; // 30 FPS
    readonly float upThresholdMs = 16.6f;   // 60 FPS


    public AdaptiveQualityManager(QualityProfile start,

Func<QualityProfile> lower,

Func<QualityProfile> higher)
    {
```

```csharp
        current = start;

        getNextLower = lower; getNextHigher = higher;

    }



    public QualityProfile Current => current;



    public void Update(GameTime gt, double
lastFrameMs, Action<QualityProfile> onChanged)

    {

        accumSeconds +=
gt.ElapsedGameTime.TotalSeconds;

        frames++;

        if (accumSeconds >= sampleWindow)

        {

            var avgMs = lastFrameMs; // you can
average over frames if you prefer

            if (avgMs > downThresholdMs)

            {

                var p = getNextLower();

                if (p != null) { current = p;
onChanged(current); }

            }

            else if (avgMs < upThresholdMs)

            {

                var p = getNextHigher();
```

```
                if (p != null) { current = p;
onChanged(current); }

        }

        accumSeconds = 0; frames = 0;

    }

  }

}
```

Invoke onChanged to resize render targets, swap in a lower atlas, lower particle budgets, and adjust physics scheduler frequencies.

Build and delivery: target assets by tier and compression

On Android use App Bundle/asset delivery or nested targeting to ship multiple texture compression variants and device-tier assets; Play's delivery system can select the right variant for each device to avoid shipping everything to every device. On iOS use app thinning and targeted asset catalogs. Preparing multiple asset tiers and letting the store—or your own installer—deliver the right set reduces install size and memory pressure.

Test on real low-end hardware and iterate

Emulators can help, but nothing replaces tests on real devices with constrained memory, slow flash, and weak GPUs. Acquire a handful of representative devices in the low tier and build a smoke test runner that automatically exercises key scenes while recording FPS, memory, and energy use. Use device farms when you need broader coverage.

Final rules you can apply immediately

Measure first and always ship a runtime quality scaler. Render to a lower resolution when necessary rather than trying to fake lower GPU cost at full resolution. Batch draws and pack atlases. Use pooled buffers to avoid GC hiccups on low RAM devices. Stream large assets and produce platform-specific compressed textures during build so devices use the right compressed format. Decouple expensive systems from the main loop and run them slower on low-end profiles. These practices, combined with a calibration pass and staged graceful degradation, will make your MonoGame title play well across the broadest range of devices.

12.5 Final QA & Debugging Checklist

Final QA is the last gate between a shipped product and angry players. Treat it as a disciplined ritual: reproduce, measure, isolate, fix, verify. This chapter gives a compact, single-page workflow you can drop into a MonoGame release cycle, plus copy-ready diagnostics and automation snippets so your team can find and fix the hard problems before they reach customers.

Begin every QA run by making the problem reproducible and measurable. If a tester reports "it crashed," collect the exact steps, the build id, the device model, OS version, and a short screen video. Try the steps yourself immediately and capture a running log and a memory/CPU snapshot. If you cannot reproduce the bug locally, create a tiny deterministic harness that reproduces the symptom; the fastest bug to fix is the one you can reproduce on your dev machine.

Ship builds that produce reproducible metadata by embedding a single build identifier and git SHA in every executable and artifact. This lets crash reports, logs, and device-farm traces point to the exact source. The snippet below shows how to produce a build stamp at compile time and expose it in your MonoGame game.

```
// File: BuildInfo.cs (add as linked code during
build)

public static class BuildInfo

{

    // Set this with a build-time property or script:
/p:BuildStamp="2025-11-30-1234"

    public static string BuildStamp { get; } =
"{BUILD_STAMP}";

    public static string GitSha { get; } =
"{GIT_SHA}";

}
```

Add your CI to replace the placeholders so every artifact prints `BuildInfo.BuildStamp` on startup and tags logs and crash reports.

Always gather structured logs and keep them small and searchable. Replace ad-hoc `Console.WriteLine` dumps with a tiny structured logger that stamps events with build id, subsystem, time and a short message. The next snippet is a minimal structured logger that writes JSON lines so logs can be ingested by centralized systems or bundled with crash uploads.

```
// File: SimpleLogger.cs

using System;

using System.IO;
```

```csharp
using System.Text.Json;


public static class SimpleLogger

{

    static readonly string path =
Path.Combine(Environment.GetFolderPath(Environment.Sp
ecialFolder.LocalApplicationData), "mygame.log");

    static readonly object sync = new();


    public static void Log(string subsystem, string
level, string message, object? meta = null)

    {

        var entry = new {

            ts = DateTime.UtcNow,

            build = BuildInfo.BuildStamp,

            subsystem,

            level,

            message,

            meta

        };

        var json = JsonSerializer.Serialize(entry);

        lock (sync) File.AppendAllText(path, json +
"\n");

    }

}
```

Integrate a crash reporter (Sentry, Firebase Crashlytics, etc.) for production. Crash reports should include the sanitized stack, the build id, the device model, and the last N lines of structured logs. If your crash tool accepts attachments, upload the last 30 seconds of logs and a small memory/GC snapshot to speed triage.

Make automated smoke tests part of your CI and release pipeline so every build runs a deterministic playthrough that covers startup, main menu navigation, a short level, and a graceful exit. A headless smoke runner should exercise key systems and emit a CSV of frametimes, allocations and load timings. The sample runner below is a simplified pattern that runs a short scripted scenario and writes a CSV; in CI it should run on each platform matrix entry.

```
// File: PerfSmokeRunner.cs (entry for CI)

using System;

using System.IO;

using Microsoft.Xna.Framework;


public class PerfSmokeRunner : Game

{

    // implement minimal loop that runs for N
seconds, exercises startup and a short scene

    protected override void Update(GameTime
gameTime)

    {

        // run scripted steps (simulate input or
call systems directly)
```

```
// collect metrics each frame

if (TotalSeconds >= RunSeconds) {

    WriteCsv("perf.csv");

    Exit();

}

}


void WriteCsv(string path) {

    // write average frame ms, max allocs,
loaded textures count

}

}
```

Automate platform-specific validation in device farms for mobile: upload a signed APK/AAB or IPA and run instrumentation tests that exercise networked flows, background/foreground cycles, permission dialogs and low-memory signals. Capture screenshots, video, logs and a device CPU/GPU trace for any failing runs. For desktop and console builds include a hardware matrix in CI that at minimum checks Windows, macOS and a representative Linux build.

Use a reproducible bug-report template so your team gets the same data every time. The template should require steps to reproduce, expected vs actual behavior, build stamp, reproduction status, attached logs/videos, and a minimal repro project or descriptive pseudocode. When a tester files a bug without a repro, mark it "needs-repro" and prioritize creating a harness before assigning it for a code fix.

When hunting performance regressions, follow the measurement-first pattern: baseline, change, re-measure. Run a short perf test before the change and after the change. If frame ms changes significantly, capture a CPU sample trace (`dotnet-trace`) and a GPU frame capture (RenderDoc or platform-equivalent) to isolate CPU vs GPU hot paths. Keep cheap in-game metrics (framerate HUD, allocation counters) enabled on debug builds and attach those numbers to the bug.

In-code assertions and runtime guards catch incorrect assumptions early. Add defensive checks that run in debug builds and log an error before a hard crash, but avoid heavy assertions in release. The helper below shows a compact runtime assert that logs, raises a debug break in development, and optionally uploads an incident marker.

```
// File: DevAssert.cs

using System;

using System.Diagnostics;


public static class DevAssert

{

    public static void Check(bool condition, string
message)

    {

#if DEBUG

        if (!condition) {
```

```
            SimpleLogger.Log("assert", "error",
message);

            Debugger.Launch(); // break into debugger
if attached

            throw new
InvalidOperationException(message);

        }

#endif

    }

}
```

Reproducers are the single most valuable artifact you can add to a bug report. When a QA report includes only a vague description, create a minimal test case that isolates the feature (UI, physics, asset load) and remove unrelated systems. Attach that minimal project to the issue tracker. A one-file repro that consistently fails often leads to a fix inside a single day.

Prioritize triage by impact and reproducibility. Crashes with high user frequency and easy repro come first, then major gameplay blockers, then visual/audio polish, then low-probability edge cases. Use tagging in your issue tracker to show reproducibility, platform, severity, and assigned owner so nothing slips through.

When fixing a bug, write (or update) an automated regression test that verifies the bug no longer reproduces. For logic and simulation bugs, unit tests are ideal. For rendering and lifecycle bugs, add device-farm automation or a headless integration test that reproduces the scenario. The process is complete only after the regression test is green in CI.

Logging can get noisy. Keep two levels of logs: a small set of structured events that are always recorded and a verbose mode used only for deep debugging. Rotate and cap log size on devices to avoid filling user storage. When an automated run fails in CI or a device farm, capture the small always-on log first; verbose logs come later if the first pass is insufficient.

Maintain a small QA checklist per platform and gate releases with it. The checklist should include a startup smoke test, scene transition memory check (no leaked textures/RTs), network disconnect/reconnect test, background/foreground lifecycle handling, audio resume behavior, input mapping sanity, localization spot-check, and a graceful handling of low-disk and low-memory conditions. Each item should map to either an automated test, a manual verification step, or both.

Finally, keep a fast feedback loop: developers should be able to reproduce top bugs locally in minutes, push a fix and see the smoke runner and unit tests pass in CI. If that loop is slow, bugs linger. Invest in small, reliable automation first even if you cannot automate everything — the return on time is immediate.

Chapter 13: Example Projects & Case Studies

You'll follow step-by-step examples: a 2D platformer, a top-down shooter, and a simple 3D demo. You'll learn tricks from real-world MonoGame projects and see how to extend them. By the end, you'll have hands-on experience building complete games.

13.1 Simple 2D Platformer — Step-By-Step

This chapter walks the reader from an empty MonoGame project to a minimal, polished 2D platformer prototype that demonstrates the pieces every platformer needs: deterministic physics (gravity + jumping), robust tile collision, sprite animation, a simple camera, level loading, and a few finishing touches (particles, sounds, debug HUD). The style below is pragmatic and compact: short conceptual paragraphs followed by copy-ready, working C# code you can paste into a MonoGame desktop project and iterate on.

The code assumes a standard MonoGame Game class (Game1) with a Content pipeline that loads Texture2D images and a bitmap font. Tile size in examples is 32×32; swap constants to match your art.

Architecture and responsibilities

Keep gameplay logic separate from rendering and platform glue. The core runtime contains: a `Player` (physics + input), a `TileMap` (collision grid + draw), an `Animator` (frame timing), and a `Camera2D` (viewport transform). This separation makes testing and later refactors — e.g., swapping tile maps for Tiled/MonoGame.Extended — straightforward.

Player physics and collision: one robust loop

The player system uses continuous velocities, discrete steps per frame and axis-separated collision resolution. Axis separation (move X, resolve with tiles; move Y, resolve with tiles) is simple to reason about and avoids sticky corner problems in many cases. The sample `Player` below is intentionally small but complete: it handles input, acceleration, gravity, jump buffering, ground detection, and tile collisions using integer tile indices.

```csharp
// File: Player.cs

using Microsoft.Xna.Framework;

using Microsoft.Xna.Framework.Graphics;

using Microsoft.Xna.Framework.Input;

using System;

public class Player

{

    public Vector2 Position;

    public Vector2 Velocity;

    public readonly int Width = 24;
```

```csharp
    public readonly int Height = 32;


    const float MoveSpeed = 180f;            //
pixels/sec

    const float AirAcceleration = 600f;

    const float GroundAcceleration = 1200f;

    const float MaxFallSpeed = 900f;

    const float JumpVelocity = -380f;

    const float Gravity = 1200f;


    bool onGround;

    float jumpBufferTimer = 0f;

    const float JumpBufferTime = 0.12f;


    Texture2D sprite;

    Animator animator;


    public Player(Texture2D texture)

    {

        sprite = texture;

        animator = new Animator(4, 0.12f); // frames,
frameTime (example)

    }
```

```csharp
    public Rectangle Bounds => new((int)(Position.X -
Width/2), (int)(Position.Y - Height), Width, Height);


    public void Update(GameTime gt, TileMap map)

    {

        float dt =
(float)gt.ElapsedGameTime.TotalSeconds;

        var k = Keyboard.GetState();


        float target = 0f;

        if (k.IsKeyDown(Keys.Left) ||
k.IsKeyDown(Keys.A)) target -= 1;

        if (k.IsKeyDown(Keys.Right) ||
k.IsKeyDown(Keys.D)) target += 1;


        float accel = onGround ? GroundAcceleration :
AirAcceleration;

        float desiredVelX = target * MoveSpeed;

        Velocity.X = MathHelper.Lerp(Velocity.X,
desiredVelX, MathHelper.Clamp(accel * dt /
Math.Abs(desiredVelX - Velocity.X + 1e-6f), 0f, 1f));


        // Jump buffer

        if (k.IsKeyDown(Keys.Space))

            jumpBufferTimer = JumpBufferTime;

        else

            jumpBufferTimer -= dt;
```

```csharp
// Gravity
Velocity.Y = MathHelper.Clamp(Velocity.Y +
Gravity * dt, -1000f, MaxFallSpeed);


// Apply movement and resolve collisions
axis-by-axis
Vector2 newPos = Position;
newPos.X += Velocity.X * dt;
ResolveCollisionsX(ref newPos, map);
newPos.Y += Velocity.Y * dt;
ResolveCollisionsY(ref newPos, map);


Position = newPos;


// Process jump after collision (grounded)
if (jumpBufferTimer > 0 && onGround)
{
    Velocity.Y = JumpVelocity;
    onGround = false;
    jumpBufferTimer = 0;
}


// Animator (very small example)
```

```
        animator.Update(dt, Math.Abs(Velocity.X) >
10f || !onGround);

    }


    void ResolveCollisionsX(ref Vector2 newPos,
TileMap map)

    {

        var bounds = new Rectangle((int)(newPos.X -
Width/2), (int)(Position.Y - Height), Width, Height);

        if (Velocity.X > 0)

        {

            int right = bounds.Right;

            int top = bounds.Top;

            int bottom = bounds.Bottom - 1;

            if (map.IsAnySolidInRect(right, top, 1,
bottom - top + 1))

            {

                // Snap to left edge of tile

                int tileX = map.WorldToTileX(right);

                newPos.X = tileX * map.TileSize -
(Width/2) - 0.001f;

                Velocity.X = 0;

            }

        }

        else if (Velocity.X < 0)

        {
```

```
            int left = bounds.Left;

            int top = bounds.Top;

            int bottom = bounds.Bottom - 1;

            if (map.IsAnySolidInRect(left, top, 1,
bottom - top + 1))

                {

                    int tileX = map.WorldToTileX(left);

                    newPos.X = (tileX + 1) * map.TileSize
+ (Width/2) + 0.001f;

                    Velocity.X = 0;

                }

        }

    }


    void ResolveCollisionsY(ref Vector2 newPos,
TileMap map)

    {

        var bounds = new Rectangle((int)(newPos.X -
Width/2), (int)(newPos.Y - Height), Width, Height);

        if (Velocity.Y > 0)

        {

            int bottom = bounds.Bottom;

            int left = bounds.Left;

            int right = bounds.Right - 1;

            if (map.IsAnySolidInRect(left, bottom,
right - left + 1, 1))
```

```
            {

                int tileY = map.WorldToTileY(bottom);

                newPos.Y = tileY * map.TileSize -
0.001f; // place on top of tile

                Velocity.Y = 0;

                onGround = true;

            }

            else onGround = false;

        }

        else if (Velocity.Y < 0)

        {

            int top = bounds.Top;

            int left = bounds.Left;

            int right = bounds.Right - 1;

            if (map.IsAnySolidInRect(left, top, right
- left + 1, 1))

            {

                int tileY = map.WorldToTileY(top);

                newPos.Y = (tileY + 1) * map.TileSize
+ Height + 0.001f;

                Velocity.Y = 0;

            }

        }

    }
```

```csharp
    public void Draw(SpriteBatch sb, Camera2D cam)

    {

        var dst = new Rectangle((int)(Position.X -
Width / 2), (int)(Position.Y - Height), Width,
Height);

        sb.Draw(sprite, dst,
animator.CurrentSourceRect(sprite.Width,
sprite.Height, Width, Height), Color.White);

    }

}
```

This Player uses TileMap helper methods we'll implement next to check for solid tiles and map coordinates.

Simple tile map and collision queries

A tiny tilemap implementation stores a 2D integer grid where value 0 = empty, >0 = solid. This is enough for prototyping before integrating Tiled/MonoGame.Extended; it also demonstrates how to write collision queries used by the Player.

```csharp
// File: TileMap.cs

using Microsoft.Xna.Framework;

using Microsoft.Xna.Framework.Graphics;

using System;


public class TileMap
```

```csharp
{
    public readonly int TileSize = 32;

    int width, height;

    int[,] tiles;

    Texture2D tileset; // assumed to contain tile
graphics laid out in a grid


    public TileMap(int w, int h, int tileSize,
Texture2D tileset, int[,] data)
    {
        width = w; height = h; TileSize = tileSize;
this.tileset = tileset; tiles = data;
    }


    public bool IsSolidTile(int tx, int ty)
    {
        if (tx < 0 || ty < 0 || tx >= width || ty >=
height) return false;

        return tiles[tx, ty] != 0;
    }


    public int WorldToTileX(int x) => x / TileSize;

    public int WorldToTileY(int y) => y / TileSize;


    // Check whether any tile in the rectangle
intersects a solid tile.
```

```csharp
    public bool IsAnySolidInRect(int worldX, int
worldY, int worldW, int worldH)

    {

        int x0 = Math.Max(0, WorldToTileX(worldX));

        int y0 = Math.Max(0, WorldToTileY(worldY));

        int x1 = Math.Min(width - 1,
WorldToTileX(worldX + worldW - 1));

        int y1 = Math.Min(height - 1,
WorldToTileY(worldY + worldH - 1));

        for (int tx = x0; tx <= x1; tx++)

            for (int ty = y0; ty <= y1; ty++)

                if (IsSolidTile(tx, ty)) return true;

        return false;

    }



    // Simple Renderer: draw each tile. For larger
maps use batched geometry or MonoGame.Extended's
TileMap renderer.

    public void Draw(SpriteBatch sb, Camera2D cam)

    {

        int tilesetCols = tileset.Width / TileSize;

        for (int x = 0; x < width; x++)

            for (int y = 0; y < height; y++)

            {

                var v = tiles[x, y];

                if (v == 0) continue;
```

```
                int tileIndex = v - 1;

                int sx = (tileIndex % tilesetCols) *
TileSize;

                int sy = (tileIndex / tilesetCols) *
TileSize;

                var src = new Rectangle(sx, sy,
TileSize, TileSize);

                var dst = new Rectangle(x * TileSize,
y * TileSize, TileSize, TileSize);

                sb.Draw(tileset, dst -
cam.WorldToScreenOffset, src, Color.White);

            }

    }


    public Point WorldToTilePoint(Vector2 world) =>
new(WorldToTileX((int)world.X),
WorldToTileY((int)world.Y));

}
```

If you later use Tiled, swap this TileMap for a loader that reads
.tmx and exposes IsSolidTile, or use MonoGame.Extended's
TiledMap APIs and query layers for collision.

Animator: simple frame-based sprite animation

An Animator returns a source rectangle from a texture atlas based
on frame index and time. Keep it tiny and data-driven.

```csharp
// File: Animator.cs
using Microsoft.Xna.Framework;
public class Animator
{
    int frames;
    float frameTime;
    float timer;
    int index;

    public Animator(int frames, float frameTime)
    {
        this.frames = frames;
        this.frameTime = frameTime;
    }

    public void Update(float dt, bool playing)
    {
        if (!playing) { index = 0; timer = 0; return;
}

        timer += dt;
        while (timer >= frameTime) { timer -=
frameTime; index = (index + 1) % frames; }
    }
```

```
    public Rectangle CurrentSourceRect(int texWidth,
int texHeight, int spriteW, int spriteH)

    {

        int cols = texWidth / spriteW;

        int sx = (index % cols) * spriteW;

        int sy = (index / cols) * spriteH;

        return new Rectangle(sx, sy, spriteW,
spriteH);

    }

}
```

Camera2D: pan and clamp to level

A minimal camera converts world to screen using a translation and optionally clamps to the map bounds.

```
// File: Camera2D.cs

using Microsoft.Xna.Framework;

public class Camera2D

{

    public Vector2 Position;

    public int ViewWidth, ViewHeight;


    public Camera2D(int viewW, int viewH) { ViewWidth
= viewW; ViewHeight = viewH; }
```

```
    public Matrix GetTransform() =>
Matrix.CreateTranslation(new Vector3(-Position, 0f));


    public Vector2 WorldToScreenOffset => new
Vector2(Position.X, Position.Y); // used for simple
draw offsets


    public void Follow(Vector2 worldCenter, int
mapPixelWidth, int mapPixelHeight)

    {

        Position = new Vector2(worldCenter.X -
ViewWidth / 2f, worldCenter.Y - ViewHeight / 2f);

        Position.X = MathHelper.Clamp(Position.X, 0,
Math.Max(0, mapPixelWidth - ViewWidth));

        Position.Y = MathHelper.Clamp(Position.Y, 0,
Math.Max(0, mapPixelHeight - ViewHeight));

    }

}
```

Use `spriteBatch.Begin(transformMatrix: camera.GetTransform())` or use the simple subtraction in draw calls as shown in `TileMap.Draw`.

Putting it together: Game1 wiring

Initialize the map, player and camera in `LoadContent` and drive them in `Update`/`Draw`. This glue is intentionally compact.

```
// File: Game1.cs (relevant excerpts)
```

```
Texture2D tilesetTex, playerTex;

TileMap map;

Player player;

Camera2D camera;

SpriteFont debugFont;


protected override void LoadContent()

{

    tilesetTex =
Content.Load<Texture2D>("tileset32"); // tileset
image

    playerTex =
Content.Load<Texture2D>("player_anim"); // horizontal
frames

    debugFont =
Content.Load<SpriteFont>("DebugFont");


    // Small sample level data (width x height)

    int w = 64, h = 20;

    int[,] data = new int[w, h];

    // Fill floor on row h-2

    for (int x = 0; x < w; x++) data[x, h - 2] = 1;

    // Add some platforms

    data[8, h - 5] = 1; data[9, h - 5] = 1; data[10,
h - 5] = 1;
```

```csharp
    map = new TileMap(w, h, 32, tilesetTex, data);

    player = new Player(playerTex) { Position = new
Microsoft.Xna.Framework.Vector2(100, (h - 3) * 32f)
};

    camera = new
Camera2D(GraphicsDevice.PresentationParameters.BackBu
fferWidth,
GraphicsDevice.PresentationParameters.BackBufferHeigh
t);

}


protected override void Update(GameTime gameTime)

{

    // usual exit

    if
(GamePad.GetState(PlayerIndex.One).Buttons.Back ==
ButtonState.Pressed ||
Keyboard.GetState().IsKeyDown(Keys.Escape)) Exit();


    player.Update(gameTime, map);

    camera.Follow(player.Position, mapWidthInPixels:
map.Width * map.TileSize, mapPixelHeight: map.Height
* map.TileSize);


    base.Update(gameTime);

}


protected override void Draw(GameTime gameTime)
```

```
{
    GraphicsDevice.Clear(Color.CornflowerBlue);

    spriteBatch.Begin(transformMatrix:
camera.GetTransform());

    map.Draw(spriteBatch, camera);

    player.Draw(spriteBatch, camera);

    spriteBatch.End();


    // debug HUD

    spriteBatch.Begin();

    spriteBatch.DrawString(debugFont, $"FPS:
{1f/(float)gameTime.ElapsedGameTime.TotalSeconds:0}",
new Vector2(8,8), Color.White);

    spriteBatch.End();


    base.Draw(gameTime);
}
```

Note: above `map.Width` and `map.Height` properties are easy to expose; add them to the `TileMap` class.

Level loading and tools

For quick prototyping use code or JSON to store tile arrays. For production levels use Tiled (TMX) and a reader (TiledSharp, TiledCS) or MonoGame.Extended's Tiled support to draw layers and mark collision objects. The `TileMap`API we used

(`IsSolidTile`, world-to-tile) is all you need to keep the player code unchanged while swapping the backend.

Polishing: particles, sound, and polish tricks

Add a tiny particle emitter triggered on jump/land, play short `SoundEffect` on jump/collision, and add a coyote-time window (allow jump shortly after leaving ground) to make controls forgiving. Always test jumps and wall collisions on worst-case framerate and tweak jump impulse/gravity until controls feel right.

Example: coyote time is implemented by setting `onGroundTimer` to a small value when grounded and decrementing it; allow jump while `onGroundTimer > 0`.

Debugging and tuning

Add a debug HUD that shows `onGround`, `Velocity`, tile under player, and frametime. Use the HUD to rapidly iterate on gravity, jump velocity and tile collision snap offsets. When collisions look jittery, draw tile boundaries and the player bounds to visualize the problem. Unit test the physics step on the desktop by driving `Player.Update` with synthetic `GameTime` and a mocked `TileMap`.

Next steps and recommended upgrades

Replace the simple array map with a Tiled map loaded via MonoGame.Extended for layered tiles and object layers. Swap the axis-separated collision for swept AABB if you need fast continuous collision with moving platforms. For many tiles, replace per-tile `SpriteBatch.Draw` with a batched vertex buffer renderer to reduce draw calls. Add an input rebinding layer and polish with animations blended from run/idle/jump states.

Minimal asset checklist

Your prototype needs at minimum: a tileset image (grid of tile sprites), a player sprite strip (frames horizontally laid out), and a small bitmap font for debug. Keep tile graphics power-of-two friendly (32×32 is common) and ensure the collision tiles are correctly marked in your level data.

Summary in one paragraph

Start small: implement axis-separated collision between a velocity-driven `Player` and a `TileMap` grid, add a compact `Animator` and `Camera2D`, then iterate: swap maps for Tiled, add batching, and polish controls with coyote time and input buffering. Keep gameplay logic isolated so rendering, asset loading, or a move to a physics engine won't force a rewrite. Use the code above as a minimal, complete baseline to build from.

13.2 Top-Down 2D Shooter Example

A top-down shooter always feels alive because everything happens at once. Enemies move toward the player, bullets cross the screen in every direction, and the pacing never stops. The secret to building one in MonoGame is learning how to coordinate simple systems—movement, shooting, collisions, and spawning—until they behave like a single, coherent organism. Once each part communicates cleanly, the gameplay loop becomes remarkably straightforward to maintain and expand.

The foundation is always the player controller. A top-down camera view removes gravity, so movement becomes a matter of reading raw directional input and normalising it to achieve smooth diagonal movement. Treat the player as a light physics object that reacts instantly. In a shooter, snappy control is the difference between flow and frustration. A minimal but responsive controller looks like this:

```
public class Player

{

    public Vector2 Position;

    public float Speed = 220f;

    public Texture2D Texture;

    public float Rotation;


    public void Load(ContentManager content)

    {

        Texture = content.Load<Texture2D>("player");

    }
```

```csharp
    public void Update(GameTime time)

    {

        float dt =
(float)time.ElapsedGameTime.TotalSeconds;


        Vector2 direction = Vector2.Zero;



        if (Keyboard.GetState().IsKeyDown(Keys.W))
direction.Y -= 1;

        if (Keyboard.GetState().IsKeyDown(Keys.S))
direction.Y += 1;

        if (Keyboard.GetState().IsKeyDown(Keys.A))
direction.X -= 1;

        if (Keyboard.GetState().IsKeyDown(Keys.D))
direction.X += 1;


        if (direction != Vector2.Zero)

            direction.Normalize();



        Position += direction * Speed * dt;

        Vector2 mouse =
Mouse.GetState().Position.ToVector2();

        Rotation = MathF.Atan2(mouse.Y - Position.Y,
mouse.X - Position.X);

    }

    public void Draw(SpriteBatch sb)

    {
```

```
        sb.Draw(

            Texture,

            Position,

            null,

            Color.White,

            Rotation,

            new Vector2(Texture.Width / 2f,
Texture.Height / 2f),

            1f,

            SpriteEffects.None,

            0f);

    }

}
```

This simple controller takes care of movement and rotation without complication. The player always faces the mouse, creating intuitive aiming. Since rotation is based on a vector difference, the player instantly "locks on" to the cursor, giving the game its characteristic twin-stick feel.

Once the player is ready, the next layer is the projectile system. A shooter without bullets is silent. A shooter with sloppy bullets is unplayable. The goal is to make projectiles fast to create, light to simulate, and easy to discard. A clean bullet class moves forward along its spawn rotation and self-deletes as soon as it travels outside the viewport.

```
public class Bullet

{
```

```csharp
    public Vector2 Position;

    public Vector2 Velocity;

    public Texture2D Texture;

    public bool IsDead;


    public Bullet(Texture2D texture, Vector2 origin,
float rotation, float speed)

    {

        Texture = texture;

        Position = origin;

        Velocity = new Vector2(MathF.Cos(rotation),
MathF.Sin(rotation)) * speed;

    }


    public void Update(GameTime time)

    {

        float dt =
(float)time.ElapsedGameTime.TotalSeconds;

        Position += Velocity * dt;


        if (Position.X < -50 || Position.X > 2000 ||

            Position.Y < -50 || Position.Y > 2000)

            IsDead = true;

    }

    public void Draw(SpriteBatch sb)
```

```
    {

        sb.Draw(Texture, Position, Color.White);

    }

}
```

Creating bullets becomes a matter of instantiating one whenever the player fires. A reliable firing system uses a short cooldown so the player cannot generate an uncontrolled stream but still feels powerful.

```
List<Bullet> bullets = new();

float fireCooldown = 0.12f;

float fireTimer = 0f;

Texture2D bulletTexture;

public void Load(ContentManager content)

{

    bulletTexture =
content.Load<Texture2D>("bullet");

}



public void UpdateShooting(GameTime time, Player
player)

{

    float dt =
(float)time.ElapsedGameTime.TotalSeconds;

    fireTimer -= dt;
```

```
if (Mouse.GetState().LeftButton ==
ButtonState.Pressed && fireTimer <= 0f)

    {

        bullets.Add(new Bullet(bulletTexture,
player.Position, player.Rotation, 620f));

        fireTimer = fireCooldown;

    }

    for (int i = bullets.Count - 1; i >= 0; i--)

    {

        bullets[i].Update(time);

        if (bullets[i].IsDead)

            bullets.RemoveAt(i);

    }

}
```

The game now has motion and firepower. The next piece is the enemy system, which breathes life into the world. A classic approach is steering behaviour where an enemy relentlessly moves toward the player. The behaviour is simple, yet the result feels aggressive and unpredictable when large numbers of enemies are spawned.

```
public class Enemy

{

    public Vector2 Position;
```

```csharp
    public Texture2D Texture;

    public float Speed = 80f;

    public bool IsDead;


    public void Load(Texture2D texture, Vector2
spawn)

    {

        Texture = texture;

        Position = spawn;

    }


    public void Update(GameTime time, Vector2
playerPosition)

    {

        float dt =
(float)time.ElapsedGameTime.TotalSeconds;

        Vector2 direction = playerPosition -
Position;


        if (direction.LengthSquared() > 1f)

            direction.Normalize();


        Position += direction * Speed * dt;

    }

    public void Draw(SpriteBatch sb)
```

```
    {
        sb.Draw(Texture, Position, Color.White);

    }

}
```

Spawning enemies at the edges of the screen ensures the player never feels overwhelmed instantly but always senses movement from the periphery. A randomised spawn manager makes encounters unpredictable and keeps pressure steady.

```
List<Enemy> enemies = new();

Texture2D enemyTexture;

Random rng = new();

float spawnTime = 1.8f;

float spawnTimer = 0f;


public void LoadEnemies(ContentManager content)

{

    enemyTexture = content.Load<Texture2D>("enemy");

}


public void UpdateEnemySpawning(GameTime time, Player player)

{

    float dt =
(float)time.ElapsedGameTime.TotalSeconds;

    spawnTimer -= dt;
```

```
if (spawnTimer <= 0f)

{

    int side = rng.Next(4);

    Vector2 spawn = side switch

    {

        0 => new Vector2(rng.Next(0, 1280), -40),

        1 => new Vector2(1320, rng.Next(0, 720)),

        2 => new Vector2(rng.Next(0, 1280), 760),

        _ => new Vector2(-40, rng.Next(0, 720)),

    };


    Enemy e = new Enemy();

    e.Load(enemyTexture, spawn);

    enemies.Add(e);

    spawnTimer = spawnTime;

}

foreach (var e in enemies)

    e.Update(time, player.Position);

}
```

Collisions complete the gameplay loop. A simple circle-based check is sufficient, cheap, and accurate enough for fast-moving bullets. Each bullet either deals damage or deletes the enemy instantly depending on your design goals. In this basic example the enemy disappears on hit, giving the player constant feedback.

```
public void HandleCollisions()

{

    for (int i = enemies.Count - 1; i >= 0; i--)

    {

        Enemy e = enemies[i];


        for (int j = bullets.Count - 1; j >= 0; j--)

        {

            Bullet b = bullets[j];

            if (Vector2.DistanceSquared(e.Position,
b.Position) < 28 * 28)

            {

                enemies.RemoveAt(i);

                bullets.RemoveAt(j);

                break;

            }

        }

    }

}
```

With all systems active, the shooter becomes a dynamic loop: the player moves, aims, fires, clears enemies, and survives wave after wave. Each subsystem remains small, readable, and isolated, so extending the game becomes a matter of adding behaviour rather than rewriting core logic. You can introduce health, different enemy types, score multipliers, bosses, power-ups, or screenshake without disturbing the underlying flow that this chapter established.

The goal of this example is not to overwhelm you with features but to show how a clean architectural approach lets a fast-paced game stay stable even as complexity rises. Build each system clearly, allow it to do one job well, let it communicate through shared world state, and a top-down shooter naturally forms around it.

13.3 Basic 3D Game Demo

A small, focused 3D demo proves the mechanics you'll need for almost every 3D MonoGame project: a camera, simple lighting, a mesh or two, textured models, input-driven movement, and a clear render loop that separates CPU work (game logic) from GPU work (draw calls). The example below is intentionally minimal but complete: everything compiles and runs in a standard MonoGame desktop project that uses the Content Pipeline. Read the short explanations, then paste the code into your project and iterate.

The demo does three things every frame: update the camera from input, update a simple actor (move/rotate), and draw the scene with BasicEffect (lighting + textures). The patterns are portable—swap BasicEffect for custom effects later without changing the high-level flow.

Project notes and prerequisites

Create a regular MonoGame DesktopGL (or Windows) project. Use the MonoGame Pipeline Tool to add a textured model (FBX/OBJ/DAE) or a simple texture if you prefer to draw a generated cube. The pipeline produces `.xnb` assets that `Content.Load<Model>("myModel")` can read. If you use plain vertex buffers (procedural cube), no model asset is required.

Camera: view and projection

A small camera class stores position and target, builds `View` and `Projection` matrices, and exposes a simple orbit and free-move control. This camera uses `LookAt` and a perspective projection.

```
// Camera3D.cs
using Microsoft.Xna.Framework;
using Microsoft.Xna.Framework.Input;


public class Camera3D
{
    public Vector3 Position;

    public Vector3 Target;

    public Matrix View =>
Matrix.CreateLookAt(Position, Target, Vector3.Up);

    public Matrix Projection { get; private set; }

    public float Distance = 10f;

    public float Yaw = 0f;
```

```
    public float Pitch = -0.3f; // slightly downward


    public Camera3D(int width, int height, float fov
= MathHelper.PiOver4, float near = 0.1f, float far =
1000f)

    {

        Projection =
Matrix.CreatePerspectiveFieldOfView(fov, width /
(float)height, near, far);

        UpdatePosition();

    }



    public void UpdateMouseOrbit(float dx, float dy)

    {

        Yaw += dx;

        Pitch = MathHelper.Clamp(Pitch + dy,
-MathHelper.PiOver2 + 0.1f, MathHelper.PiOver2 -
0.1f);

        UpdatePosition();

    }



    public void Zoom(float delta)

    {

        Distance = MathHelper.Clamp(Distance + delta,
2f, 100f);

        UpdatePosition();

    }
```

```
    void UpdatePosition()

    {

         var rot = Matrix.CreateRotationX(Pitch) *
Matrix.CreateRotationY(Yaw);

         Position = Vector3.Transform(new Vector3(0,
0, Distance), rot) + Target;

    }


    public void Pan(Vector3 offset)

    {

        Position += offset;

        Target += offset;

    }

}
```

Use small orbit controls during development (mouse-drag to rotate, wheel to zoom) and a keyboard pan for scene positioning.

Simple textured cube (procedural geometry)

If you want a guaranteed-works demo without importing models, create a cube via a VertexBuffer and a BasicEffect. The code below builds a cube with positions, normals and UVs and draws it with a texture and a single directional light.

```csharp
// CubePrimitive.cs

using Microsoft.Xna.Framework;

using Microsoft.Xna.Framework.Graphics;


public class CubePrimitive

{

    GraphicsDevice gd;

    VertexBuffer vbo;

    IndexBuffer ibo;

    BasicEffect effect;

    Texture2D texture;


    public Vector3 WorldPosition = Vector3.Zero;

    public Quaternion Rotation = Quaternion.Identity;

    public float Scale = 1f;


    public CubePrimitive(GraphicsDevice graphics,
Texture2D tex)

    {

        gd = graphics;

        texture = tex;

        BuildBuffers();

        effect = new BasicEffect(gd)

        {
```

```csharp
            TextureEnabled = true,

            Texture = texture,

            LightingEnabled = true,

            AmbientLightColor = new Vector3(0.3f),

            DiffuseColor = new Vector3(1f)

        };

        effect.DirectionalLight0.Enabled = true;

        effect.DirectionalLight0.Direction =
Vector3.Normalize(new Vector3(-1, -1, -1));

        effect.DirectionalLight0.DiffuseColor =
Vector3.One;

    }



    void BuildBuffers()

    {

        var verts = new
VertexPositionNormalTexture[24];

        var indices = new ushort[36];



        // Build 6 faces, 4 verts each (position,
normal, uv)

        // Front face

        verts[0] = new
VertexPositionNormalTexture(new Vector3(-1, -1, 1),
Vector3.Forward, new Vector2(0,1));
```

```csharp
        verts[1] = new
VertexPositionNormalTexture(new Vector3(1, -1, 1),
Vector3.Forward, new Vector2(1,1));

        verts[2] = new
VertexPositionNormalTexture(new Vector3(-1, 1, 1),
Vector3.Forward, new Vector2(0,0));

        verts[3] = new
VertexPositionNormalTexture(new Vector3(1, 1, 1),
Vector3.Forward, new Vector2(1,0));

        // Back

        verts[4] = new
VertexPositionNormalTexture(new Vector3(1, -1, -1),
Vector3.Backward, new Vector2(0,1));

        verts[5] = new
VertexPositionNormalTexture(new Vector3(-1, -1, -1),
Vector3.Backward, new Vector2(1,1));

        verts[6] = new
VertexPositionNormalTexture(new Vector3(1, 1, -1),
Vector3.Backward, new Vector2(0,0));

        verts[7] = new
VertexPositionNormalTexture(new Vector3(-1, 1, -1),
Vector3.Backward, new Vector2(1,0));

        // Left

        verts[8] = new
VertexPositionNormalTexture(new Vector3(-1, -1, -1),
Vector3.Left, new Vector2(0,1));

        verts[9] = new
VertexPositionNormalTexture(new Vector3(-1, -1, 1),
Vector3.Left, new Vector2(1,1));

        verts[10] = new
VertexPositionNormalTexture(new Vector3(-1, 1, -1),
Vector3.Left, new Vector2(0,0));
```

```csharp
        verts[11] = new
VertexPositionNormalTexture(new Vector3(-1, 1, 1),
Vector3.Left, new Vector2(1,0));

        // Right

        verts[12] = new
VertexPositionNormalTexture(new Vector3(1, -1, 1),
Vector3.Right, new Vector2(0,1));

        verts[13] = new
VertexPositionNormalTexture(new Vector3(1, -1, -1),
Vector3.Right, new Vector2(1,1));

        verts[14] = new
VertexPositionNormalTexture(new Vector3(1, 1, 1),
Vector3.Right, new Vector2(0,0));

        verts[15] = new
VertexPositionNormalTexture(new Vector3(1, 1, -1),
Vector3.Right, new Vector2(1,0));

        // Top

        verts[16] = new
VertexPositionNormalTexture(new Vector3(-1, 1, 1),
Vector3.Up, new Vector2(0,1));

        verts[17] = new
VertexPositionNormalTexture(new Vector3(1, 1, 1),
Vector3.Up, new Vector2(1,1));

        verts[18] = new
VertexPositionNormalTexture(new Vector3(-1, 1, -1),
Vector3.Up, new Vector2(0,0));

        verts[19] = new
VertexPositionNormalTexture(new Vector3(1, 1, -1),
Vector3.Up, new Vector2(1,0));

        // Bottom

        verts[20] = new
VertexPositionNormalTexture(new Vector3(-1, -1, -1),
Vector3.Down, new Vector2(0,1));
```

```
        verts[21] = new
VertexPositionNormalTexture(new Vector3(1, -1, -1),
Vector3.Down, new Vector2(1,1));

        verts[22] = new
VertexPositionNormalTexture(new Vector3(-1, -1, 1),
Vector3.Down, new Vector2(0,0));

        verts[23] = new
VertexPositionNormalTexture(new Vector3(1, -1, 1),
Vector3.Down, new Vector2(1,0));


        // Indices (two triangles per face)

        ushort[] faceOrder = {

            0,1,2, 2,1,3,

            4,5,6, 6,5,7,

            8,9,10, 10,9,11,

            12,13,14, 14,13,15,

            16,17,18, 18,17,19,

            20,21,22, 22,21,23

        };

        indices = faceOrder;



        vbo = new VertexBuffer(gd,
typeof(VertexPositionNormalTexture), verts.Length,
BufferUsage.WriteOnly);

        vbo.SetData(verts);

        ibo = new IndexBuffer(gd,
IndexElementSize.SixteenBits, indices.Length,
BufferUsage.WriteOnly);
```

```
        ibo.SetData(indices);

    }


    public void Draw(Matrix view, Matrix proj)

    {

        effect.World = Matrix.CreateScale(Scale) *
Matrix.CreateFromQuaternion(Rotation) *
Matrix.CreateTranslation(WorldPosition);

        effect.View = view;

        effect.Projection = proj;

        effect.Texture = texture;


        gd.SetVertexBuffer(vbo);

        gd.Indices = ibo;


        foreach (var pass in
effect.CurrentTechnique.Passes)

        {

            pass.Apply();

gd.DrawIndexedPrimitives(PrimitiveType.TriangleList,
0, 0, 12);

        }


        // reset state as SpriteBatch may rely on
defaults
```

```
        gd.SetVertexBuffer(null);

        gd.Indices = null;

    }

    public void Dispose()

    {

        vbo?.Dispose();

        ibo?.Dispose();

        effect?.Dispose();

    }

}
```

This cube shows textured normals and responds to the directional light set in BasicEffect. Use Scale and Rotation to animate.

Loading and drawing a Content Pipeline Model

If you prefer artist-authored models, add an .fbx/.dae/.obj to the pipeline and load it like this. Model objects often contain skin/mesh parts with their own Effect instances—replace or configure them for consistent lighting.

```
// in Game1.cs LoadContent

Model model = Content.Load<Model>("myModel"); // pipeline asset name

// in Draw()
```

```
Matrix world = Matrix.CreateScale(1f) *
Matrix.CreateRotationY(myRotation) *
Matrix.CreateTranslation(new Vector3(0,0,0));

foreach (ModelMesh mesh in model.Meshes)

{

    foreach (BasicEffect be in mesh.Effects)

    {

        be.World = mesh.ParentBone.Transform * world;

        be.View = camera.View;

        be.Projection = camera.Projection;

        be.EnableDefaultLighting(); // convenience,
sets directional lights

        be.TextureEnabled = true;

        // be.Texture =
Content.Load<Texture2D>("myModelTexture"); //
optional override

    }

    mesh.Draw();

}
```

If a model's effect is not BasicEffect (custom shaders), you will need to set parameters according to that effect's API.

Input and simple actor movement

Move an actor with WASD and rotate it slowly. This keeps collision and physics trivial while demonstrating transform updates.

```
// Simple actor update in Game1.Update

var ks = Keyboard.GetState();

Vector3 move = Vector3.Zero;

if (ks.IsKeyDown(Keys.W)) move += Vector3.Forward;

if (ks.IsKeyDown(Keys.S)) move += Vector3.Backward;

if (ks.IsKeyDown(Keys.A)) move += Vector3.Left;

if (ks.IsKeyDown(Keys.D)) move += Vector3.Right;

if (move != Vector3.Zero) move.Normalize();

float speed = 6f; // units per second

actorWorldPosition += move * speed *
(float)gameTime.ElapsedGameTime.TotalSeconds;

actorRotation += 0.6f *
(float)gameTime.ElapsedGameTime.TotalSeconds; //
example spin
```

World space units are arbitrary; tune speed and camera distance until the feel is right.

Simple collision hint: ray/plane or bounding-sphere

For small demos, use bounding spheres for cheap collision tests (e.g., bullets hitting models) or a raycast against a ground plane for mouse picking. Sphere checks are two lines and cheap:

```
// sphere collision check

bool IntersectsSphere(Vector3 aPos, float aRadius,
Vector3 bPos, float bRadius)
```

```
{
    return Vector3.DistanceSquared(aPos, bPos) <=
(aRadius + bRadius) * (aRadius + bRadius);

}
```

For mouse picking use `Viewport.Unproject` with near/far points and build a ray; intersect against model bounding spheres or triangles for precise hits.

Performance and practical tips

Prefer `BasicEffect` for small demos because it gives normals, three directional lights, per-pixel lighting toggle and texture support without authoring HLSL. For larger projects move to precompiled shader effects. Keep large meshes in `Model` assets and avoid recreating vertex/index buffers every frame. Dispose GPU resources on exit and keep draw calls low: merge static geometry where possible and use frustum culling (skip `mesh.Draw()` when its bounding sphere is outside the camera frustum).

When importing models, remember the MonoGame Content Pipeline uses Assimp under the hood and common formats are FBX and COLLADA; textures must be present and referenced to be processed. If a model appears untextured, check the mesh `Effect` and `Texture` assignments in the pipeline output.

Minimal Game1 wiring

Below is the minimal skeleton for Game1 showing startup, input, update, and draw using the cube primitive and camera.

```
// Game1.cs (excerpt)

protected override void LoadContent()

{

    spriteBatch = new SpriteBatch(GraphicsDevice);

    camera = new
Camera3D(GraphicsDevice.PresentationParameters.BackBu
fferWidth,


GraphicsDevice.PresentationParameters.BackBufferHeigh
t);

    Texture2D tex = Content.Load<Texture2D>("crate");
// small texture for cube faces

    cube = new CubePrimitive(GraphicsDevice, tex);

    cube.WorldPosition = new Vector3(0, 0, 0);

}



protected override void Update(GameTime gameTime)

{

    var mouse = Mouse.GetState();

    if (mouse.LeftButton == ButtonState.Pressed)

    {

        // rotate camera by dragging (example)

        camera.UpdateMouseOrbit(-mouseDeltaX * 0.01f,
-mouseDeltaY * 0.01f);
```

```
    }

    camera.Target = new Vector3(0, 0, 0); // keep
orbiting this point

    cube.Rotation *=
Quaternion.CreateFromAxisAngle(Vector3.Up, 0.6f *
(float)gameTime.ElapsedGameTime.TotalSeconds);

    base.Update(gameTime);

}


protected override void Draw(GameTime gameTime)

{

    GraphicsDevice.Clear(Color.CornflowerBlue);

    cube.Draw(camera.View, camera.Projection);

    base.Draw(gameTime);

}
```

Add a small debug HUD that prints camera position and frame ms so you can tune distances and speeds.

Next steps and expansion ideas

Replace BasicEffect with a custom lighting effect, add normal maps and specular terms, import skinned animated models and set their bone transforms, implement a first-person controller with collision against a simple NavMesh, or add post-processing (bloom, tone mapping) via render targets. Each step reuses the same update/draw separation: CPU updates transform, GPU renders with prepared matrices and effect parameters.

13.4 Lessons from Real MonoGame Projects

Real projects teach faster than any tutorial: they force tradeoffs, expose platform differences, and reveal the engineering choices that scale from prototype to release. This chapter condenses those lessons into a short, practical guide you can apply immediately. It emphasises patterns that repeatedly solved real-world problems: clear separation of concerns, predictable asset handling, pragmatic performance hygiene, cross-platform testing, and simple automation that prevents regressions. Each idea is explained with why it matters and a compact, copy-ready example when code helps.

Start by separating *engine* from *game*. Teams that survive long development cycles keep gameplay logic in pure C# libraries with no MonoGame plumbing — physics, rules, AI and save/load live in testable assemblies. Rendering, input adapters and platform services sit in thin adapters that the core consumes through interfaces. That separation makes unit testing trivial and reduces the "it works on my machine" syndrome because most bugs move into small adapter layers that are easy to inspect.

Real projects often adopt scene-scoped content ownership to make resource lifetime explicit. Create a `ContentManager` per level or scene so you can call `Unload()` and free native GPU memory

528

deterministically when a scene ends. The snippet below shows the pattern: create, use, unload.

```csharp
// SceneContentHelper.cs — create a scene
ContentManager, load a texture, then unload on scene
exit

public class SceneContentHelper : IDisposable

{

    public readonly ContentManager SceneContent;

    public SceneContentHelper(IServiceProvider
services, string root = "Content")

    {

        SceneContent = new ContentManager(services,
root);

    }


    public Texture2D LoadTexture(string assetName) =>
SceneContent.Load<Texture2D>(assetName);


    public void Dispose() { SceneContent.Unload();
SceneContent.Dispose(); }

}



// Usage

using(var sceneAssets = new
SceneContentHelper(game.Services)) {

    var bg = sceneAssets.LoadTexture("level1/bg");

    // run scene...
```

```
} // Unload automatically here
```

Assets and the content pipeline are a frequent pain point in real projects. Use the pipeline for production assets because preprocessed build artifacts load faster and reduce runtime parsing cost. But design your loaders so they can swap between pipeline XNBs and raw runtime loaders (PNG/JSON) for modding or downloadable content. Many teams keep the same `IAssetLoader` interface and provide pipeline and runtime implementations to avoid branching logic deeply in game code.

Loading must be non-blocking where possible. Real teams moved heavy I/O and decode off the main thread and only finalize GPU uploads on the render thread. The pattern we used earlier — background read + `Texture2D.FromStream` on the main thread — is cheap to implement and prevents startup jank on slower devices.

Performance matters earlier than you think. Real projects that postponed profiling hit a wall late in development. Measure first, then optimise the real hotspots. Start with a cheap in-game metrics HUD (FPS, frame ms, GC allocations) and run a short CI smoke test that records frametimes for critical scenes. Avoid premature micro-optimisations; focus on allocation hot paths, excessive draw calls, and large texture uploads. The community consistently reports that GC churn from tiny per-frame allocations and uncapped draw-call counts are the most common causes of poor runtime behaviour.

Memory and native resources bite teams that forget to `Dispose`. Many postmortems name leaked textures, unreleased render targets, or unreleased audio buffers as the cause of OOM crashes on mobile. Use scene content managers, explicit `Dispose()` on manually created GPU objects, and keep a small debug helper to list live resources during scene transitions.

Cross-platform testing isn't optional. MonoGame projects target a wide spectrum of devices; consoles and iOS/macOS builds require specific signing and runner setups. Run a CI matrix that builds and runs unit tests on Windows, macOS and Linux. For mobile, add scheduled device-farm runs (or a small in-house device lab) to catch lifecycle, memory and touch-specific issues. Many teams caught critical bugs only after device testing revealed differences in texture formats, driver quirks, or lifecycle behaviour (suspend/resume).

Keep your pipeline and build process reproducible and fast. Real teams invested in build scripts and Fastlane/FOSS equivalents to automate signing, compressing textures for each platform and publishing. Packing multiple compressed texture sets per target device reduces memory and improves load times, but it requires build-time automation to be viable.

Automate regressions. A core lesson is: if fixing a bug doesn't add an automated regression test, the bug usually returns. For logic bugs add unit tests; for rendering or lifecycle problems add small deterministic smoke runners and run them in CI (or device farms). Capture CSVs of perf runs so you can detect regressions in frametime, allocations or load times across builds.

Keep an opinionated—but small—runtime debug toolkit. A compact logger that writes line-delimited JSON, a build stamp embedded at compile time, and a short diagnostics HUD provide huge value during triage. Use the build stamp everywhere: logs, crash reports, and device-farm uploads. It's trivial to implement and saves days of manual tracking when a crash report lands.

Lean on the community and the showcase. MonoGame is mature and battle-tested; many teams reuse samples, libraries, and workflows. Look at shipped MonoGame titles and community posts to avoid reinventing solutions for content workflows, input mapping, and platform packaging. Developers reported big wins by reusing proven tools (content pipeline automation, sprite atlas tools, renderdoc for GPU captures) rather than building one-off solutions.

Simplify platform-specific code with small adapter layers and feature detection. Instead of branching game logic for each OS, provide platform capability flags early (supports ASTC? has hardware tangent-space? can run background audio?) and use them to pick assets and shaders. This keeps the core codebase clean and makes it much easier to add new platforms later.

Finally, expect and plan for iteration. Shipping a minimal playable core quickly, then polishing systems with measurement-driven changes, is how many MonoGame projects reached release. Build tools to make iteration cheap: hot-reload content where possible, scriptable levels, and a fast feedback loop from editor to device. The fastest teams shipped frequent internal builds and used smoke runners and simple telemetry to guide tradeoffs.

Short, practical checklist (apply today)

One: move pure game logic into platform-agnostic libraries to enable unit tests. Two: use scene-scoped `ContentManager` objects and dispose native resources explicitly. Three: push heavy I/O off the main thread and finalize GPU uploads on the render thread. Four: measure before you optimise — use a HUD and automated smoke runs. Five: run cross-platform builds and device tests early and often. Six: automate asset compression/packaging in your CI. Seven: add regression tests for any real bug you fix. Eight: embed a build stamp and structured logging to make triage fast.

13.5 Tips to Extend & Customize Your Games

Extending a MonoGame project is about making change cheap and safe. When your codebase is easy to adapt, artists can iterate faster, designers can ship new levels without a rebuild, and modders can extend the game without talking to you. This chapter shows practical, production-minded patterns you can drop into your code: plugin/mod loading, safe runtime scripting, hot-reload workflows, data-driven assets, input rebinding, shader variant handling, CI/packaging hints, and small code examples that actually work in modern .NET/MonoGame projects. Read the short explanations, copy the snippets, and use them as building blocks — each example is intentionally small so you can integrate it and expand it to your needs.

Make an explicit extension surface (plugin interface)

Define a tiny, versioned contract that plugins implement. Keep the interface minimal and stable: initialization, update, shutdown and a small metadata object. Load plugins from a Mods or Plugins folder at runtime; use an AssemblyLoadContext so you can unload and reload plugin assemblies during development.

```
// File: IGamePlugin.cs
```

```
public interface IGamePlugin

{

    string Id { get; }              // stable id of
the plugin

    string Version { get; }         // semantic
version string

    void Initialize(Game game);     // called once
when plugin is loaded

    void Update(GameTime dt);       // called from
your main Update loop

    void Shutdown();                // called when
plugin unloads

}
```

Load plugins with a small loader that isolates assemblies so you can unload them when needed. The example below loads all DLLs in Mods/, instantiates types implementing IGamePlugin, and keeps a reference to the custom AssemblyLoadContext so you can unload later.

```
// File: PluginLoader.cs

using System;

using System.Collections.Generic;

using System.IO;

using System.Linq;

using System.Reflection;

using System.Runtime.Loader;
```

```csharp
public class PluginLoader : IDisposable

{

    class PluginEntry { public IGamePlugin Plugin;
public AssemblyLoadContext Alc; }


    readonly List<PluginEntry> loaded = new();

    readonly string modsFolder;


    public PluginLoader(string modsFolder = "Mods")
=> this.modsFolder = modsFolder;


    public void LoadAll(Game game)

    {

        if (!Directory.Exists(modsFolder))
Directory.CreateDirectory(modsFolder);

        var dlls = Directory.GetFiles(modsFolder,
"*.dll", SearchOption.TopDirectoryOnly);

        foreach (var dll in dlls)

        {

            try

            {

                var alc = new
AssemblyLoadContext(Path.GetFileNameWithoutExtension(
dll), isCollectible: true);

                using var fs = File.OpenRead(dll);

                var asm = alc.LoadFromStream(fs);
```

```
                var types = asm.GetTypes().Where(t =>
typeof(IGamePlugin).IsAssignableFrom(t) &&
!t.IsAbstract);

                foreach (var t in types)

                {

                    var plugin =
(IGamePlugin)Activator.CreateInstance(t)!;

                    plugin.Initialize(game);

                    loaded.Add(new PluginEntry {
Plugin = plugin, Alc = alc });

                }

            }

            catch (Exception ex)

            {

                Console.WriteLine($"Failed loading
plugin {dll}: {ex.Message}");

            }

        }

    }


    public void UnloadAll()

    {

        foreach (var e in loaded)

        {

            try { e.Plugin.Shutdown(); } catch { }
```

```
            e.Alc.Unload(); // request unload; may
take time until GC collects

        }

        loaded.Clear();

    }

    public void Dispose() => UnloadAll();

}
```

This pattern gives modders a clear entry point and lets you add permissions (e.g., deny direct file I/O) later by wrapping the interface with safe facades.

Embed scripting for safe runtime logic (C# scripting or Lua)

Scripting makes customization accessible without compiling C# DLLs. You can embed a modern C# scripting engine (Roslyn scripting via `Microsoft.CodeAnalysis.CSharp.Scripting`) for power users, or embed a lightweight Lua runtime (MoonSharp) for wide adoption. C# scripting lets designers write strongly typed glue that can reference your safe API; Lua is tiny, portable and familiar to modders.

A tiny C# scripting example that runs sandboxed logic and can call a safe API:

```
// Requires NuGet:
Microsoft.CodeAnalysis.CSharp.Scripting

using Microsoft.CodeAnalysis.CSharp.Scripting;
```

```csharp
using Microsoft.CodeAnalysis.Scripting;

public class ScriptRunner

{

    readonly ScriptOptions options =
ScriptOptions.Default

        .WithImports("System",
"Microsoft.Xna.Framework")

.WithReferences(AppDomain.CurrentDomain.GetAssemblies
()

            .Where(a => !a.IsDynamic &&
!string.IsNullOrEmpty(a.Location)));


    public async Task RunScriptAsync(string code,
object globals = null)

    {

        // For safety, only expose a limited set of
types via the 'globals' object

        await CSharpScript.RunAsync(code, options,
globals);

    }

}
```

The globals object is how you pass a small API surface (for example methods to spawn entities, play sounds, query time). Limit what you expose to avoid giving scripts full app control.

For Lua, MoonSharp is a good choice (embedding example omitted here), or pick your preferred Lua CLR bridge. Use scripts for AI behaviors, item effects, or level triggers rather than core systems.

Hot-reload assets and code to speed iteration

Developer productivity accelerates with hot-reload. For assets, watch files and re-import or reload them in-place. For managed code, .NET Hot Reload and community tools (MonoGame.Reload) let you change code without restarting the whole game. Integrate a debug-only hot-reload toggle so artists can iterate on sprites and designers can tweak script files live.

A practical asset hot-reload pattern is simple: watch a folder and enqueue changed file paths, then finalize re-creation of GPU resources on the main thread:

```
// File: AssetWatcher.cs

using System;

using System.Collections.Concurrent;

using System.IO;


public class AssetWatcher : IDisposable

{

    readonly FileSystemWatcher watcher;

    readonly ConcurrentQueue<string> changed = new();


    public AssetWatcher(string path)

    {

        watcher = new FileSystemWatcher(path) {
IncludeSubdirectories = true, EnableRaisingEvents =
true };
```

```
        watcher.Changed += (s,e) =>
changed.Enqueue(e.FullPath);

        watcher.Created += (s,e) =>
changed.Enqueue(e.FullPath);

        watcher.Renamed += (s,e) =>
changed.Enqueue(e.FullPath);

    }



    // Call from Game.Update on main thread to
process changes safely (recreate textures/effects
there)

    public IEnumerable<string> DequeueAll()

    {

        while (changed.TryDequeue(out var p)) yield
return p;

    }



    public void Dispose() => watcher.Dispose();

}
```

For code hot-reload, try the community hot-reloader packages
during development or use `dotnet watch`/Visual Studio's Hot
Reload for immediate feedback. Keep hot-reload developer-only
and toggleable.

Data-driven architecture: config, content packs and mod manifests

Make data formats first-class citizens: JSON or YAML for level definitions, behavior tables, and UI layouts. Keep business logic in code and data in files so content creators can tweak values without touching code. Version your data schemas and include a small migration step so older mods can still load on newer game versions.

A minimal mod manifest (JSON) and loader pattern:

```
// mods/examplemod/manifest.json

{

  "id": "examplemod",

  "name": "Example Mod",

  "version": "1.0.0",

  "assets": ["sprites/player_new.png",
"sfx/blast.ogg"],

  "entry": "scripts/init.csx"

}
```

Load the manifest, register its assets (mount into your asset manager with an override priority), and run the script in `entry`. This predictable pattern keeps mods isolated and makes conflict resolution straightforward (last-wins or explicit overrides).

Input rebinding & profile persistence

Allow players to rebind controls and save presets per input device. Store bindings as a simple JSON mapping from semantic actions to hardware inputs and expose a small UI for editing. Keep an abstraction `IInputProvider` in your game logic so you read actions (Jump, Fire) instead of raw keys.

```csharp
// File: InputMap.cs

using System.Collections.Generic;

public class InputMap

{

    public Dictionary<string, string> Bindings =
new(); // action -> input token (e.g.,
"Keyboard:Space" or "Gamepad:ButtonA")


    public void Save(string path) =>
File.WriteAllText(path,
JsonSerializer.Serialize(this));

    public static InputMap Load(string path) =>
JsonSerializer.Deserialize<InputMap>(File.ReadAllText
(path));

}
```

Translate tokens to platform checks inside a single adapter and keep legacy mappings for users migrating between control schemes.

Shader variants & fallback effects

Author shader variants for high/medium/low quality and choose them at runtime. Keep a small shader manager that maps semantic effects (UI, Sprite, PBR) to compiled effect files and allows runtime swapping. For artist iteration, watch compiled effect files the same way you watch textures and reload Effect objects on the main thread.

```csharp
// File: ShaderManager.cs (conceptual)

public class ShaderManager

{
```

```
    readonly GraphicsDevice gd;

    readonly Dictionary<string, Effect> effects =
new();


    public void LoadEffect(string key, byte[]
compiledBytes)

    {

        using var ms = new
MemoryStream(compiledBytes);

        effects[key] = new Effect(gd, ms.ToArray());

    }

    public Effect Get(string key) => effects[key];

}
```

Provide a cheap fallback (BasicEffect or simpler pass) so devices that don't support a feature will still run.

Asset bundles and streaming for mods & DLC

Don't force every modder to follow the Content Pipeline. Support raw asset packs (zip, tar) with a small manifest and a resolver that looks for mod assets before the base game. At runtime, mount the pack by reading its index and mapping virtual asset names to streams. This keeps mod distribution simple and avoids rebuilding .xnb files.

```
// Pseudocode: lookup order

// 1. Mods overlay (modA -> mod assets)

// 2. User override folder
```

Use stream-based loading and finalize GPU resources on the main thread to avoid blocking frames.

Use small extension-friendly systems: events and service locators

Avoid sprawling global state. Use a minimal ISeviceLocator for rare cross-cutting services (audio, asset manager, input) and an event bus for loose coupling between plugins and core systems (e.g., OnLevelLoaded, OnPlayerDamage). Keep event payloads small and prefer explicit registration/unregistration so you don't leak references when unloading mods.

Provide a debug / editor mode

Expose a debug console, live level editor, and a simple UI to spawn entities, toggle systems, and toggle quality settings. These tools let designers and QA iterate without a full build. If you offer hot-reload, wire the editor to re-run scripts and reload assets in-place.

Packaging, CI and distribution for extensible games

Automate multi-tier asset building in CI: produce platform-specific texture compression sets, build optional mod bundles, and produce signed test artifacts for device farms. Use Fastlane or equivalent to automate iOS/Android distribution, and keep a test channel for mod-enabled builds. Automate smoke tests that exercise mod loading so regressions in the plugin surface are caught early.

Security and sandboxing

Treat untrusted mods and scripts as untrusted input. Limit file system access, network, and reflection in third-party scripts. For C# scripting, avoid exposing `System.IO` directly; instead expose a controlled API object that mediates allowed operations. For plugins, document the risks and provide a "trusted plugin" flag for signed extensions.

Small, practical examples you can drop in now

A safe API wrapper you expose to scripts might look like this: `IGameApi { void Spawn(string entityId, Vector2 pos); void PlaySound(string name); float Time { get; } }` — pass a small `GameApi` object as `globals` to Roslyn scripts so scripts can only perform these operations. Keep the implementation thin and safe.

For hot asset reload, combine `FileSystemWatcher` (as shown earlier) with your asset manager's `ReloadAsset(string path)` method; always finalize GPU uploads on the main thread and swap references atomically so systems see either the old or the new asset consistently.

For input rebinding, persist JSON and map tokens to checks; for example `Keyboard:Space` maps to `Keys.Space` and `Gamepad:ButtonA` maps to `Buttons.A`. The game's input adapter converts tokens to boolean checks each update.

Make extension discoverability easy

Provide a short "mod README" template, a tiny manifest generator, and a sample plugin project that demonstrates the `IGamePlugin` interface and how to register event handlers. Ship a "mod kit" with example assets, sample scripts and clear instructions; lowering the friction to start modding multiplies the community.

Monitor and evolve the API

Version the plugin/scripting API and add deprecation warnings. When you change the contract, keep compatibility shims (or migrate scripts in the mod loader) so existing mods don't immediately break. Log clear messages when a plugin fails to load and provide a compatibility report to help mod authors update.

Final checklist (implement these incrementally)

Start by adding a small plugin interface and a script runner for designers. Next add an asset hot-reload watcher and a simple mod manifest loader. Provide input rebinding and a small shader manager with fallbacks. Automate platform packaging and CI so you can ship mod-enabled builds to testers. Secure untrusted code by exposing a minimal API surface. Ship a mod kit and example plugin so the community can get started quickly.

Conclusion & Next Steps

This final chapter closes your journey through MonoGame with clarity, confidence, and forward momentum. By now, you've built foundational knowledge, mastered practical workflows, and explored full project examples that mirror the structure of professional games. This conclusion does three things: it reviews what you've learned, shows how to continue beyond this book, and equips you with a roadmap for publishing, practicing, and staying connected to the community.

Recap of Skills & Knowledge Gained

You began with MonoGame's essential architecture and gradually built the habits and technical depth required to create stable, extensible, multi-platform games. You learned how the game loop works, how drawing and updating form the backbone of every project, and how content is imported, processed, and optimized. You explored input systems, physics foundations, camera movement, UI, audio, and even unit testing.

From there you stepped into more advanced topics such as memory management, shader programming, asynchronous loading, profiling, modular architecture, data-driven design, cross-platform deployment, and mobile performance. Each concept was supported by practical code examples so you could see not only what to do, but *how* to do it without guesswork.

You then built complete mini-projects — a 2D platformer, a top-down shooter, and a beginner-friendly 3D demo — to prove your mastery by applying everything at once. Finally, you looked at lessons from real MonoGame projects and learned how to customize and extend your own games through modding, scripting, plugin systems, and tool-building.

You now have the practical, reusable mental models that game developers rely on daily.

Further Learning & Publishing Your Games

As you grow, your work naturally shifts from "how do I build this?" to "how do I refine, package, and release this?" Publishing is both technical and creative. To prepare for it, expand in three directions.

Learn distribution pipelines.
Experiment with exporting builds to Windows, Linux, macOS, Android, and the web. Learn how each platform handles input, asset compression, threading, and file access. Understand store requirements such as signing, device compatibility, packaging formats, and build automation. This gives you the control you need to ship updates confidently.

Study game design and production.
Beyond code, polish comes from iteration, readability, timing, and player psychology. Learn to tune game feel, communicate visually, and structure your gameplay loops. Read design books, follow postmortems, and practice tuning small prototypes.

Immerse yourself in tools and engines beyond MonoGame.
Not to replace it, but to broaden your thinking. Investigate how Godot, Stride, Unreal, or Unity approach scene management, rendering, and resource pipelines. Understanding multiple

perspectives makes you a stronger developer and helps you design better architectures in MonoGame.

Recommended Practice Projects

Your long-term skill growth depends on structured practice. Here are project types that reinforce the lessons from this book while pushing you slightly outside your comfort zone.

A physics-heavy arcade game.
Build a breakout clone, a pinball system, or a simple platform physics sandbox. Implement collision categories, custom physics responses, and debug drawing. This strengthens your spatial reasoning and optimization discipline.

A content-driven RPG slice.
Prototype tile-based movement, dialogue, inventory, and a small quest chain. Use JSON or YAML for content, build a clean state machine, and support hot-reload of data. This teaches you the value of data-driven design.

A shader playground.
Create a small application that visualizes and compares shader techniques: lighting models, post-processing, palette shifts, and texture distortions. Build a UI to tweak parameters at runtime. This will make you far more confident with graphics programming.

A mobile-optimized endless runner.
Focus on framerate stability, object pooling, asset memory limits, touch controls, and ultra-fast scene transitions. This helps you learn how to ship to low-end devices without frame drops.

Each project is intentionally small. Small projects let you iterate faster, learn more deeply, and finish what you start.

Resources, Community, & Continuing Development

The MonoGame community is supportive, open, and filled with developers willing to share code, workflows, and guidance. To keep growing, stay plugged into active spaces where people build, experiment, and collaborate.

Study real production repositories to understand architectural patterns. Watch conference talks, devlogs, and postmortems. Read source code — MonoGame itself is open source, and the best way to understand engines is to see how they're made.

Most importantly, keep shipping small things. Each finished game teaches more than ten unfinished ones. Build a habit of releasing prototypes, sharing demos, and learning from feedback. When something sparks your curiosity, follow it — whether it's rendering, tooling, networking, or storytelling. Your interests will naturally guide your specialization.

A Note to the Reader

If this book has supported your learning journey, I'd appreciate you taking a moment to share your honest thoughts in the form of a review or comment on the store where you purchased it. Your feedback — whether positive, neutral, or critical — helps other readers discover the book and helps guide improvements for future editions. Thank you for being part of this learning process and for contributing to a growing community of developers.

Final Thoughts

You now have the confidence, tools, and technical grounding to build games you can share proudly with the world. You've learned how to organize projects, write clean code, build efficient systems, test across devices, optimize performance, and release multi-platform builds. You've also learned how to extend your work with modding, scripting, editors, and data-driven workflows — skills that scale from small indie titles to professional productions.

The next step is simple: take everything you've learned and build something that excites you. Start small, aim for completion, and give yourself permission to grow through mistakes and iteration. With MonoGame — and with the fundamentals you now understand — you can create games of any style, scope, or ambition.